Network Function Virtualization

Network Function Virtualization

Ken Gray

Director, CTO and Architecture Group, Cisco Systems

Thomas D. Nadeau

Chief Architect, Open Source and Distinguished Engineer,
Brocade Communications Systems

AMSTERDAM • BOSTON • HEIDELBERG • LONDON
NEW YORK • OXFORD • PARIS • SAN DIEGO
SAN FRANCISCO • SINGAPORE • SYDNEY • TOKYO

Morgan Kaufmann is an imprint of Elsevier

British Library Cataloguing-in-Publication Data
A catalogue record for this book is available from the British Library

Library of Congress Cataloging-in-Publication Data
A catalog record for this book is available from the Library of Congress

ISBN: 978-0-12-802119-4

For Information on all Morgan Kaufmann publications
visit our website at https://www.elsevier.com/

Working together
to grow libraries in
developing countries

www.elsevier.com • www.bookaid.org

Publisher: Todd Green
Acquisition Editor: Brian Romer
Editorial Project Manager: Amy Invernizzi
Production Project Manager: Priya Kumaraguruparan
Designer: Victoria Pearson

Typeset by MPS Limited, Chennai, India

Contents

Foreword by Dave Ward xi
Foreword by Chris Wright xix
Preface xxi
Acknowledgments xxix
Introduction xxxi

CHAPTER 1   Network Function Virtualization 1
Introduction 1
Background 1
Redrawing NFV and Missing Pieces 3
Defining NFV 4
Is NFV SDN? 5
NFV Is The Base Case 6
Strengthening "NFV as SDN Use Case" 8
    Improving Virtualization 8
Data Plane I/O and COTS Evolution 9
Standardizing an NFV Architecture 11
The Marketplace Grew Anyway 11
Academic Studies Are Still Relevant 12
NFV at ETSI 12
NFV—Why Should I Care? 14
Enabling a New Consumption Model 15
Conclusions 16
End Notes 17

CHAPTER 2   Service Creation and Service Function Chaining 19
Introduction 19
Definitions 19
The Service Creation Problem 22
    A Quick History 22
Virtual Service Creation and SFC 29
    Varying Approaches to Decomposition 32
Metadata 35
What Can You Do with SFC? 36
    Logical Limits 41
NFV Without SFC 46

Conclusion 46
End Notes...47

CHAPTER 3   ETSI NFV ISG...**49**
Introduction..49
Getting Chartered 49
European Telecommunications Institute..49
NFV at ETSI...50
Organization...51
Impact on 3GPP..52
Digesting ETSI Output 52
Output 52
Terminology..53
Architecture—General...53
Architecture—Big Blocks and Reference Points..55
Use Cases...59
Virtualization Requirements...62
Gap Analysis...65
PoC Observations 67
A Look Back—White Paper 3 69
Future Directions 70
Open Platform for NFV..70
Repatriation/ISG2.0 (and 3.0) 71
Conclusion 73
End Notes...75

CHAPTER 4   IETF Related Standards: NETMOD, NETCONF, SFC
and SPRING...**77**
Introduction..77
Service Function Chaining 78
Problem Statement..78
SFC Architecture 79
NSH Header..82
Source Packet Routing in Networking...88
A Demonstration..90
Next for SRv6...91
Network Modeling...91
The Yang Data Modeling Language 92
The NETCONF Protocol 93
Operations..94
Message Layer...95

Secure Transports 96
The RESTCONF Protocol 96
The Public Github Yang Repository 96
Conclusions 98
Appendix A 99
Example of Yang Model Usage 99
End Notes 101

CHAPTER 5   **The NFV Infrastructure Management** **103**
Introduction 103
NFV Virtual Infrastructure Management (VIM) 104
OpenStack 105
Network Controllers 111
Controller Architecture 112
OpenDaylight 114
ODL and OpenStack Collaboration 116
Open Network Operating System (ONOS) 117
PaaS, NFV, and OpenStack 120
OpenStack Cue 121
The Impact of PaaS on NFV 121
Conclusions 123
End Notes 124

CHAPTER 6   **MANO: Management, Orchestration, OSS, and**
                Service Assurance **127**
Introduction 127
The VNF Domain 128
The OSS/BSS Block 129
Reimagining the OSS (and BSS)—Brownfield Partnership 131
Reimagining the OSS—Opportunities in SA 132
Interpretations from the Architectural Diagram Reference Points 134
NFV Orchestration (General) 134
Service Graphs 134
Network Service Descriptors and MANO Descriptors 135
The Network Service Catalog 136
Generic Resource and Policy Management for Network Services 137
The VNFM Demarcation Point 138
Open Orchestration 138
Tacker 139
Open-O 147

Open MANO 148
OpenBaton 149
Architecture on Steroids 150
Conclusions 152
End Notes 153

CHAPTER 7 The Virtualization Layer—Performance, Packaging, and NFV 155
Introduction 155
Evolving Virtualization Techniques 156
The VM-Centric Model 158
Containers—Do We Need Hypervisors? 160
Unikernels 165
Hybrid Virtualization 165
Security Trade-offs 167
Security—The Lowest Common Denominator 169
Current Packet Handling 170
Application Processing 171
Background—Context Switch/Data Copy Reduction 172
Background—Scalar Versus Vectorization 173
Ongoing—Intel Advancements (and Academic Work) 173
Netmap and vhost-User 178
Turnkey Optimization (Is There an EASY Button?) 180
fd.io (None of the Above?) 182
Conclusions 184
End Notes 185

CHAPTER 8 NFV Infrastructure—Hardware Evolution and Testing 191
Introduction 191
Evolving Hardware 192
CPU Complex 192
Extending the System 200
ARM 209
Performance Measurement 210
Measuring Performance 210
Power Efficiency 211
Conclusion 212
End Notes 213

CHAPTER 9   **An NFV Future** 217
    Introduction 217
    What Is NFV (Restated)? 217
    The Current NFV Model 218
        The Cost of NFV 218
        A First Order Change 221
    The Role of Standards and Open Systems 222
    Consumer Behavior 223
    Changing Your Spots 224
    Parting Thoughts 225
    End Notes 226

Index 227

Foreword by Dave Ward

Lift and Shift Is Necessary but not Sufficient

This book by Ken and Tom on Network Function Virtualization is perhaps the first time they have laid out both a fantastic review of the vast landscape of technologies related to virtualized networking, and woven in a subtle argument and allusion to what the future of this technology holds. I may be drunk on my own Koolaid, but I certainly read the book with a specific lens in which I asked the question "Where are we on the maturity continuum of the technology and how close is it to what operators and customers need or want to deploy?" The answer I believe I read from Tom and Ken is that "We've only just begun." (Now try and get Karen Carpenter out of your head while reading the rest of this ☺). What I mean by this is that over the last say 6 years of trade-rag-eye-ball-seeking articles, the industry has lived through huge hype cycles and "presumptive close" arguments of download-install-transition-your-telco/mso to a whole new business.

What K/T lay out is not only an industry in transition but one that is completely dependent on the pace being set by the integration of huge open source projects and proprietary products, proprietary implementations of newly virtualized appliances, huge holes in the stack of SW required to make the business: resilient, anti-fragile, predictable, supportable, able to migrate across DCs, flexibly rearrangeable, a whole mess of additional x-ilities and most importantly ... operate-able and billable. This transition MUST happen for the industry and it MUST happen in many networking-dependent industries. Why? Because the dominant architecture of many SPs is one in which flexible data centers were not considered part of the service delivery network. On-demand user choice was not the norm. Therefore, trucking in a bunch of compute-storage-switching (aka data centers) does not by itself deliver a service. SPs build services in which there are SLAs (many by regulation in addition to service guarantees), guarantees of experience, giving access to any and all new devices that arrive on the market and as a goal focus on building more and more uses of their network. The key message this book lays out is that: it's complex, there are a ton of moving parts, there are layers upon layers, there are very few people—if in fact any—that can hold the entire architecture in their head and keep track of it. And most importantly; we are closer to the starting line than the finish line.

Thankfully as K/T have laid out in another book, we have made it through the SDN-hype cycle and it's being rolled out across the industry. We watched the movie "Rise of the Controllers" and the industry is settled down and deploying the technology widely. Now we are to the point where virtualizing everything is the dominant topic. Technology progresses. It requires a lot of "stack" and all that is necessary in that stack does not exist today and is in various stages of completeness, but not integrated into something consistent or coherent yet. Also, when someone says VNF (virtualized network function) or NFV (network function virtualization): (1) it applies to more than networking related stuff, see video production and playout services and (2) the terms were defined when hypervisors where the only choice for virtualization. Now that containers are available; we

have to clearly set the industry goal that "cloud native" (which is basically a synonym for container-
ized applications) is the ultimate endpoint; until the next wave comes in. The real point is that
lifting and shifting of physical appliances to hypervisor based VNFs (necessary first step but not
sufficient) led to one particular stack of technology, but cloud-native leads to a different variant.
One in which use of DC resources is dramatically lower, time to boot/active service is faster and
parallelism is the central premise. For the love of all the G*ds, I truly hope that the industry does
not stall prematurely. Without knowing what Ken and Tom are up to next; it's an easy prediction
to make that this book will have a potential for 42 versions of publication as today it documents
the first steps toward this industry revolution.

The implicit argument that I read throughout the book is that we are seeing the end of the feudal
reign of silo-ed organizations and technical structure of long lasting beliefs of the architecture of
the Internet. The next conclusion I came to is that we are at the point where the OSI model should
only be taught in history books. It's close to irrelevant and assumptions that do not hold water
today. What K/T lay out (although they do not spell it out this way so I will take the liberty) is that
there are now so many more explicit first-class citizens in the Internet architecture that our old
notions of layering have to be wholesale rejected. What are these new first-class citizens? Identity,
encapsulation/tunneling, specific application treatment, service chains, security, privacy, content as
endpoint, dependent applications performing as workflows, access agnosticism, multi-homing, location independence, flat addressing schemes, unique treatment/augmentation per person, and a desire
that the network and the service someone or some business requested reacts to repair itself and
reacts to experience that is desired . . . to name a few.

Ok, let me dial it back a little and try and explain how I got this worked up. I reached the same
point K/T discuss in the book that the stack to virtualize networks goes way beyond the concepts
of SDN. As the reader probably understands, SDN is a key ingredient to enable NFV but alone it
only does part of the job. I am going to switch terms from what K/T use and describe the high-
level goal as "Reactive Networking"

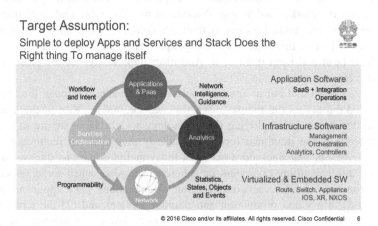

The industry has been making progress toward this target in the open source community and
somewhat in standards bodies (eg, MEF, IETF, ETSI). Services orchestration now includes SDN

controllers. Many are working toward an implementation of MANO, the orchestration framework that can create virtualized services per tenants or customers. There are service orchestration products on the market; I lumped them all together in the bubble on the left. The network can now be built around strong, programmable forwarders. Providing a solid analytics platform is needed immediately and work is already underway. This is so key because in this day and age we cannot actually correlate a network failure to video quality analytics. For example, did a country full of video viewers just have their content halt because a link went down somewhere and no one has any idea what caused it? Yep, it's the case right now we cannot correlate any networking or NFV event to service quality analytics. It all exists in silos. Everything today is compartmentalized to its fiefdom or rigidly stuck in its OSI layer. One of the magical cloud's most important contributions to the industry is the notion of a PaaS. Request a service and voila, it's working. We need to get NFV to the PaaS and cloud designs for relevancy. But, at the same time we have to make networking relevant in the PaaS layer. Today you can dial up/request CPU, RAM, and storage but not networking (even bandwidth) in any cloud.

That last fact is horribly depressing to me, but I understand some of the reasons why. In cloudy DCs available today, the Internet is considered ubiquitous and infinite. The services put in the cloud are built on that assumption and are most often not I/O constrained (note that there are just about no VNFs available either); they are CPU, RAM, and storage constrained. They are built for webservices-type workloads. When they are I/O bound, you pay for it (aka $) in a big way via massive egress bandwidth charges. As mentioned, you can pay for it but you cannot provision it. But read what I wrote way above, in SP cloudy DCs; the Internet is also ubiquitous but they have a big business around SLAs, best of class experiences and are stuck dealing with regulations. Therefore, in an SP network the Internet is also infinite, but it is purposefully engineered to meet those goals of best in class, on-all-the-time and guaranteed. VNFs in an SP cloud are sources and sinks of mostly I/O and the VNFs are chained together and orchestrated as a complete service. For example, a virtual router, load balancer, firewall, anti-DDOS, anti-malware, IPS, cloud storage are all one bundle for the end customer. For the SP, it's a service chain per tenant (yes, it could also be deployed as a multitenanted service chain) who also fundamentally bought a 1 or 10 Gig end-to-end access and security service++. Therefore, the virtualized services are directly tied to a residential or business customer who is buying a complete turnkey service. And they want something new tomorrow—not only more and more bandwidth but services available that are cool, valuable, and going to solve their problems. The fact the SP uses VNFs to reduce cost, add more flexibility to service delivery (aka new stuff all the time) is great for the end customer, but the SP has to build an end-to-end service from access through to VNFs and to the Internet seamlessly. The DC has to be orchestrated as a part of the complete network and not as an island. The stack to do this is across domains, as K/T explain, is very complex.

That last note on complexity is the key to the point of the picture above. The stack for NFV has to be fully reactive and do the right thing to manage itself. Elastic services (expanding and contracting on demand), migrating workloads (aka, VNFs), lifecycle management, low-cost compute and storage failures, constantly changing load in the network, load engineering in the DC all require the bus between the analytics platform and orchestration to be functioning well or we are going to end up with an old-school event->alarm->notify->trouble ticketing system of the last decades all over again.

As K/T explain throughout the book and really do a great job at simplifying; the stack is complex. Toward that end, there is another concept in the industry of the "whole stack" developer. This concept is that for an app developer or service designer in the NFV space, to do their job well; they need to understand the "whole stack" of orchestration++ infrastructure below their app or service to get their job done. The goal for the NFV industry hopefully is not going to be toward this end. This tangent is a moderately interesting argument in the intro of a book that attempts to describe the whole stack and how important it is to understand. Where I differ, and I suspect that the authors might agree, is that the industry target has to be to a "No Stack" developer. That is the point of having a fully reactive, do-what-I-need, do-what-I-want set of orchestration and analytics software. A service designer for NFV probably does not want to know the goop and infinite layers below and should not care less. It's all being swapped out and upgraded to the latest and greatest new set of tools and services tomorrow anyway. I posited above that there are very few, if any people that could fit the entire architecture at any point in time into their heads anyways. Let alone all the APIs, function call flows, events, triggers and fubars that are happening underneath at any point in deployment.

So, I offer this diagram derived from the chapters of the book and my own hallucinations:

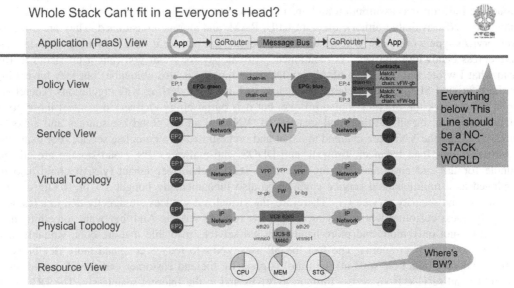

Everything below that blue (big) line represents all the networking layers that the NFV stack has to config/provision, spew telemetry data, collect and correlate in the analytics platform, react to changes in the network, reprogram the network, spin up elastic VNFs, lifecycle manage them, create service chains, apply to tenants changing service requests, etc, etc, etc. Please see the book referred to the introduction for details ☺.

All the service designer or app developer or the SP's OSS/BSS should see as a result is way up at the top programmed and managed via the Service Platform. In industry terms it's a PaaS layer (which today does not exist for NFV but IT is exactly the target the industry needs to hit). The history of SDN, controllers, changes to embedded OS that enable generic apps to run on them, orchestration platforms and biggest data platforms is one of chasing the developer. The industry chased each new building block during the creation of the stack believing that developers would be attracted to their API set and developer platform. Apps on the router/switch, apps on the SDN controller, analytics apps... in fact they all were right in the end and all wrong. But to date, none have emerged as more than pieces of infrastructure in the stack and as application platforms for very specific outcomes. This point is often really hard to explain. An SDN controller is both infrastructure and an app platform? Yes. In an overall NFV or orchestration stack, it's infrastructure. It's the thing that speaks SDN protocols to program the virtual and physical topologies and ultimate resources. As an app platform, it's unbelievably awesome for an IT pro or engineer trying to debug or program something very specific. But, it may not be the right tool for an overall NFV lifecycle manager and service orchestrator. Rinse and repeat the argument for the on-box apps or analytics platform. Great for certain types of apps in specific scenarios, but awesome as infra in an overall infrastructure orchestration stack. And perfect if linked together by high performance message busses to enable reactive networking.

Here is a picture of the situation:

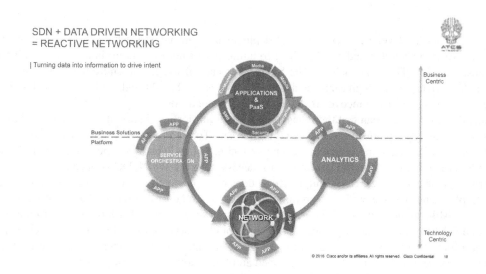

Assume the dashed line in this picture is in the same location as the solid line in the previous picture. The more technology-centric you get, the more the apps become very specific for a task or job. All the action for an SP or Enterprise to deliver a business outcome or service is at the PaaS layer. The reason I say this is that dragging all the APIs and data models from lower layers in the layered stack all the way to the NFV service designer or app developer == dragging every single feature, event, trigger and state to the top. No one builds a cloud service that way and it would be a modification to the old saying and now be "Luke, use the 1 million APIs."

Projecting forward to future versions of K/T's book, the argument I read and conclusion I came to could be a world that looks something like this:

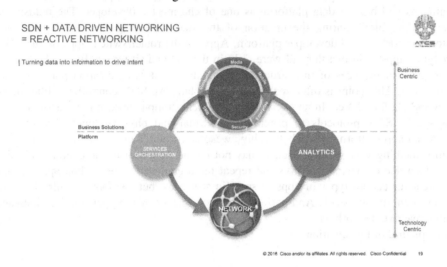

SDN + DATA DRIVEN NETWORKING
= REACTIVE NETWORKING

| Turning data into information to drive intent

The "No Stack" developer, designer, and deployer is in an industry where there is a PaaS that has a rich catalog of VNFs and VxFs (I hate to admit it, but not everything is networking related; eg, transcoders for JIT, CDN caches). The Stack takes care of itself. The entire network (including DCs) is load, delay, jitter engineered as a whole; services are bought and sold on demand and the entire system reacts and can recover from any change in conditions.

Note this does NOT mean that there has to be a grand-unification theory of controllers, orchestration systems, analytics platforms to achieve this. Ken and Tom go to great lengths to describe access ! = WAN ! = DC ! = peering policy ! = content caching policy. This does mean there is room for NNI interfaces inbetween specific controllers for access, campus, WAN, DC as each of the resource, physical, and virtual devices, etc is unique. But it does mean that a crossdomain orchestration system that can place and manage VNFs on-prem, in a CO or head end or centralized DC, is a reality. As much as I dislike grand-unification theories, I dislike centralized versus distributed and on-prem versus cloud debates. As the authors describe, they are pointless arguments and really boring conversations at a dinner party. All of the scenarios are going to emerge. The sooner we face up to it, the sooner we can get building it and not get wrapped around the axle of use-case jousting.

This being said, there are some fundamentals that make this challenging and a ton of work to round out the different mechanisms to orchestrate VNFs wherever they may be placed. Let me give a couple of examples. How much resource does a VNF need? What I mean is in terms of: CPU cores/cycles, RAM, storage, and what are the capabilities and attributes of the VNF? Can it fling 10 Gpbs? 1? 100? How/where can we describe this? That "manifest" format does not exist yet, although there is work being done specifically for VNFs. Note that it does not really exist for anything virtualized via hypervisors or containers in general either. Virtualized forwarding (switching or routing) recently was a trouble area but this status has recently changed with the introduction of fd.io. The platform for network data analytics is just about to emerge as I write this. Most VNFs are not cloud-native yet and are stuck in the lift and shift model and in heavyweight hypervisors. Yes, the industry is making it work but for how long before economic and complexity collapse?

Can I reduce the overlay/underlay operational headache to a single flat layer with a flat addressing scheme like IPv6 could provide? Probably yes. Linkages to OSS/BSS and other management systems have not been defined. Is the PaaS I describe above really the new (re)formulation of an SPs OSS/BSS? Some operators are alluding to it. As a customer am I going to have the cloud-based experience to see the state of my entire network and/or services? I say this because most often a customer has no way of verifying except packets are flowing or not. What about the user experience of different roles within the enterprise or SP? Thankfully, the notion of bring this to a PaaS layer means these different questions appear to have some answers as the orchestration and analytics platforms can both be utilized at the "outcome" services of PaaS. This enables someone to rerender the data into an operational experience that meets the different roles of an operator and necessary information to an end customer. The earlier diagrams Jedi-mind trick "these are not the layers you are looking for" into an outcome like this:

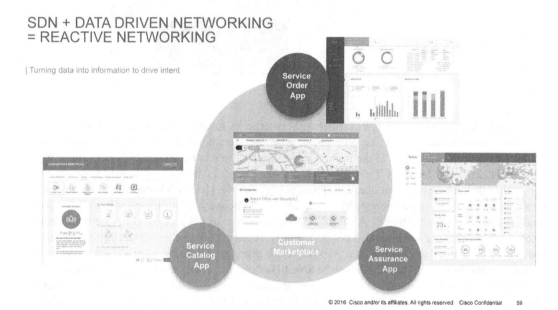

This is all the same data available at the PaaS to enable:

- an on-demand customer marketplace for the end-user,
- service catalog app for the service designer,
- service order app for the product manager (what is the status of my customer's deployment),
- service assurance app for the operator (in which the layers and services have been identified and tracked to render the data from resource to policy and every way of viewing inbetween).

Ok, I have been riffing and ranting for a while and you really want to get to the book, so let us start bringing this to a close. The overall goal, drawn slightly differently again, is to deploy VNFs as a part of an engineered end-to-end service. There are physical resources of compute, switching storage (hopefully orchestrated in a "hyper converged manner") which is enabled by a cloud platform using hypervisors, containers, both programmed by SDN controllers with telemetry data spewing out to the Model Driven orchestration and analytics platforms.

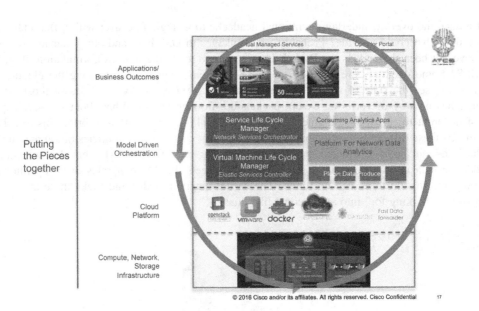

Topped off by a service-rich PaaS that may emerge in future revisions of the book as being segment specific because of service differences. Also, we already know some of the immediate next scenes in this screenplay. One of the immediate scenes required is an answer to the question "What do I need to install to deploy X Tbps of Y NFV service?" Today, there are no academic or engineering models that can answer that question. Particularly with the lack of IO optimized computer platforms on the market. As mentioned, NFV services are IO bound and not necessarily cycle or RAM (and certainly not storage) bound. A lift and shift architecture to get a physical device into a hypervisor is not particularly hard but also not particularly efficient. So another scene is going to be how fast are VNFs enabled as cloud-native. Another one is going to be around common data models that have to emerge in the standards bodies to be able to orchestrate a rich ecosystem of suppliers.

As mentioned right up front, this is a fast moving space with a lot of details and coordination that has to occur which MUST be simplified to "No Stack" delivery. BUT the whole purpose of continuing on with the book is to get the details of why, how, where, what-were-they-thinking with respect to the big NFV story from Ken and Tom. I certainly hope the authors have great success and I fully predict they have a great career writing the next 41 revisions of the book as this area of technology is moving FAST.

Dave Ward

Dave is Chief Architect at Cisco Systems, responsible for architectural governance, defining strategy, development of new technology and leading use-inspired research. Working via tight partnerships with customers, partners, developers and academia he is also leading co-development and co-innovation initiatives. He has been the Routing Area Director at the IETF and chair of four Working Groups: IS-IS, HIP, BFD and Softwires and worked with the ITU-T, ONF and several Open Source consortia. David was also a Juniper Fellow and Chief Architect working on the operating system and next-generation routing systems. Dave has a small vineyard in the Santa Cruz Mountains, an heirloom tomato farm along the St. Croix River in Somerset, Wisconsin.

Foreword by Chris Wright

With network functions virtualization (NFV) we are transforming the global communications network. Let me say that again: we are transforming the global communications network. This network, or really collection of networks, is retooled maybe once every ten or more years. Given that, it is a rare opportunity to be involved in such a broad scale network transformation. This is why I get so excited by NFV. NFV is a disruptive trend in the networking industry, and Tom and Ken are bringing you all the details you will need to find your way through this industry scale transformation. Whether you are a software developer, a network architect or engineer, or a network operator, this book will help you find your way through this transformation. At the core, business realities are behind the NFV movement. The networks built by communications service providers (CSPs) are under a relentless growing strain by ever-increasing data traffic. Both businesses and consumers are always connected to the network, serving and consuming data as we share information and services across the internet. Staggering growth in data traffic is largely driven by video streaming. One CSP cited 150,000% growth in data traffic from 2007–15 in the recent OpenStack Summit in Austin in April 2016. Many of the services consumers use are over the top (OTT) of the CSP's network. OTT services such as messaging, voice, and video are a source of network strain but not a source of network revenue. Demand outpacing revenue represents an existential business risk for CSPs. To remain relevant and competitive it is time for CSPs to reinvent themselves.

Meanwhile, the IT industry is exploding with innovation. Technology shifts such as virtualization and the cloud, a focus on application programming interfaces (APIs) and automation, and services that are being continuously improved and updated fuel the IT industry's ability to rapidly respond to changing business needs. This business agility is what draws consumers to these new services. Services that evolve quickly and converge on serving customers' real interests have allowed the IT industry to push ahead and capture marketshare with OTT services. This same business agility is also the key to CSPs success. CSPs are looking to reinvent themselves by applying the innovation and learning from the IT industry to how they build and operate their own networks. The networking industry has historically worked through standards bodies to define the CSPs requirements and enable interoperability. This process is relatively slow. It can take years to go from initial Standards discussions to formal Standards to functional implementations to deploying those implementations in CSPs' networks. While Standards and interoperability are still important, the process is too slow to be the only engine behind network innovation. But what does this mean in practice? It is time for the industry to collaborate more directly on not just the definition of the requirements, but also the actual underlying implementation. This is something that open source software and specifically the open source software development model excels at: fostering industry collaboration. It is no secret that the IT industry's innovation is largely driven by open source software. Tom and Ken look at open source software projects such as OpenStack, OpenDaylight, and Open vSwitch as key building blocks for NFV. Fundamental to the NFV transformation is moving network functions trapped in function specific hardware to a more flexible fabric of compute, storage and network built from general purpose hardware — a cloud. This environment is software defined, meaning it can be quickly adjusted to new workloads using APIs and software automation. A network function becomes a piece of software executing like an application in a cloud. A simplistic view of NFV is simply virtualizing these hardware based applications, sometimes known as a "physical to virtual migration" or simply p2v. However, p2v alone is just a starting point. One challenge presented by NFV is providing sufficient packet processing efficiency in a cloud to make the transformation financially viable. A network service is typically composed of multiple network functions. Orchestrating the launch of a network service including directing network traffic through each of the network functions also provides some interesting challenges for NFV. Another challenge is providing the network Service Assurance expected by users when building from commodity infrastructure. Tom and Ken delve into these challenges in detail, looking at different industry efforts in both standards and open source.

What's most exciting to me is that NFV is just the beginning. Significant industry trends such as Internet of Things (IoT) and 5G will be built on these next generation networks that are set in motion by NFV. Mainstream introduction of new technologies such as self-driving cars, augmented and virtual reality, and smart cities are examples of the kind of impact this new network will have on society. So coming up to speed on the terminology, the history, and evolution of NFV, and the details of how the industry is solving the challenges presented by NFV will serve you well. Tom and Ken have brought all of this information together, and I hope you enjoy learning from them as much as I have!

Chris Wright

Chris Wright is Vice President and Chief Technologist at Red Hat where he is leading engineers who work on cloud computing, distributed storage, software defined networking and network functions virtualization, containers, machine learning, and continuous delivery. During his more than 20 years as a software engineer he has worked in the telecom industry on high availability and distributed systems and in the Linux industry on security, virtualization, and networking. He has been a Linux developer for over 15 years, most of that time spent deep in the Linux kernel. He is passionate about open source software serving as the foundation for next generation IT systems. He lives in sunny Portland, Oregon, where he is happily working with open source projects such as OpenDaylight, Open vSwitch, OPNFV, OpenStack, Open Container Initiative, and Cloud Native Computing Foundation.

Preface

About three years ago, we attempted to capture the state of the art in one of the most game changing technological shifts in the networking industry since Multiprotocol Label Switching (MPLS) came onto the scene. This meant the capture, corraling, and definition for the reader of the fabled unicorn of Software Designed Networks (SDN). We continue to lobby *hard* for the glitter-horned unicorn because we did see it then and now as necessary technology.

This time the unicorn is called Network Function Virtualization (NFV). Unsurprisingly, many of the issues, questions, concerns and confusion around its definition and efficacy paint the same background as when we wrote on SDN. Again, have set out with the goal to clearly define first what NFV is, and then to give the reader a clear and concise survey of the technical playing field.

NFV and Service Function Chaining (SFC) concepts have advanced and progressed as a technology driven by network operators and vendors that wish to build and deploy it—with an emphasis on using components derived using open source techniques. The starting point of their ideas is the ETSI NFV framework, which we will delve into in detail. It was one of the first documented efforts by network operators and potential NFV users to specify what this new unicorn looks like. A thumbnail sketch of the cat wearing the unicorn was produced. It is not quite the unicorn we were looking for, as we will see after our in-depth investigation is complete, but we are iterating on the picture as an industry—and continue to do so. As with SDN before it, we will refine the details of the picture to the point where this thing will work—and be a true unicorn we can get on and ride.

With that image in your mind—and hopefully a chuckle—we want to point out that there is real evidence that NFV has finally emerged. We are seeing real deployments of this technology. We hope you see that in this book.

At the time of writing this book, Thomas D. Nadeau was a Distinguished Engineer and Chief Architect of Open Source at Brocade, and Ken Gray was a Senior Director at Cisco Systems. We both also have extensive experience that spans roles both with other vendors and service providers, such as BT and Bell Atlantic (now Verizon).

It is important to note that this is a vendor-independent book. We are not commissioned by our present employers to write this book or espouse their viewpoints. The opinions expressed here are our own, and only our own. In some cases, we have relied on references or examples that came from our experiences with our most recent employers in the text. In no case do we intend to promote our specific company's wares or approaches.

This work is targeted to benefit the networking industry and not necessarily our employers, although in both of our cases we are working on these technologies as part of our day jobs.

We hope the reader finds any bias to be accidental and not distracting or overwhelming. If this can be corrected or enhanced in a subsequent revision, we will do so. We both agree that there are likely to be many updates to this text going forward given how young the technology we describe herein, and how frighteningly rapidly it continues to evolve.

We have tried our best to be inclusive of everyone that is relevant in the NFV and SFC space without being encyclopedic on the topic, and still providing enough breadth of material to cover the space.

This book was another effort on our part to define what NFV and SFC are based on our real world experiences and dialogues with customers and colleagues as well as our observation of the networking industry as a whole.

Finally, we both happily work for employers who encourage us to develop and express our own opinions. We hope the reader finds the depth and breadth of information presented herein to be interesting and informative, while at the same time evocative. We give our opinions about topics, but try to present material that describes the pros and cons of a topic in what we think is as unbiased a manner as possible. We readily acknowledge there may be divergent viewpoints—our hope is that you will be aided in forming your own opinions by exposure to our viewpoint.

We do hope you find unicorns, fairy dust, and especially lots of interesting insight and information in this book!

ASSUMPTIONS

NFV is a new approach to the current world of networking, but it is still networking. As you get into this book, we are assuming a certain level of networking knowledge. You do not have to be an engineer, but knowing how networking principles work—and frankly, do not work—will aid your comprehension of the text.

This topic has its own terminology, which you will discover in the book, but the following terms should be familiar before you read the book:

OSI model
    The Open Systems Interconnection (OSI) model defines seven different layers of
    technology: physical, data link, network, transport, session, presentation, and application.

This model allows network engineers and network vendors to easily discuss and apply technology to a specific OSI level. This segmentation lets engineers divide the overall problem of getting one application to talk to another into discrete parts and more manageable sections. Each level has certain attributes that describe it and each level interacts with its neighboring levels in a very well-defined manner. Knowledge of the layers above layer 7 is not mandatory, but understanding that interoperability is not always about electrons and photons will help.

Switches

These devices operate at layer 2 of the OSI model and use logical local addressing to move frames across a network. Devices in this category include Ethernet in all its variations, VLANs, aggregates, and redundant forms.

Routers

These devices operate at layer 3 of the OSI model and connect IP subnets to each other. Routers move packets across a network in a hop-by-hop fashion.

Ethernet

These broadcast domains connect multiple hosts together on a common infrastructure. Hosts communicate with each other using layer 2 media access control (MAC) addresses.

IP addressing and subnetting

Hosts using IP to communicate with each other use 32-bit addresses. Humans often use a dotted decimal format to represent this address. This address notation includes a network portion and a host portion, which is normally displayed, for example, as 192.168.1.1/24.

TCP and UDP

These layer 4 protocols define methods for communicating between hosts. The Transmission Control Protocol (TCP) provides for connection-oriented communications, whereas the User Datagram Protocol (UDP) uses a connectionless paradigm. Other benefits of using TCP include flow control, windowing/buffering, and explicit acknowledgments.

ICMP

Network engineers use this protocol to troubleshoot and operate a network, as it is the core protocol used (on some platforms) by the ping and traceroute programs. In addition, the Internet Control Message Protocol (ICMP) is used to signal error and other messages between hosts in an IP-based network.

Data center

A facility used to house computer systems and associated components, such as telecommunications and storage systems. It generally includes redundant or backup power supplies, redundant data communications connections, environmental controls (eg, air conditioning, fire suppression), and security devices. Large data centers are industrial scale operations using as much electricity as a small town.

MPLS

MPLS is a mechanism in high-performance networks that directs data from one network node to the next based on short path labels rather than long network addresses, avoiding complex lookups in a routing table. The labels identify virtual links (*paths*) between distant nodes rather than endpoints. MPLS can encapsulate packets of various network protocols. MPLS supports a range of access technologies.

Northbound interface

An interface that conceptualizes the lower-level details (eg, data or functions) used by, or in, the component. It is used to interface with higher-level layers using the southbound interface of the higher-level component(s). In any architectural overview, the northbound interface is normally drawn at the top of the component it is defined in, hence the name northbound interface. Examples of a northbound interface are JSON or Thrift.

Southbound interface

An interface that conceptualizes the opposite of a northbound interface. The southbound interface is normally drawn at the bottom of an architectural diagram. Examples of southbound interfaces include I2RS, NETCONF, or a command-line interface.

SDN

SDN encompasses a number of key concepts including a logically centralized data plane that is externalized from a data plane. The control plane may or may not exists as part of an externalized SDN Controller. Rapid and application-friendly Application Programming Interfaces (APIs) also are often part of the equation as they play a critical role in extending and interacting with the externalized control planes, as well as traditional ones.

Network topology

The arrangement of the various elements (links, nodes, interfaces, hosts, etc.) of a computer network. Essentially, it is the topological structure of a network, and may be depicted physically or logically. *Physical topology* refers to the placement of the network's various components, including device location and cable installation, while *logical topology* shows how data flows within a network, regardless of its physical design. Distances between nodes, physical interconnections, transmission rates, and/or signal types may differ between two networks, yet their topologies may be identical.

APIs

A specification of how some software components should interact with each other. In practice, an API is usually a library that includes specification for variables, routines, object classes, and data structures. An API specification can take many forms, including an international standard (eg, POSIX), vendor documentation (eg, the JunOS SDK), or the libraries of a programming language.

WHAT IS IN THIS BOOK?

Introduction

This text introduces and frames the conversation this book engages in around the concepts of NFV, where they came from, and why they are important to discuss.

Chapter 1, *Network Function Virtualization*

In this chapter, we define what NFV is in our view. We also take the time to discuss what its key components are and more importantly, are not.

Chapter 2, *Service Creation and Service Function Chaining*

Here we define what goes into defining a service today and the need for change that is inspiring NFV. We discuss the components that are needed to define the salient components of a service, as well as discuss the pitfalls of some definitions. We discuss the concepts of service paths, and how services can be defined as composites of other subservices, as well as how these components can be chained together.

Chapter 3, *ETSI NFV ISG*

In this chapter, we consider the contribution of the ETSI NFV ISG group's work (with focus on the charter period ending in December 2014—which we will refer to as Phase 1—and an update on its later phase) as it pertains to NFV and the potential future of the ISG. The main focus of this work is around decoupling service software from network hardware, creating flexible deployments and dynamic operations—the stated benefits of NFV in their architecture framework.

Chapter 4, *IETF Related Standards: NETMOD, NETCONF, SFC and SPRING*

This chapter introduces the notion of other relevant and useful standards efforts going on in the industry. In particular, we focus here on the Internet Engineering Task Force's (IETF's) efforts in this space, both failed and current. Here we define and describe what the NETMOD, NETCONF, SFC, and SPRING working groups are up to and why it matters to NFV and SFC technology.

Chapter 5, *The NFV Infrastructure Management*

In this and the succeeding chapters we will look a little bit more closely at the major building blocks of the ETSI-prescribed NFV architecture. Here we revisit the high-level architecture framework we described in Chapter 3. We begin with a discussion of the NFV-I functional area as it relates to management and control of the virtualized compute, storage and network components that together realize all virtualized functions on a given hardware platform—the VIM. We do this within the context of various open source projects such as OpenStack, and OpenDaylight. We introduce the concept of PaaS versus IaaS approaches to NFV and begin to ask questions about the ETSI architecture.

Chapter 6, *MANO: Management, Orchestration, OSS, and Service Assurance*

In this chapter, we discuss the orchestration of services and introduce elements that are now becoming more common in both current ETSI and open source solution dialogs. We also explore the practicality of moving to NFV en masse across an existing network, which will introduce a number of its own challenges.

Chapter 7, *The Virtualization Layer—Performance, Packaging, and NFV*

In this chapter, we will look at the evolution of virtualization techniques and software network I/O acceleration to satisfy these application requirements. We will also look at how the constant evolution in the compute component of the (ETSI-labeled) "NFVI" might affect the current aggregated, VM-centric NFV model, our concept of SFC and the potential economic assumptions behind the NFV proposition.

Chapter 8, *NFV Infrastructure—Hardware Evolution and Testing*

In this chapter, we will look in detail at the architectural evolution in the Intel Architecture (IA) for NFV including the increased dependence on cache efficiency for performance of NFV on CPU cores. We also look at the strategy of hardware augmentation that is opening the market for complimentary hardware acceleration through PCIE expansion. As with the software evolution in the preceding chapter, this leads to questions about our current architecture.

Chapter 9, *An NFV Future*

Here we wrap things up with conclusions and opinions on the topics discussed. We consolidate the big questions around NFV from the earlier chapters and offer our opinions on a path forward.

CONVENTIONS USED IN THIS BOOK

The following typographical conventions are used in this book:

Italic
> Indicates new terms, URLs, email addresses, filenames, file extensions, pathnames, directories, and Unix utilities.

`Constant width`
> Indicates commands, options, switches, variables, attributes, keys, functions, types, classes, namespaces, methods, modules, properties, parameters, values, objects, events, event handlers, XML tags, HTML tags, macros, the contents of files, and the output from commands.

`Constant width bold`
> Shows commands and other text that should be typed literally by the user, as well as important lines of code.

`Constant width italic`
> Shows text that should be replaced with user-supplied values.

USING CODE EXAMPLES

This book is here to help you get your job done. In general, you may use the code in this book in your own configuration and documentation. You do not need to contact us for permission unless you are reproducing a significant portion of the material. For example, deploying a network based on actual configurations from this book does not require permission. Selling or distributing a CD-ROM of examples from this book does require permission. Answering a question by citing this book and quoting example code does not require permission. Incorporating a significant amount of sample configurations or operational output from this book into your product's documentation does require permission.

> NOTE: The web page for this book, http://sdnprogrammability.net hosts a *.txt* file of the complete configurations used in Chapter 9's use case. You may download the configurations for use in your own lab.

We appreciate, but do not require, attribution. An attribution usually includes the title, author, publisher, and ISBN, for example: "Network Function Virtualization" by Ken E. Gray and Thomas D. Nadeau, Copyright 2016 Ken E. Gray and Thomas D. Nadeau, 978-0-12-802119-4.

If you feel your use of code examples falls outside fair use or the permission given here, feel free to contact us at permissions@elsevier.com.

COMMENTS AND QUESTIONS

For more information about our books, courses, conferences, and news, see our website at www.store.elsevier.com

We have a web page for this book. You can access this page at:
  http://sdnprogrammability.net
  http://networkprogrammability.net

Follow us on Twitter:
  http://twitter.com/tdnjunisco
  https://twitter.com/GraymatterKen

Acknowledgments

ACKNOWLEDGMENTS FROM KEN GRAY

I would like to thank my amazing wife, Leslie. She is my balance amidst the craziness of being a geek in an ever-evolving occupation.

For my children, Lilly and Zane, I hope that my continued urge to write will stimulate yours.

The space here cannot contain the list of customers, colleagues, and friends whose conversations over the last 3 years have shaped my views on this topic. Some of those colleagues are noted directly in the text. I do not want to take credit for their ideas, but point to them instead as being people who helped shape my opinions about what is important in NFV.

I want to thank all of our technical reviewers for their insights.

I would finally like to give great thanks to my coauthor, Thomas Nadeau. We no longer work in the same company, but still manage to agree on topics (even agree to disagree) though we come from separate viewpoints. I hope THAT is inspirational to our readers.

ACKNOWLEDGMENTS FROM THOMAS D. NADEAU

I would like to first thank my wonderful wife, Katie, and two sons, Thomas Peter "monkey pants" and Henry Clifford. I cannot imagine being happy without you guys. Life is a journey, and I am glad you guys are walking the road with me. I would also like to thank my parents, Clement and Janina. Without your support and encouragement, I would likely have never made it as an engineer—or at least without Dad's instruction at a young age, I would not be so adept at soldering, tinkering, and exploring new concepts now. It is important to not miss my best friend John LaPadula, who taught me that there is permanence in change, and that is one of those rules to live your life by.

Thank you to my many colleagues, present and past, who pushed me to stretch my imagination in the area of SDN. These folks include but are not limited to David Ward, Dave Meyer, Chris Wright, Sam Aldrin, and our too-soon departed friend Ping Pan.

There are many others from my journey at Cisco, Juniper, CA, and my current employer Brocade Communications who are too numerous to mention. I would like to thank the larger SDN and NFV community and my colleagues at the IETF, ONF, OpenStack, OPNFV, and Open Daylight Project. Thank you to Amy, Brian, and the rest of the staff at Elsevier. It's been a longer-than-expected haul on this one, and we appreciate you supporting and encouraging us along the way.

Thank you to Vishwanathan Jayaraman, Sridhar Ramaswamy, Margaret Chiosi, Anton Ivanov, and Andrew McLachlan for their detailed technical reviews which made the book a whole lot better. Thank you to David Ward and Chris Wright for their insightful Forewords.

Last, but surely not least, I would like to give my heartfelt thanks to Ken Gray, my coauthor on this book. Without you grabbing the other oar of this boat, I am not sure I would have been able to row it myself to the end. Your contributions truly enhanced this book beyond anything I would have imagined myself. You pushed me beyond my limits now for a second time, and since it's not killed me, I think I am better for it!

Introduction

About four or five years ago the basic ideas that comprise what we now commonly refer to as Software Defined Networks (SDN) became popular.

SDN was invented because early proponents of SDN saw that network device vendors were not meeting their needs, particularly in the rapid feature development and innovation spaces. These devices were programmable only through the canonical command line interface or using The Simple Network Protocol; neither met the evolving requirements for rapidly accessible, malleable, application-friendly interfaces.

A few engineers from Stanford University created a protocol called OpenFlow that could be implemented in an architecture comprised of a number of devices containing only data planes to respond to commands sent to them from a logically centralized controller that housed the single control plane for that network. The controller was responsible for maintaining all of the network paths, as well as programming each of the network devices it controlled. The commands and responses to those commands are described in the OpenFlow protocol.

OpenFlow was SDN—or so the mantra of the ONF went. At the time, OpenFlow could even "transmogrify" these platforms to be other devices (eg, firewalls, NAT). Approaches to make a "hybrid" environment with the existing network world went nowhere.

We documented this tectonic technological shift in the networking industry in our first book entitled *SDN: Software Defined Networks, An Authoritative Review of Network Programmability*.[1]

Our book explained that SDN was more than control and data plane separation and more than a single protocol. Our position was that SDN was about the problems of Network Programmability and that SDN solutions could be achieved through a polyglot of protocols.

Since then, SDN technologies have advanced quite a bit and the advent of what we merely scratched the surface on is now being deployed in production networks.

In writing about SDN, we agreed with the need for network programmability to solve the problems of network operators, but we broke with the common, current definition of SDN. Instead, we discussed a concept called Software Driven Networks as opposed to SDN. In the Driven approach, OpenFlow and that architecture was a distinct subset of functionality that is possible.

We pointed out that the purist approach of headless machines replacing every network element generally does not scale well or work well operationally in practice. Behind these observations were concerns in terms of both CAPEX and OPEX with a "clean slate" approach that required network operators to rip and replace all of their gear with newer ones in order to realize any of the benefits of the bold new SDN world.

The large majority of SDN deployments today are in fact "brownfield" networks that evolved by starting as "SDN ready" rather than having SDN enabled. This allowed operators to evolve not only their equipment but also more importantly, their operational control and management systems that interacted with these devices on a schedule that was more amenable to their cost constraints. This meant that much of their existing equipment was preserved until its scheduled lifespan was complete, while SDN capabilities were slowly added.

In that book, we correctly postulated that an SDN use case based on the rapidly growing availability of low cost COTS compute, Network Function Virtualization (NFV), would be the future evolutionary direction of SDN. These two technologies are the primary focus of state-of-the-art networking today.

Writing about NFV today, we find ourselves in the same position—agreeing with the fundamental justifications for NFV, but (as you will see throughout the book) not necessarily with the first-generation architecture proposed for NFV.

In this book, we hope to guide you through the labyrinth of early technology adoption so you can form your own opinions about NFV today and in the future.

Along the way, we will visit the motivations that make NFV so necessary for network operators, the architecture as it was mandated by the ETSI NFV ISG, the ongoing roles of various standards bodies and open source organizations in both setting and realizing the NFV architecture (as it is today) and the evolution of both technology and mindset that might make the NFV solutions of the future.

As with our prior book, we strive to present a vendor neutral viewpoint on the topics we cover.

END NOTE

1. http://shop.oreilly.com/product/0636920027577.do

NETWORK FUNCTION VIRTUALIZATION

INTRODUCTION

Arguably, Network Function Virtualization (NFV) builds on some of the basic and now salient concepts of SDN. These include control/data plane separation, logical centralization, controllers, network virtualization (logical overlays), application awareness, application intent control, and the trend of running all of these on commodity (Commercial Off-The-Shelf (COTS)) hardware platforms. NFV expands these concepts with new methods in support of service element interconnectivity such as Service Function Chaining (SFC) and new management techniques that must be employed to cope with its dynamic, elastic capabilities.

NFV is a complex technical and business topic. This book is structured to cover the key topics in both of these areas that continue to fuel the discussions around both proof-of-concept, and ultimate deployments of NFV.

In this chapter, we will first review the evolution of NFV from its origins in physical proprietary hardware, to its first stage of evolution with the onset of virtualization, and then SDN concepts to what exists at present. We will also demonstrate how these most recent requirements for SDN and specifically NFV requirements have evolved into a consistent set of requirements that are not appearing on any network operator RFP/RFQs over the short course of two years.

By the end of the chapter, we will define what NFV is fundamentally about (and support that definition through the material in the remaining chapters).

As was the case with SDN, our definition may not include the hyperbolic properties you hear espoused by invested vendors or endorse the architectures proposed by ardent devotees of newly evolved interest groups attempting to "standardize" NFV. Rather, we will offer a pragmatic assessment of the value proposition of NFV.

BACKGROUND

In 2013, in our first book covering SDN[1] we described NFV as an application that would manage the splicing together of virtual machines that were deployed as virtualized services (eg, vFirewall) in collaboration with an SDN controller. While the NFV concept continues to have Enterprise application relevance, the evolution of the idea was triggered by a broader set of political/economic realities in the Service Provider industry and technical innovations in areas adjacent and critical to NFV (shown in Fig. 1.1).

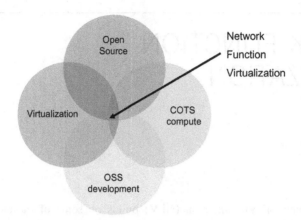

FIGURE 1.1

The innovations that make NFV compelling.

The acceleration of pressure that network operators began to see when we wrote about SDN in 2013 grew into real challenges to their businesses.

- What began as an Over The Top (OTT) video and social media incursion into their broadband customer base expanded into OTT service offerings to their business customers. The outsourcing of Enterprise IT to cloud providers positioned these new competitors as potentially more relevant IT partners. Many were now seeing competition in traditional services like virtual private networking (VPN).
- Wireline operators in particular faced large and long-delayed transitions in copper-based services.
- Wireless operators were also facing a potentially expensive architecture change in the move to LTE to accommodate the growing demand for data services. Complicating this was the growing presence of WiFi while competition put pressure on pricing.

These circumstances led to pressure from investors on traditional service providers to increase operational agility, particularly around service agility (reducing costs through automation, just in time provisioning, resource pooling, etc.) and innovation (create new, sticky, and potentially individualized services). The intended result would be twofold—to compete (or at least find a stable position) with the OTT threat and avoid relegation as mere transport providers and to provide new revenue sources.

Many operators had both wireline and wireless operations that they were seeking to consolidate to cut costs and increase efficiency. Here the impacts are seen largely in reducing operational and capital expense (OPEX and CAPEX).

Meanwhile, virtualization concepts evolved from more Enterprise-centric virtual machine operations (eg, VM-motion) to more compose-able and scalable constructs like containers (in public and private clouds) and open source alternatives in orchestration matured.

Optimized performance for virtualization infrastructure started to receive a huge push through efforts like Intel's Dataplane Development Kit (DPDK)-enabled version of Open vSwitch (OVS)—making the potential throughput of virtualized network functions more attractive.

During this time, cloud computing continued to attract enterprise customers. This not only continued the reduction in COTS costs, but also created an environment in which potentially more service outsourcing may be palatable.

Some highly computer-centric network applications were already beginning to appear as ready-to-run on COTS hardware (eg, IMS, PCRF and other elements of mobile networks), either from incumbents or startups that sensed an easy entry opportunity. Network operators, particularly Tier 1 telcos, were encouraged by the technological gains in virtualization and orchestration over this period and chastened by these business challenges. They responded by working toward establishing what they called next generation network evolutions. Some declared these publicly (eg, AT&T Domain 2.0 or Verizon's SDN/NFV Reference Architecture (https://www.sdxcentral.com/articles/news/verizon-publishes-sdnnfv-reference-architecture/2016/04/)) while others held their cards closer to their vests. In either case, these approaches were all predicated on the promises of SDN and NFV.

REDRAWING NFV AND MISSING PIECES

In our previous book, the functionality spawning the interest in NFV was depicted as the intersection of technological revolutions (Fig. 1.2).

The difference between the view projected in 2013 (Fig. 1.2) and today (Fig. 1.1) is explained by the growth of open source software for infrastructure and some oversights in the original NFV discussion.

Since 2013, there has been an expansion of interest in highly collaborative, multivendor open source environments. Open source software emerged as a very real and viable ingredient of networking and compute environments. This was the case both in the development of orchestration components and SDN controllers based on the Linux operating system, which was already a big

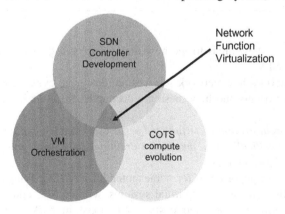

FIGURE 1.2

Our 2013 depiction of the drivers of the NFV use case for SDN.

part of cloud compute. Open source environments are changing the landscape of how compute and network solutions are standardized, packaged, and introduced to the marketplace. So much so, that this interest is often co-opted in what we refer to as "open-washing" of products targeted at NFV infrastructure. To put a point on this, many of these first phase products or efforts were merely proprietary offerings covered by a thin veil of "open" with a vendor-only or single vendor dominant community that used the term "open" as a marketing strategy.

This growing "open mandate" is explored more fully in Chapter 5, The NFV Infrastructure Management (OpenDaylight and OpenStack), Chapter 6, MANO: Management, Orchestration, OSS, and Service Assurance (MANO), and Chapter 7, The Virtualization Layer—Performance, Packaging, and NFV (virtualization) and has replaced the SDN component of the original drawing (as a super-set).

Other chapters will deal with some missing pieces from the original concept of NFV:

- While the virtualization aspects of those early NFV definitions included the concepts of orchestrated overlays (virtual networking), they did not have a firm plan for service chaining. It was the addition of the SFC concept that finally offered a true service overlay (this is covered in Chapter 4: IETF Related Standards: NETMOD, NETCONF, SFC and SPRING).
- Another critical area that was not included in the original calculus of NFV proponents was the Operations Support Systems (OSS) used to operate and manage the networks where NFV will be used. While a very old concept dating back to networks in the 1960s and 1970s, the OSS is undergoing a potential rebirth as an SDN-driven and highly programmable system (this is covered in Chapter 6: MANO: Management, Orchestration, OSS, and Service Assurance).

Without these critical components, NFV is merely virtualized physical devices (or emulations thereof) dropped down on COTS hardware. Ultimately it is the *intersection and combination* of the advancement of the OSS, plus advances in COTS computing to support virtualization and high speed network forwarding at severely lower cost points coupled with the latest trend in open source network software components, and virtualization that together form the complete NFV (and later SFC) story.

DEFINING NFV

Before we explore each of these areas to see how they combine together as the basis for NFV, we should start by defining NFV.

NFV describes and defines how network services are designed, constructed, and deployed using virtualized software components and how these are decoupled from the hardware upon which they execute.

NFV allows for the orchestration of virtualized services or service components, along with their physical counterparts. Specifically, this means the creation, placement, interconnection, modification, and destruction of those services.

Even though there is an opportunity for some potential CAPEX savings and OPEX reduction due to the elasticity of these orchestrated virtual systems, without SFC and a requisite OSS reboot, the same inherent operational issues and costs would exist in NFV that plagued the original services, systems, and networks supporting them.

At its heart, NFV is about service creation. The true value of NFV, particularly in its early phases, is realized in combination with SFC and modernization of the OSS. This may also involve the deconstruction and reconstructed optimization of existing services in defiance of box-based component-to-function mappings dictated by standards or common practice today. Ultimately, it may result in the proliferation of Web-inspired Over-The-Top service implementations.

IS NFV SDN?

SDN is a component of NFV. In some ways it is a related enabler of NFV, but one is not the other, despite some currently confused positioning in the marketplace. With the advent of SDN, orchestration techniques and virtualization advances in COGS hardware, NFV is now being realized albeit slowly. Indications of its utility are the numerous early deployments in production networks today.[2] Just as it caused some rethinking about the control plane, SDN concepts and constructs press service providers and users to rethink the assumptions built into the current method of providing a service plane or delivering services using new virtualized, flexible, and COGS hardware-based service platform. The existence of SDN also affords service providers potentially more flexible ways of manipulating services than they had before.

Virtualization alone does not solve all service deployment problems and actually introduces new reliability problem vectors that a service orchestration system or architecture has to mitigate. Virtualization, like any tool, put into nonskilled hands or deployed improperly, can result in unexpected or disastrous results.

While virtualization is the focus of the NFV effort, the reality is that the orchestration and chaining involved needs to have a scope that includes present and future fully integrated service platforms (at least up to the point where the I/O characteristics of fully virtualized solutions eclipse them and some "tail" period in which they would amortize). Here, SDN can provide a "glue" layer of enabling middle-ware.

Even though the role of SDN in the control of service virtualization appears to be universally accepted, the type of control point or points have been, and will continue to be, much debated. This is a vestige of earlier debates about the nature of SDN itself; whether SDN was single protocol or polyglot and whether SDN was completely centralized control or a hybrid of centralized and distributed. In NFV this manifests in debates around stateless and proxy control points, or when inline or imputed metadata is employed.

Orchestration may allocate the service virtual machine or containers while SDN provides the connectivity in these NFV architectures or models, including some potential abstractions that hide some of the complexity that comes with elasticity.

SDN will be a key early enabler of the IETF Network Service Header (NSH) for service chaining (see Chapter 4: IETF Related Standards: NETMOD, NETCONF, SFC and SPRING).

Orchestration and SDN components will have to work cooperatively to provide high availability and a single management/operations view. In particular, the concepts of services models that abstract away (for network operators) the details of the underlying network are coming onto the scene independent of, but certainly applicable to the NFV movement.

NFV IS THE BASE CASE

The original NFV SDN use case was born from the issues surrounding the construction and composition of new services, or the modification or decomposition of existing ones on traditional proprietary network hardware, or the often-proprietary platform operating systems that ran on these platforms. The challenge of service creation is covered in depth in Chapter 2, Service Creation and Service Function Chaining.

At the time when the "NFV as an SDN use case" was initially proposed, most, if not all, service providers owned and operated some sort of cloud service. Their cloud was used to offer public services, internal services or both. A common theme was the use of some form of virtual machine that hosted a duplicate of a service that used to run on proprietary hardware. To make an even finer point, the service was often really a virtualized image of an entire router or switch.

The basic network orchestration to support this service was built around one of the obvious and new commercial hypervisor offerings on the market, but the provisioning systems used to actually manage or provision these services was often the same one that had been used in the past. These services usually ran on commodity hardware with processors and basic designs from either Intel or AMD.

An example of this is shown in Fig. 1.3 where an EPC that was traditionally offered on proprietary hardware has been broken into its constituent software components and offered to execute on commodity hardware within the Service Provider Cloud.

While orchestration and management of the system is shown here to use some more modern components in order to facilitate control and management of the constituent components, if they were offered as a simple virtualized version of the proprietary hardware offering of the EPC, this could easily be managed by the traditional management software from that vendor—except that it would need to deploy the virtual machine that executed the EPC system software.

End-to-end NFV-vEPC Service Orchestration

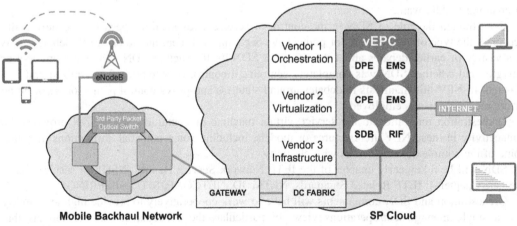

FIGURE 1.3

A virtualized EPC offered as NFV functions within a SP Cloud.

The motivations for that trend were more or less straightforward in that the network operators wanted to reduce their CAPEX expenses by moving from proprietary hardware to commodity hardware. They also wanted to try to reduce operational expenses such as power and cooling, as well as space management expenses (ie, real estate). In this way, racking servers in a common lab consolidates and compacts various compute loads in a more efficient way than services dedicated to a specific service, or proprietary routers and switches before this. This easily can reduce the amount of idle resources by instituting an infrastructure that encourages more efficient utilization of system resources while at the same time powering-down unused resources.

The economics of the Cloud were an important basis of the NFV use case, as was the elasticity of web services.

However, as we all know and understand, the key component missing here is that simply taking an identical (or near identical) copy of, say, the route processor software that use to run on bespoke hardware and now running it on commodity hardware, has relatively small actual cost savings. The point is that in that model, the operator still manages and operates essentially the same monolithic footprint of various processes within a single, large container. The road to optimal bin packing of workloads and its corresponding cost savings, can only be achieved through disaggregation of the numerous services and processes that execute within that canonical envelope, so that only the ones necessary for a particular service are executed. Another perhaps less obvious component missing from this approach is the way these disaggregated components are orchestrated.

One could argue that the NFV marketplace, at least virtualization of services, predated the push made by operators in 2013. Virtualization of a singleton service (a single function) was not a foreign concept, as pure-software (non-dataplane) services like Domain Name Service (DNS) servers were common (at least in service provider operations). Services like policy and security were also leaning heavily toward virtualized, software-only implementations.

The low-hanging fruit that we pointed to in 2013 were processes like Route Reflection (generally speaking, control and management processes), but this was still far from a "virtual router" (Fig. 1.4) that may have a considerable dataplane component. Similarly, the virtual Firewall appliance provided an easy "victory" for first deployments, providing the dataplane requirements were low (applicable to managed security services for small and medium businesses).

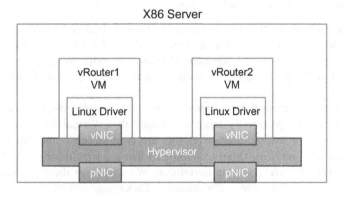

FIGURE 1.4

An example of the simplified NFV base case—a multitenant vRouter implementation using a hypervisor (no bypass).

This actually is only the beginning of what is possible with SDN and NFV. While one could argue that technically speaking, moving composite services from proprietary hardware to COGS hardware in a virtualized form is in fact a decomposition of services, what made the decomposition even more interesting was the potential flexibility in the location and position of these individual components that comprised the service running on those platforms. These fledgling virtualized services enjoyed the added benefit that SDN-based network controls offered, providing the missing link between the original concepts of Software Engineered Paths[3] and virtualization that became NFV. It is the latter that is the real key to unlocking the value of disaggregated service components, by allowing operators (or their operational systems) to optimally and maximally load commodity servers with workload components thereby maximizing their utilization while at the same time enjoying the flexibility of rapid deployment, change or destruction of services components.

STRENGTHENING "NFV AS SDN USE CASE"

What really made the use case seem more viable in such a short time were the aforementioned improvements in virtualization and dataplane performance on COTS compute. The combination of the two should theoretically place downward pressure on the cost per bit to process network traffic in a virtualized environment.

IMPROVING VIRTUALIZATION

In 2013, we showed the following taxonomy for virtualizing services (shown in Fig. 1.5):

- services implemented in a machine with multiple/compartmentalized OS(s)
- services implemented within the hypervisor
- services implemented as distributed or clustered as composites
- services on bare metal machines
- services implemented in Linux virtual containers

At the time, we pointed out that virtual machines provide tremendous advantages with respect to management,[4] and thus were pursued as a primary vehicle for NFV, but also had some hurdles to be considered (eg, contention, management visibility, security, resource consumption). Since then, the two most significant changes have occurred in the rise of alternative service virtualization and orchestration.

Containers have now entered the mainstream and have recently begun forays into true open source. Although they face potentially more challenges than Virtual Machines in shared-tenant environments, they offer packaging alternatives that are more efficient and can be used to (potentially) more compose-able services. Other technologies that use hybrids of the VM/container environments and micro-kernels have also been introduced. We will cover these alternatives as a section of Chapter 7, The Virtualization Layer—Performance, Packaging, and NFV.

The orchestration of virtual compute solidified over this timeframe, with multiple releases of OpenStack Nova and other projects giving NFV planners more confidence in an Open Source

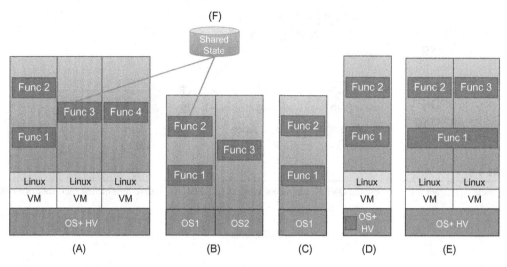

FIGURE 1.5

Our now-in complete taxonomy of virtualization options for NFV from 2013: hypervisor partitioned (A), compartmentalized OS (B), bare metal (C), hypervisor imbedded (D), and distributed/clustered composite functions (E). Two of these methods (A and B) also are depicted sharing state through shared storage (F).

alternative to the traditional Enterprise orchestration dominance of companies like VMware. The additions of projects like Tacker have real potential to give operators all the tools necessary to realize these goals. These technologies are discussed in detail within the context of the OpenStack movement in Chapter 6, MANO: Management, Orchestration, OSS, and Service Assurance and Chapter 7, The Virtualization Layer—Performance, Packaging, and NFV.

DATA PLANE I/O AND COTS EVOLUTION

In our last book we made the statement that "Generally speaking, advances in data-plane I/O have been key enablers to running services on COTS hardware." The original leverage of DPDK against the hypervisor virtual switch (OVS) performance overhead we cited (OVDK via https://01.org/) has evolved—multiple times (Fig. 1.6).

The DPDK[5] is Intel's innovation in I/O virtualization improvements. DPDK provides data plane libraries and optimized (poll-mode) NIC drivers (for Intel NICs). These exist in Linux user space providing advanced queue and buffer management as well as flow classification through a simple API interface (supported via a standard tool chain—gcc/icc, gdb, profiling tools). These all have been shown to vastly improve performance of nonoptimized systems significantly.

When we released our SDN book in August 2013, the version at the Intel sponsored site was 0.5. Eight releases later, 1.1 shipped (August, 2014). Intel subsequently ceased their fork of OVS and sought to integrate into the main distribution of Linux. That version integrated the 1.7 release

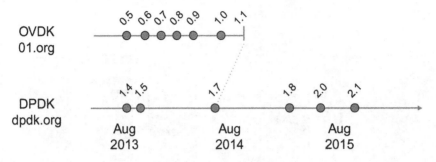

FIGURE 1.6

Intel made significant improvements in OVDK, ultimately integrating DPDK 1.7 before terminating their fork of OVS.

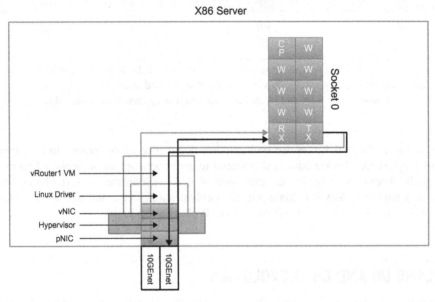

FIGURE 1.7

Our hypothetical vRouter (illustrating the base NFV use case) using multiple threads on multiple cores to scale performance.

of the DPDK, which continues development. This has been aided by an Intel processor architecture that has evolved through a full "tick-tock" cycle[6] in the intervening 2 years.

In 2014, Intel introduced their Haswell micro-architecture and accompanying 40 Gbps and 4×10 Gbps NICs, increasing core density and changing cache/memory architectures to be more effective at handling network I/O.[6]

This has been particularly useful and influential in driving the scale-up performance of the virtualized router or switch in our base use case. In Fig. 1.7, the appliance uses ten cores in a socket to support 20 Gbps throughput (a core/management thread, seven worker threads, a receive and a transmit thread). Another important advance has been how other processor vendors have entered the picture and positioned themselves as PCIe-based offload engines for the Intel architecture or directly challenging Intel as THE processor for NFV.

These advancements are described in Chapter 8, NFV Infrastructure—Hardware Evolution and Testing.

Both Intel and software vendors using their architecture are claiming support of theoretical dataplane throughput in excess of 100 Gbps (typically, 120 Gbps for SandyBridge and up to 180 Gbps for IvyBridge variants). Alternative "forwarders" for the dataplane have also emerged (both proprietary and open).

The evolution of state-of-the-art in forwarding (and its continuing challenges) on the Intel architecture is described in both Chapter 7, The Virtualization Layer—Performance, Packaging, and NFV and Chapter 8, NFV Infrastructure—Hardware Evolution and Testing.

STANDARDIZING AN NFV ARCHITECTURE

The most critical standards for NFV are only now evolving and some may never evolve in a traditional SDO environment (but through Open Source projects and de-facto standardization).

Today, from a standards perspective, the horizon has broadened. As the original ETSI NFV process concluded with no real API definitions or standards, work on some of the necessary gaps has begun in the IETF (see Chapter 4: IETF Related Standards: NETMOD, NETCONF, SFC and SPRING), starting with SFC.

The data modeling part that we predicted would be a critical outcome of MANO work in 2013 is being realized more in OpenDaylight and IETF NETMOD than anywhere else (and is now trickling into other projects like OpenStack). If fact, an explosion of modeling is occurring as of 2015 in functionality like routing and service definition.

Many of the same actors that participated in that early ETSI work moved into the ONF to propose architecture workgroups on L4-L7 services in attempt to define APIs for service chaining and NFV (albeit around the single protocol, OpenFlow).

The growth of neo-SDOs like the ONF and the attempt to move work of groups like the ETSI NFV WG into "normative" status, along with the rise of open source communities, brings forward the question of governance. Many of the newly minted "open" products are readily verified through third parties (or the use of tools like "git") to actually be closed (all or most of the contributions are made and controlled by a single company positioning itself as sole-source of support/revenue from the project).

A great talk on the need for the cooperation of standards and open source as well as governance was given by Dave Ward at the IETF 91 meeting, and is captured in his blog.[7]

THE MARKETPLACE GREW ANYWAY

In 2013, we noted that the existence of the ETSI workgroup should not imply that this is the only place service virtualization study and standards development are being conducted. Even then, without standards, production service virtualization offerings were already coming to market.

This remains the case, although we have already gone through some early progression in virtualization of traditional network products and some shakeout of startups focused on this market. For example:

- The startups we mentioned in our previous book, LineRate and Embrane, have both been acquired (by F5 Networks and Cisco Systems, respectively) and their products and, to some degree their teams, appear to be assimilated into the operations of these companies. The controllers they were originally positioning for Layer 2 through Layer 7 that worked with their own virtualized services have yet to gain market traction or disappeared entirely.
- Almost every vendor of routing products now offers a virtualized router product. In fact, VNFs for most service functions now proliferate and new startups are being acquired by larger, existing vendors or named as partners to build VNF catalogues in market segments that they may not have competed before (eg, Brocade acquires Connectem giving them a vEPC product[9] and Juniper partners with Acclaim).
- Service orchestration products like Tail-F (acquired by Cisco Systems) that leverage the aforementioned service-model concept saw widespread adoption.
- Interest in VIM-related open source components like OpenDaylight and OpenStack emerged.

ACADEMIC STUDIES ARE STILL RELEVANT

"Middlebox" studies that we pointed to in 2013[9,11] in the academic community continue to inform ongoing NFV work in the areas of service assurance, performance, and placement. Some of these studies[12] provide hints that may be applicable to compose-ability in the future and making the concept of "function" more fungible.

While academic studies can at times make assumptions that are less applicable in actual operation, academic work buttressing NFV understanding has expanded in the areas of resource management (including bandwidth allocation in WAN), telemetry/analytics, high-availability[13] and policy—all of which were under-explored in early NFV work.

NFV AT ETSI

The attempt by network operators (largely from the telco community) to define NFV architecture is covered in detail in Chapter 3, ETSI NFV ISG. Be forewarned—it is an ongoing story. While many of its contributors may refer to ETSI NFV as a "standard," it is (at best) an "incomplete" architecture.

In our original description of the activity we pointed with hope to three workgroups as the keys to success of the architecture effort—MANO, INF, and SWA (Fig. 1.8).

Today, even though desired functionality has been defined, much of the necessary practical definitions expected in these architectural components remains undone—particularly in the challenge areas of performance, resource management, high-availability, and integration.

Some of these may be settled in a future phase of ETSI work, but a timing issue for early adopters looms.

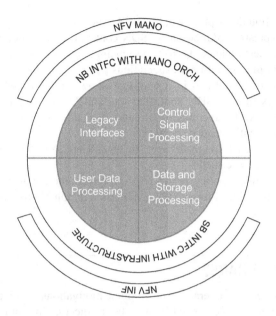

FIGURE 1.8

Our original depiction of the relationship between MANO, SWA, and INF workgroups.

Management and Orchestration (MANO) work did not lead directly to new management tools to augment traditional OAM&P models to handle virtualized network services. Chapter 6 covers the oversights in NFV Orchestration related to interfaces with legacy OSS/BSS and the complete lack of Service Assurance. Individual vendors and their customers are sorting through this today. The roles of various managers (VIM and NFVO) are still being debated/defined in an ongoing phase of ETSI work.

Resource management that was envisioned as part of the orchestration layer was defined in terms of capacity but not capability—the latter a problem that emerges in the heterogeneous environments described in Chapter 7, The Virtualization Layer—Performance, Packaging, and NFV and Chapter 8, NFV Infrastructure—Hardware Evolution and Testing.

Minimization of context switching happened organically as a requirement to expand Intel's market (previously described), through research projects in academia uncoupled from the influence of ETSI NFV Infrastructure (INF) workgroup and through competition. The identification of a "best practice" has proven to be a moving target as a result.

ETSI Software Architecture (NFV SWA) published work remained VM-centric. While they chanced into describing the decomposition of functions into subcomponents they did not define the anticipated descriptors that would used to communicate the relationships and communication between the parts, operational behavior, and constraints (eg, topology). The approach here was anticipated to be model driven, and follow-on "open source" activities in MANO have attempted to define these. A number of examples such as the Open-O effort. More details on these are given in Chapter 7, The Virtualization Layer—Performance, Packaging, and NFV.

These anticipated function descriptors would act like the familiar concept of policies attached to SDN "applications" as expressed-to/imposed-on SDN controllers. Such policies specify each application's routing, security, performance, QoS, "geo-fencing," access control, consistency, availability/disaster-recovery, and other operational expectations/parameters.

Such descriptors were to be defined in a way that allows flow-through provisioning. That is, while the orchestration system and SDN controller can collaborate on placement, path placement and instantiation of the network functions, their individual and composite configurations can be quite complex—and are currently vendor-specific.

Much of this ultimately fell through to work in OpenStack, YANG modeling in other SDOs, projects in OPNFV or is still undefined.

Some basic attempts to inject policy in the NFV process came about through the Group Based Policy project in the OpenDaylight Project and an experimental plugin to OpenStack Neutron.

NFV—WHY SHOULD I CARE?

The potential benefits to network operators are implicit motivations to adopt NFV. Again, in this book we are not questioning whether NFV will be a success in both Service Provider and Enterprise networks, but rather the forms of its architecture and evolution, the original assumptions behind it and how they have changed, the degree to which it is or can be standardized (and other topics). Most importantly we are concerned with increasing your understanding of the topic.

For the individual reading this book, you are more than likely directly or indirectly affected by the future of NFV.

The personnel implications of these initiatives cannot be ignored within the companies that champion NFV. To be successful, the employee bases of companies aggressively deploying NFV have to transition mindset and skills from Network Operator to Network DevOps.

The idea is to "do more with less" to cope with scale and agility competitive pressures via automation. NFV will affect careers in networking at both enterprises and service providers going forward. Though there may be other observable ways to measure the impact of NFV, because OPEX is the largest contributor to costs for operators and OPEX is often equated with "people costs," perhaps the most visible realization of NFV will be through the reduction of headcount.

Similarly, the industry serving these companies will also have to change.

For equipment manufacturers, software companies and integrators, the implications are just as potentially drastic. Different research firms show the market for NFV related products and services.

Though analysts divide the attribution of revenue differently between SDN, VNFs, Infrastructure software (SDN), and Orchestration, the movement has been steadily "up and to the right" for market predictions. The more recent the estimate, the more optimistic the predictions get.

Growth is estimated to rise from a $1B market in 2014 at a combined aggregate growth rate north of 60% over the next 5 years leading (in the most optimistic case) to a double-digit billion dollar overall market (Fig. 1.9).[14-16]

Parts of the underlying predictions are not quite what one would expect from the early discussions of NFV.

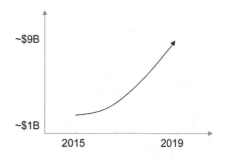

FIGURE 1.9

Up and to the right. Analysts predict big growth for an NFV market.

- Physical infrastructure (switches, compute, storage) represents a small part of these revenues. The overall market shift for equipment from traditional purpose-built service appliances to NFV based equipment is of the same relative magnitude (ie, the overall market shift for network equipment is about the same). The projected magnitude (between a 10% and 20% shift), while not as drastic as some NFV advocates imagine, is enough to get the attention of the incumbent vendors.
- The big expenditures are expected in MANO and the VNFs themselves. It is humorous to note that most of the discussion in 2015 is around Infrastructure software components (SDN and virtualization management), perhaps since it is the only well-understood section of the proposed NFV architecture and vendors may feel it is a key control point (to control competitive ingress into accounts). While SDN and Orchestration are not insignificant, the lion's share of the predicted software market is driven by VNFs, particularly wireless service virtualization (IMS, PCRF, EPC, and GiLAN components like DPI).
- There is a significant amount of separately tracked revenue associated with outsourcing services approximately equivalent to the Infrastructure piece (with similar growth rates) that goes hand-in-hand with the personnel problems of the target NFV market.

The analysts seem to converge around that fact that (contrary to the belief that NFV is creating vast new market segments) NFV represents a "shift" in expenditure largely into already existing segments.

ENABLING A NEW CONSUMPTION MODEL

For the provider, a side effect of NFV is that it enables a new consumption model for network infrastructure. By moving services off their respective edge termination platforms (EPG, BNG, CMTS), providers are positioned to transition to the consumption of "merchant" based network equipment.

Although the definition of "merchant" is contentious, it is not associated with high touch feature capabilities or high session state scale. Instead, the focus of this equipment becomes termination, switching and transport with a minimum feature capability (like QoS and multicast) to support the services in the service overlay. Arguably, providers cannot consume "merchant" without a parallel NFV plan to remove features and states from their equipment.

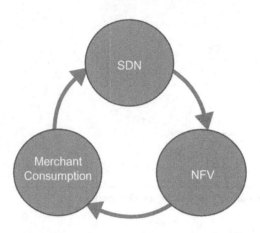

FIGURE 1.10

The SDN—NFV—Merchant cycle.

Strangely enough, once this consumption begins, the control plane and management plane flexibility (mapping control and management 1:1 or 1:N in a merchant underlay) potentially brings us back to SDN (this cycle is illustrated in Fig. 1.10).

Often, the move to NFV and the subsequent realization of merchant platforms—coupled with SDN control—makes the network more access agnostic and leads to end-to-end re-evaluation of the IP network used for transport. In turn, this leads to new means of translating its value to applications like Segment Routing.[17]

CONCLUSIONS

Providers are currently announcing the pilot implementations of what are mostly "low hanging fruit" transformations of integrated service platforms emulating existing service offerings.

None of it is yet the transformative service creation engine that portends a true change in operation and competitiveness.

Deployment of the first functions and some NFVI has indeed started, yet NFV standardization is incomplete and its future is now spread across multiple non-ETSI initiatives for more practical definitions—including open source.

The pace of COTS and virtualization innovation is outstripping the ability of any organization to recommend a relevant "best practice" for deployment.

And, while "service chaining" is often conflated with NFV, we have been clear to define NFV as the base case of any service chained NFV component. In this way, a single NFV service is a Service Chain with a single element connected to a network at least once. As straightforward as this observation may be, getting that base case right is critical to the efficacy of SFC.

The improvements of NFV currently leveraged are primarily in the scale up and down (in situ) of services. We will discuss this further in the chapter on SFC, but for now we hope that we have given you a sufficient and detailed introduction to NFV.

The overall number of functional elements, service chains and the constraints on how those chains are constructed and operate need to be defined and may only be known through trial deployments and experimentation.

However, these chains will have to incorporate both virtual and nonvirtual service elements. There is no ready greenfield for most NFV deployments unless they are incredibly simple monotonic functions.

All the while, behind the scenes, traditional OSS/BSS is not really designed to manage the highly decomposed services of NFV, and the NFV Orchestration/SDN pairings will have to provide a transition. These systems will need to evolve and be adapted to the new future reality of virtualized network services that NFV promises.

More than two years have elapsed since operators began announcements detailing Next Generation business and architecture plans that hinged on NFV.

This discontinuity between readiness—the absence of standards, the apparent incomplete understanding of the complexities in service chaining and OSS integration, a potential misunderstanding of the actual market—and willingness (planned rapid adoption), lead to the conclusion that the process of "getting NFV right" will be iterative.

Throughout the coming chapters, a number of important questions arise (hopefully reading the book will help you develop your own answers). Here are a few high-level questions around the NFV proposition for the end of our first chapter:

- Are the assumptions and model originally behind NFV still valid?
- How big will the ultimate savings be and how much of the costs will just be shifted?
- With so much unspecified or under-specified, how "fixed" is the architecture of NFV after ETSI and is dogmatic pursuit of its architecture adding any value? Are we "crossing the chasm" too soon? Will the missing definitions from the phase one ETSI model be somehow defined in a later phase in time for consumers to care?
- What will be the role of Open Source software going forward?
- Are network operators REALLY going to change fundamentally?

We cannot promise to answer them all, but will hopefully provide some observations of our own and pointers to material that will help you form your own opinions.

END NOTES

1. http://shop.oreilly.com/product/0636920027577.do
2. https://www.sdxcentral.com/articles/news/how-att-honed-its-sdn-nfv-plan-code-first-tweak-later/2015/05/
3. Guichard et al.
4. A short list of management benefits: VM lifecycle management, storage management, VM placement optimization, VM snapshots, VM migration, disaster recovery, performance monitoring, compliance management and capacity management.
5. Intel has developed a DPDK-enhanced version of OVS for the public domain and works with major virtualization projects (KVM, Xen, UML, xVM).
6. On the "tick," Intel releases a new micro-architecture and on the "tock" improves process technology. At the time we wrote the book on SDN, Sandy Bridge micro-architecture had just been introduced.

7. The Haswell architecture moved the Intel Xeon product family from version 2 to version 3 and increased the range of cores from 6 to 10 per socket to 8 to 12 (depending on the model).
8. This was presented by David Ward at both the lunchtime speaker spot at IETF 91 http://recordings.conf. meetecho.com/Playout/watch.jsp?recording=IETF91_SPEAKER_SERIES&chapter=LUNCH&t=1024 and in his blog http://blogs.cisco.com/news/open-standards-open-source-open-loop.
9. http://www.bizjournals.com/sanjose/blog/techflash/2015/03/brocade-acquires-software-company-connectem. html
10. http://minds.wisconsin.edu/bitstream/handle/1793/61606/stratos_tech_report.pdf?sequence=3
11. http://www.opennetsummit.org/pdf/2013/research_track/poster_papers/final/ons2013-final28.pdf
12. http://www.opennetsummit.org/pdf/2013/research_track/poster_papers/final/ons2013-final51.pdf
13. http://www.cs.berkeley.edu/~justine/ftmb-final.pdf
14. Some of these projections are from private/paid services and cannot be directly quoted here. Public prognostications are listed in the next few links.
15. http://www.lightreading.com/author.asp?section_id=222&doc_id=705403&piddl_msgid=148524&piddl_msgposted=yes - msg_148524
16. http://www.analysysmason.com/About-Us/News/Insight/NFV-SDN-forecasts-Jun2014-RMA16/
17. Segment Routing is being defined in the IETF SPRING workgroup. It affords a label based forwarding paradigm for path control that can be managed via a centralized or distributed control plane without the need for tunnel state in the network. Further, the path can be determined by setting a label stack at the source.

SERVICE CREATION AND SERVICE FUNCTION CHAINING

INTRODUCTION

Whether we're talking about corporate/enterprise/IT applications and networks that support them (in order to provide competitive advantage within a vertical business grouping), or the services created by carriers in support of, or to entice/secure the business of, enterprise or broadband subscribers, network operators (enterprise or service provider) differentiate through service creation.

In this chapter we will take a preliminary look at the historical problems in service creation that drive the ideas behind service function chaining (SFC) and the potential of the SFC solution. In latter chapters, these will be refined in our discussion of efforts to standardize and optimize the solution space of SFC.

DEFINITIONS

Anyone involved with one of the numerous Standards Development Organizations grappling with Network Function Virtualization (NFV) will notice that there is a lot of debate over simple terminology. This often leads to arguments, confusion and a general lack of understanding of what is trying to be accomplished.

For the sake of making this book easier to follow, we will choose a set of terminology and (hopefully) remain consistent throughout the text. Because we will go into greater detail on both the ETSI and IETF work around SFC, this will not yet be exhaustive, nor is it necessarily authoritative. We are sure our editors will hound us for future updates to this text in order to keep up with the evolution in this space.

Network Service—A network service is any computational service that has a network component. Some of these functions can discriminate or otherwise manipulate individual network flows. Or as the IETF SFC Architecture document defines it: "An offering provided by an operator that is delivered using one or more service functions."

Service Function—Again, the IETF document does a good job here in its definition: "A function that is responsible for specific treatment of received packets." Of course, a network element providing a service function, be it virtual or the traditional, highly integrated device (described below) may provide more than one service function—in which case we would call it a "composite" service function.

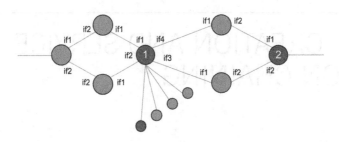

FIGURE 2.1

Chains, paths, and instances.

In the illustration in Fig. 2.1, the service may be an access application that requires two distinct functions for the service. If it helps to give a more concrete example, think of these functions as a firewall identified as the node numbered "1" and a Network Address Translation function as the node numbered "2." These virtualized network functions are connected together and may forward traffic to and from each other as if they were real devices with physical cabling connecting each.

Service Chain—A Service Chain is the ordered set of functions that embody a "service." This is generally the case excluding the derivative cases where a "service" can be delivered via a single function or a single composite function (eg: our "base" case in the preceding chapter). Services that are chained also imply an ordering or *direction* of traffic flow across service functions. That is, services can be chained in a unidirectional or serial fashion, where traffic enters on the left-hand side, traverses the services left-to-right and exits at the right-most service point.

However, Services can be chained in arbitrary ways too. Given the example from Fig. 2.1, one can imagine traffic entering on the left side of service function 1, being processed, and leaving via one of the links to its right and being passed to service function 2. However, we strongly recommend that the service definition include not only the functional definitions but also *order* of their traversal in the definition of the chain. So, using Fig. 2.1 as an example, we could define the traffic flow as { <if1> → function1 → <if2> function2 → egress <if3> } meaning that traffic enters function 1 via interface 1, is processed, exits via interface 2, goes to function 2 and is processed, and finally exits via interface 3. Also please keep in mind that as we previously mentioned, this does not have to be a linear progression, as some services can and do "branch" (eg, depending on the result of the function operation), so more complex definitions are possible.

Fig. 2.2 illustrates a hypothetical branching service chain. Initial classification may direct the flow to service function 1. Normal processing would result in the forwarding of the network flow to service function 2 via the lower interface. However, when function 1 is executed, the flow might exceed an operational threshold or fail some inspection step that results in redirection to an anomaly treatment service function using the upper interface towards 2′. (For example, function 1 could be a DPI service that detects an embedded attack and forwards the traffic to a mitigation/logging function—which may be located more centrally in the network.)

The expression of this chain might look like { <if1> →lambda (function1) → (<if2> function2 → egress <if3>, <if3> function 2′ → egress <null>)}.[1]

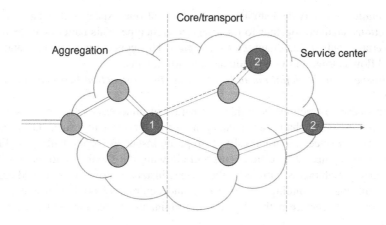

Core/transport

Aggregation

Service center

FIGURE 2.2

A "branching" service chain.

Service Path—The Service Path is the logical path within the forwarding context between the service functions. The actual path is determined by the classification of a flow at any given point in time. The service path identifies the service and thus the chain of service function points that the flow traverses for inspection, processing or treatment if any exists other than default forwarding. Note that there is nothing in the definition of the service path that says how the flow should get from ingress to the first entity in the path, the first entity to the second entity, or the second entity and egress. The purpose in this ambiguity is to allow the operator to deploy a number of networking strategies: VLAN segmentation, overlay routing, etc. and if they choose, to simply allow for a default "shortest path" forwarding.

In our example (Fig. 2.1), the service path identifies specific network entities that the flow should visit in order to experience the defined service {address_function1, address_function2}. Conversely, the set of resulting nodes can vary and depend on the actual run time state of the system as is shown in Fig. 2.2.

Service Instance—A Service Instance is a further logical construct that combines with the service path to allow for service elasticity. The path should get the flow forwarded to a particular location in the network that in the abstract we call a "node." A node may in turn share through a number of potential mechanisms, an address. This in fact can be implemented as a pool of instances of a function if one considered "cloud" instantiations of the functions as separate servers, Virtual Machines (VMs) or containers that are managed to scale with demand.

In our example (Fig. 2.1), the first identified function (function1) may be managing a larger pool of devices that execute its associated function. The highlighted device is an *instance* of the service, and as such a number of them may actually exist at any given time. For example, in a multi-tenant cloud environment, different instances of a firewall function might exist and be instantiated to process traffic per tenant. In this way, the service description, definition and chain can be viewed much in the way as service *templates*. The selection of the instance and its management can be done locally by the macro entity identified in the path or globally/centrally (eg, by a controller).

Service Templates—A Service Template is simply what one expects—it is pattern of one or all of Service Functions, chained together to for a service archetype. This pattern can be instantiated at will, within a certain context (ie, tenant, customer, etc.). This concept is similar to, and often implemented as, workflow automation in operational support systems.

The critical aspects in the definition of SFC include the abstraction between "chains," "paths" and "instances."

The power of these abstractions is in the elimination of unnecessary friction in service management. For example, a single chain can manifest as many service paths such that a large operator (eg, multinational) may select geographically appropriate instances for the path thus eliminating the need to manage geographically specific chains and allowing the flexibility to use instances from a wider range of function elements. Similarly, the service instance allows a single addressable service function to become logical—hiding an expanding and contracting pool of instances that are not explicitly exposed in the service path. This in turn eliminates the requirement to manage a service path per instance.

What we have not yet defined, but is just as critical to SFC, are the roles played by management and policy. These include considerations such as business, security, and network elements in the creation of "paths" from "chains." This part of the picture will fill out more when we get to the details of work in various standards bodies related to SFC.

THE SERVICE CREATION PROBLEM

Until the advent of formalized SFC, most service offerings required highly integrated devices that were typically packaged as a single physical network element. By leveraging some clever tricks in DNS and IP addressing, some services started to appear as a more loosely coupled group of network elements (providing some lateral scalability) while remaining still highly pipelined or chained from a networking perspective. However by combining the virtualization of NFV with the locational independence of SFC, we can create, destroy and modify *very* loosely coupled services at very rapid rates. Moreover, we can augment those services on the fly in some cases, with a few keystrokes or even in an automated fashion.

Examples of this evolution are depicted in Fig. 2.3.

A QUICK HISTORY

Historically, when a service was deployed, each of the physical service elements comprising the service had to be manually coupled together, most often by deploying new/more devices and physically connecting them together. While these configurations were closed, proprietary, and limited to a small set of specific functions, a network operator was free to arbitrarily chain them together as needed.

An evolution of this approach occurred when some products could support multiple service functions on a single physical device. These services were sometimes "sliced" in that multiple copies of the same service could execute within rudimentary environments that were the precursor to the modern hypervisor. Inside of these offerings was (arguably) the start of NFV as well as SFC.

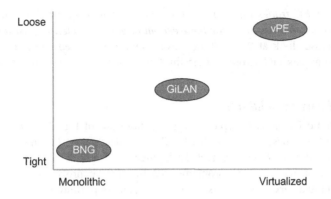

FIGURE 2.3

Integration and virtualization. The evolution from tightly integrated services to highly virtualized and decoupled with some examples of actual services.

Since functions were colocated on a single device, this at first limited most physical changes to things such as running short cables between line cards on the same box, and ultimately eliminated physical change by moving the cabling to internal connections that could be programmed in software.

While network services could be manipulated arbitrarily on these devices, they were still limited to the confines of that device and functions offered. So network services implemented within these closed, proprietary systems that needed to be chained with those on other devices to create services, ultimately still required physical intervention.

While generally rare and not obvious to most at the time, the Virtual Network Function did exist. For example, a few cases such as DNS, DHCP, and Radius could execute on general compute, but were generally not viewed as a virtualized service function, nor were those services viewed as "chained" together with others.

Most recently, modern NFV generalized such specialization into virtualized service functions that execute within a virtualized environment on Commercial Off The Shelf (COTS) compute. These environments are connected via networks that allow for easy and seamless multi-tenancy, in many cases without the network functions being aware that they are executing in such environments.

Since these virtualized elements all run within the context of a virtual environment, including the networks that attach them, operators are now free to move or change them without the burden of physically doing anything. What the virtualized storage, compute and network environment now represents is a general substrate in which to position and manipulate these resources. Of course, these virtualized elements are at some point, connected to at least one physical network element, and in some cases are connected multiple times in heterogeneous configurations but the point is that an entire virtualized world can be created to create and maintain the services that requires nearly no physical cabling or manual intervention to standup, modify, or destroy.

What was just described is referred to as Network Service Chaining (NSC) or SFC. SFC and NSC expand the reach of NFV, by allowing autonomy in the physical placement of the elements, enabling the concept of a Service Overlay.

In doing so, NSC/SFC trades off some performance that was afforded in more tightly coupled service architectures, as compensation for the freedom of general function positioning.

We can take a closer look at the evolution from tightly integrated solutions and "loosely coupled appliance" techniques and explore their limitations to appreciate what a virtualized service overlay might offer.

Tightly integrated service solutions

In a tightly integrated offering as is depicted in the bottom left of Fig. 2.3, the problems in service creation are many. We discussed some of these earlier in this chapter, but they are generally related to increased friction and cost around services deployment.

There are several business-related problems that impact the profitability of service providers that use tightly integrated service solutions to create revenue opportunities:

- An operator could be locked into certain services architecture by going with a particular vendor. If one vendor prefers one type of provisioning mechanism and supports some set of functions, and a new one comes along that supports one that is needed for a new service, this introduces undue friction in deploying that service.
- A vendor might employ a pricing strategy that might incentivize customers to purchase certain well-packaged solutions that work well within the confines of those supported, prepackaged service functions, but not with others. This also introduces potential friction to services deployment.

At the macroeconomic level, tightly integrated solutions can impact customer−vendor relationships. Purchasing leverage is constrained where a lack of competition exists towards the bottom left of Fig. 2.3, or may be enabled by competition towards the top right. In general, network service solutions have come from a handful of vendors, and they have dominated the service function market with their often proprietary and invariably antiquated interfaces to their equipment that dictate behaviors in the OSS.[2] However, as we move towards the world depicted in the upper right of the figure, the disruption of challengers emerges.

There is a laundry list of operational concerns with highly integrated service architectures, including:

- The chosen vendor may not have expertise in all the related functions resulting in weaker implementations.
- The vendor implementation may not be at all modular or interoperate with other vendors' offerings.
- The vendor software maintenance strategies may not allow easy patching and fixing (Service Software Upgrade).
- Time to market constraints due to the fact that service functions must exist on proprietary hardware. Solutions must be implemented by the vendor and thus cannot be deployed until such time as said vendor implements the function.

The overall combination of a poor vendor architecture/development cycle and an operator upgrade cycle that is spread out to minimize risk and churn can at best create undue resistance to service deployment velocity, but at worst, create a bottleneck to innovation and evolution of services.

Implementations of tightly integrated service platforms often have to balance the management of state with network forwarding capacity, resulting in somewhat rigid designs that balance service

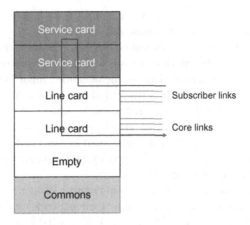

FIGURE 2.4

Highly integrated service element—typical of traditional BNG.

blades and network blades connected to a common fabric. The result of such a trade-off is that service deployment flexibility and agility suffers.

For the broadband network gateway (BNG) example (Fig. 2.4) typical designs are implemented as a modular chassis containing blades that implement different service functions. One generation of service blades may be designed and used to scale a certain number of control sessions (Radius/PCEF), subscriber state management, address assignment services (DHCP), DPI (APPID), and NAT (this is a nonexhaustive list).

As generations progress, subsequent generations are often designed with more scalable versions of these existing services, but sometimes less scale is possible as a sacrifice to supporting some newly introduced service function.

The internal connectivity between a service card and the forwarding line card may be (worst case) statically allocated through a command line interface (CLI) or dynamically allocated through a management demon in the bundled operating system.

Operators calculate and size these devices to support services they sell (such as broadband subscriber access) that are mapped onto the aforementioned functions that are chained together on the BNG.

If the operator miscalculates the nature of service uptake at a particular point of presence or if the vendor provides poor matches because of internal environmental limits that exist on the service cards such as chassis power or mismatches in the line/service card capacities, these capacity limits can result in unrealized opportunity or valuable assets stranded. Worse, service providers might continue to miss opportunities to sell new services when delays are encountered racking and stacking a new device.

The operator is not spared the challenges of elasticity or high availability by this high level of integration, although some of these architectural hurdles can be internalized within the vendor architecture through high availability of these systems such as dual control processors for the platform, active–active/active–standby state management across cards within a system or external system pairing using a heartbeat mechanism and some protocol that asserts a common next-hop IP address. These additions sometimes require additional hardware such as monitors within the chassis and redundant physical elements.

Note that one of the "features" (satirically speaking) of the highly integrated elements is the inability to pool resources between multiple elements.

With these tightly coupled elements, it should be obvious that new services (eg, requiring a new function that can be used in a different combination with existing service elements) are predominantly implemented by the device vendor. That is, the operator cannot build this himself/herself on the device, nor can they purchase the function from another vendor and run that on this hardware.

As the demand for features (functions required to implement an additional or enhanced service) across a vendor's customer base for a device grows, production of any one feature may slow, resulting in another related problem with tightly integrated systems called *feature velocity friction.*

This results in a similar service deployment velocity at customers using those devices as they wait for new software and hardware to be delivered.

A network operator can choose to purchase an alternative device from another vendor, but at the added expense of integrating a new system into their network and operations. Depending on how "sticky" a vendor can make their device, this can lead to what is often called a *vendor lock-in.*

Loosely coupled—toward NFV/SFC

Like the BNG, the Gi-LAN was originally a very tightly coupled service (Fig. 2.5). Until approximately 2010, the Gi-LAN designs were like those in the (A) section of the drawing. The chain per

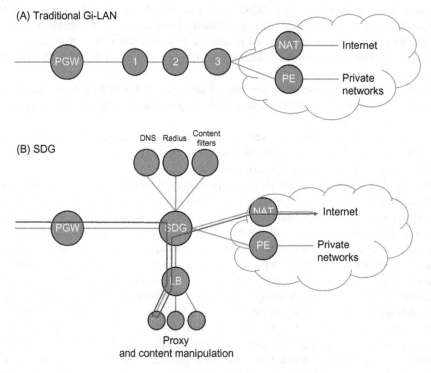

FIGURE 2.5

The Gi-LAN of a wireless network service center: (A) as an original conceptual implementation and (B) with a SDG.[3]

customer from the Packet Gateway (PGW) was varied in the functions themselves, unshared and physically rigid.

Around 2010, the Service Delivery Gateway (SDG)[4] allowed for a loose coupling for more specialization in the functions, albeit still with dedicated appliances. Over time, further evolution of the mobile architecture (in general) has occurred to take advantage of SFC.

Note that in the illustration above, the SDG is working as a classifier and implements policy. All of the subsequent functions are constrained to a logical one-hop radius, creating a physical pipeline in a constrained topology with basic service steering by the aforementioned policy.

In solving some of the problems of tightly integrated solutions, however, a few new problems in service creation are introduced.

The first of these new problems is configuration complexity.

This affects operational costs. If each function supports a different methodology for configuring the service and managing the device, integration becomes even more difficult. Naturally, there should be less of a concern if the products come from the same vendor, but this is not always the case (eg, acquired products can take a while to normalize themselves to the acquiring vendor's CLI semantic and syntax or OSS methodologies and hooks). This can leave the operator with the same potential vendor lock-in and services deployment velocity dilemma described in the tightly integrated solution.

There are lesser complications arising from the configuration complexity around the capability of the functional components to process configuration changes, which can be limited but not eliminated both by chosen protocol and vendor-implemented methodology. Historically, these arcana led to the rise of intermediary mitigation systems such as solutions from BNG, CA, Op-Net, and Tail-F. These systems masked the proprietary command lines and configuration quirks of various vendor devices through the insertion of extensible middleware and superimposed a transaction-processing framework for commits that spanned multiple devices. These innovations are examples of the start of the loosely coupled service architecture.

The second problem introduced is the "passing a clue problem," which we refer to later as metadata.

Logically, when we broke apart the highly integrated system, we also removed any proprietary/internal methodology used to route the packets (flows) between service functions and/or provide accumulated information between the services (eg, subscriber/session ID). In the tightly integrated solution, this may have been accomplished using nonstandard extensions to fabric/buffer headers, using process shared memory pointers or an inter-process pub/sub data distribution service. Once externalized, these functions will reside in different machines and need to use standard transfer protocols for such information exchange as they no longer share common process space/environment.

In some loosely coupled solution spaces, this has been addressed through external arbitration (eg, policy servers and radius/diameter—as in Fig. 2.5). These schemes have their own architectural considerations for dealing with signal density and data distribution issues such as scale and the ubiquity of client software. This often introduces issues of openness and complexity.

A third problem arises by distributing the burden of classifying the traffic—mapping a flow to a subscriber and/or service.

- Classification engines within a forwarding device create additional overhead both in table memory and operations/cycles per packet. Without the deployment of costly, always-on classification tooling such as Deep Packet Inspection, all traffic traverses the pipeline as is shown in Fig. 2.5A.

- In multiple function, multiple vendor environments, the ability to classify traffic (more specifically, the ability to process a certain number of tuples at line rate), and the speed and method of updating classification rules can vary.
- On some platforms, particularly COTS/x86 compute, this is particularly onerous. While numerous tricks such as flow caching can be deployed to accelerate classification, there is a session startup cost and associated cache management concerns. Both the performance and scale of caching and flows are the focus of several recent research works.[5]
- Finally, in an increasingly encrypted world that is in part motivated by a backlash to the NSA headlines of today, classification in the service pipeline will become increasingly difficult if not nearly impossible. This is true particularly for flows that are classified by looking into the application-specific headers.

Both loosely coupled and highly integrated service solutions are also burdened by a lack of topological independence.

That is, they depend on the physical location of a physical device, and how it is connected to other physical devices. This static nature manifests itself as an impediment to deployment. That is, the envisioned service must be carefully planned in terms of not only capacity and performance of the service, but also as a physical device provisioning exercise as well as a geographical planning exercise.

These additional planning steps drive significant deployment cost that will be assumed in target markets by placing the device(s) with some preliminary scale. For an example, see the balancing problem above for highly integrated devices and imagine the additional calculus required in determining the initial scale and service component ratios within the device for a new market deployment.

The loosely coupled solution is arguably more flexible when coupled with the abstraction of a programmable overlay—commonly VLAN stitching or Layer 3 overlay. However service chain changes (which will require synchronization) or new service additions require topology changes and may present logical scale problems (eg, reaching the VLAN limit for per-customer services when using VLAN stitching[6]) (Fig. 2.6).

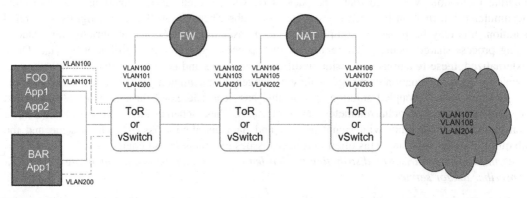

FIGURE 2.6

VLAN stitching. Tenant FOO hosts two apps that require separate treatment and BAR hosts one—all launched into the service chain as individual VLANs.

As an example of the previously mentioned "calculus", imagine an operator decides to deploy a security service that requires vendor X's firewall and vendor Y's Intrusion Detection System (IDS). The operator's research points to 10 markets where the service should be introduced, each with a varying percentage of existing/new subscribers that may want to purchase the service offering and with different historical service up-take patterns. Appliance X comes in two and four slot variants, each capable of 10 Gbps/slot, while appliance Y has two nonmodular versions, one capable of 20 Gbps and one capable of 40 Gbps. Also as is typical, the per-port cost of the four slot modular chassis will be cheaper than that of two of the two-slot model.

- Does the operator go solely with deployments with the four-slot model of X only to more effectively manage inventory and the upfront cost, even though 2 of the 10 markets are projected to take a very long time to grow to that amount of throughput? Consider the time it takes to actually fill those devices at full utilization and the cost depreciation model coupled with year-over-year price reductions of the device.
- Does the operator go solely with the larger appliance Y for similar reasons or multiple smaller instances to grow incrementally but at a higher base cost? What if that incremental growth is impossible to equally balance from appliance X—potentially requiring another appliance to effect load balancing?
- What if either model's growth slows or increases mid-way through the service history?

If the service device in question does not directly terminate the subscriber circuit, it had to be deployed inline with the normal SPF routing/forwarding progression from the terminating device to ensure proper flow traversal as well as proper application of the service.

Arguably, overlay/tunnel technology coupled with the use of anycast addressing or SDN control can be leveraged to loosen these planning and placement constraints and limitations. It is fair to point out that these could be at the potential cost of bandwidth efficiency (the flow "trombones" back to original path post-service), network churn (if the provider desired elasticity) and potential synchronization issues during reconfiguration.

Even with the evolution of these designs to incorporate a greater degree of topological freedom, both suffer from Least Common Denominator scale in functions in the pipeline created.

For example, in our SDG (Fig. 2.5), if the capacity of a component saturates at 20% of the line rate of bandwidth, the entire service pipeline (after that point) will likewise be limited to 20% throughput overall. In the loosely coupled environment, services can be made more elastic but at the same time more complex through the introduction of load balancing for the individual devices. The fundamental underlying problems (prior to NFV) being inventory and furnishing, as each service element is potentially a highly specialized piece of equipment. This is demonstrated in the Load Balanced proxy or content optimization service in our example.

VIRTUAL SERVICE CREATION AND SFC

At this point in the discussion, what NFV potentially introduces is a much greater degree of dynamic elasticity since the functions share a common hardware/software base ... theoretically, substitutable infrastructure. This can lead to lower service deployment friction, and at the same time a higher degree of service "bin packing" on devices that are already deployed and in service. While having the potential for less optimal traffic routing by virtue of being forced to locate a service function instance somewhere further away, but available, this approach also results in far fewer stranded or under-utilized resources. This model also makes for a potentially far easier service cost/benefit calculus for the network operator.

The role of SFC is to not only render the service path from the service chain by virtue that it creates true topological independence, but also in doing so to give the operator a bridge to the missing functionality of the highly integrated solution set.

Transport technologies like MPLS and/or SDN-associated technologies (eg, VXLAN or NVGRE abetted by Orchestration or DevOps tooling) allow the network operator to create orchestrated overlays.[7] Whether you use Layer 2 (VLAN-stitching) or Layer 3 (VRF-stitching or tunnel-stitching), transport-only solutions lack the additional functionality that address the entire service creation problem directly. For example, these solutions do not address the specifics of the placement of the virtualized network elements or the lifecycle management of those constructs.

Although operators have been creating services with these technologies, just as they have through "brute-force" physical chaining, the attraction of SFC is in yet-to-be-created services that take advantage of the additional information that can be passed in the creation of a true service overlay.

Fig. 2.7 demonstrates two service chains, A (A1, A2, A3) and B (B1, B2, B3), but also shows service function reuse service in that both chains traverse the same service function A2. In this figure we demonstrate how SFC should also provide the additional benefit of service component reuse where it makes sense. That is a single component/function can be utilized by more than one chain or path. Thus SFC will help an operator manage both the physical and logical separation of service functions, and at the same time, compressing together and optimizing resources.

Ultimately, the problem of configuration complexity will have to be solved outside of SFC.[8] Note that by "configuration" we intend that more than the network path is configured. This is best expressed as the logical operation of the function itself when it is applied to a specific flow, affecting not only forwarding of the flow but also embedding state/policy dependencies.

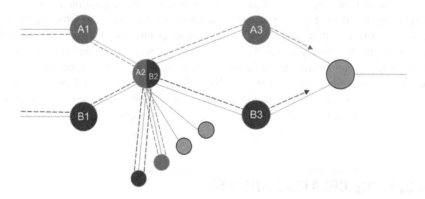

FIGURE 2.7

Two service chains (A and B) with two separate paths while reusing service function 2, which provides an additional abstraction in the form of multiple instances.

This can be accomplished through the use of common service models, which can eliminate or obscure the CLI of individual vendor implementations. This can be achieved using a standards-based (or de facto standard derived from open source) REST API call that is locally translated into a configuration. The next step here will likely involve some sort of evolution from vendor-specific to community-wide multivendor models. An early example of this normalization is the use of service models in the IETF NETMAP WG, or even The OpenDaylight project's northbound API for SFC.

Note that service chaining still has to deal with architectural requirements around bidirectional flows. This is particularly true for stateful services where the restrictions imposed by highly integrated and loosely coupled services implicitly avoid these issues.

For stateless service functions, high availability will be realized through the "swarm" or "web-scale"[9] approach.

This paradigm relies on orchestration and monitoring to eliminate failed members of a swarm of servers (ie, far more than a few servers) that scale to handle demand and simple load distribution. The collection of servers is either dictated in overlay network directives through central control, or managed inline. In the latter case, the abstraction between chain-and-path and function-and-instance are critical to scale.

For stateful service functions (eg, proxy services: any service that maps one communication session to another and thus has the reverse mapping state or monitors the status of a session in order to trigger some action), traditional HA mechanisms can be leveraged. These have traditionally been active/active or active/passive, 1:1 or 1:N, and with or without heartbeat failure detection.

Admittedly, traditional stateful function redundancy schemes have a cost component to be considered as well.

These traditional mechanisms have been labeled "weak" by recent academic work[10] (or at least "nondeterministic" regarding the state synchronization, which can lead to session loss on failover). Potential mitigation techniques for "nondeterministic state sharing" have their own potential costs in delay and overall scale (eg, requirements to write to queues instead of directly to/from NIC, freezing the VM to snapshot memory) that need to be balanced.

New system design techniques such as those used in high scale distributed systems can be used to decouple these applications from a direct linkage to their state store (common store for worker threads) or their backup (if the state store is necessarily "local" by design), potentially enabling the web-scale availability model while reducing cost.[11] This "nonmigratory" HA, like the recommendations to solve determinism problems in other schemes, assumes a rewrite of code in the transition from appliance to VM providing an opportunity to improve HA.

The traditional stateful HA approaches often include a scheme to appear as a single addressable network entity, thus masking their internal complexities (an abstraction that collapses detail).

In Fig. 2.8, the service chain "A" is bidirectional and the function A2 is stateful and elastic. The service path for both the forward and reverse direction for a flow distributed by A2 to a virtual instance of its function must transit the same instance. Here A2 is shown as an HA pair with A2'.

To some degree, SFC might actually provide relief for common network operational problems through limited geographical service function or service path redundancy. The seemingly requisite distribution function whether centralized or locally available, may ultimately be leveraged to allow operational flexibility (eg, A/B software upgrade schemes or "live migration").

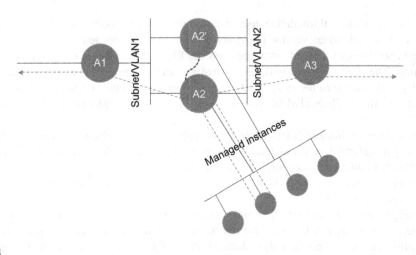

FIGURE 2.8

High availability of stateful service functions.

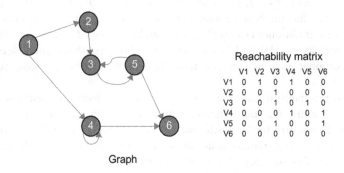

FIGURE 2.9

Service graphs.

Ultimately, our view of a "chain" has to change from a linear concept to that of a "graph" (Fig. 2.9) whose vertices are service functions and edges can be IP or overlay connectivity—with less focus on the network connectivity and more on the relationship of the functions.

VARYING APPROACHES TO DECOMPOSITION

As we transition from the tightly coupled, through loosely coupled and on to full virtualization, it is important to note that different vendors may chose widely varying decomposition, scale, and packaging strategies to a service.

While the "base use case" (referenced in Chapter 1: Network Function Virtualization) is an "atomic" function that does not decompose (it may "multi-thread" to scale), and is thus relatively simple, some integrated service platforms are far more complex and potentially decompose-able.

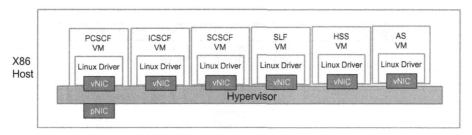

FIGURE 2.10

IMS decomposition in default, function-per-VM mode.

Consumers and vendors often refer to this decomposition as creating "micro services" allowing them to either sell/consume a service in a formerly bundled "macro service" (eg, GiLAN may have an integrated NAT or Firewall service, which can now be "parted out" into a service chain) independently, allowing "best of breed" consumption. However, true "micro services" go beyond decomposition to the function/service level and can approach the process/routine level as an enabler of software agility, which we will touch on in a later chapter.

This is particularly well illustrated in the area of mobility with the GiLAN and vIMS (both of which we pointed to in Chapter 1: Network Function Virtualization, as a service that was well on its way to virtualization prior to the NFV mandate, and thus "low hanging fruit").

For its part, the GiLAN decomposes into more readily-identifiable services/atoms IMS is a much more interesting study.

In a 2014 IEEE paper on cloudified IMS,[12] the authors propose three possible solutions/implementation designs to address the scale requirements of a cloud implementation of IMS: a one-to-one mapping (or encapsulation of existing functionality, see Fig. 2.10), a split into subcomponents (completely atomic) and a decomposition with some functions merged. Each of these architectures preserves (in one way or another) the interfaces of the traditional service with minimal alteration to messaging to preserve interoperability with existing/traditional deployments.

These views illustrate the complexity involved and decision making in decomposing highly integrated functions that make a service—outside of the mechanisms used to chain the components together (the networking piece)!

In the one-to-one mapping, each function of a traditional IMS would be placed in its own VM (they do not have to be in the same host, this is a simplification). Note that some of the functions are stateful (and some are not). In this decomposition, 3GPP defines the discovery, distribution, and scaling of the individual functions.

In the split decomposition, each function has a function specific load balancer (Fig. 2.11). In this imagining, each function is rendered into a stateless worker thread (if it is not already stateless) in a container, with any shared state for the function being moved to shared memory. Even the load balancing is stateless, though it has its own complexities (it has to implement the 3GPP interfaces that the function would traditionally present).

The last decomposition (Fig. 2.12) combines a subset of functions in the same VM (as threads) to reduce communication costs between them. It also removes the state in a common webscale

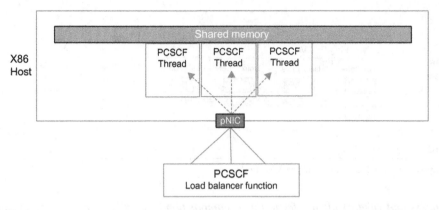

FIGURE 2.11

The PCSCF function split decomposition with its own load balancer and back-end state sharing.

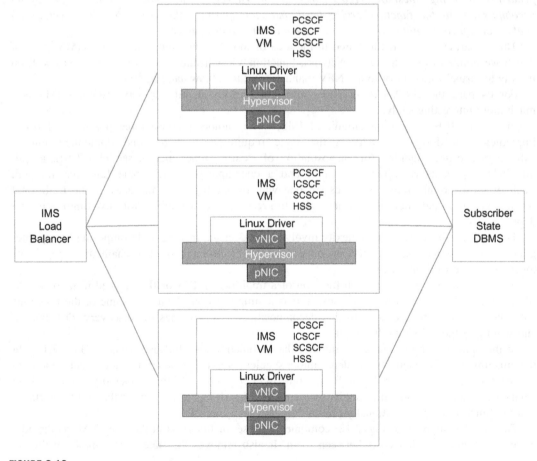

FIGURE 2.12

The IMS "merged" decomposition proposition.

fashion into a back-end database and replaces function-specific load balancing with a simple proxy (the proxy has to support one of the traditional IMS interfaces, Mw).

These choices in decomposition were the grist of some debate in the ETSI work, and ultimately were left undefined (with respect to how they would be managed and orchestrated) in their early work (see Chapter 3: ETSI NFV ISG).

Ultimately, many of the scale techniques use architectures that work within the limits of the von Neumann architecture that dominates COTS compute. We pick up on this theme in Chapter 7, The Virtualization Layer—Performance, Packaging, and NFV and Chapter 8, NFV Infrastructure—Hardware Evolution and Testing.

METADATA

Metadata is literally "data about data." It is a context pertinent to a set of data.

Arguably, metadata might be more critical to the success of SFC than the creation of service overlays for virtual functions.

It is possible to create a service represented by a chain of service functions that do not need to pass any information, just as you might be able to create a service chain without an overlay—but these mechanisms (service overlay and metadata) are powerful and compelling.

Examples of compelling metadata include[13]:

- Forwarding information (such as VRF): the ingress VRF of the packet on the first classifier. Using this encoded VRF the last node in the chain can place the (post service(s)) packets into the right forwarding context. This way the service chain is "vrf enabled" without the service participating in the routing topology, and there is no need to return the packets, after chaining, to the original classifier
- Application ID: if the first classifier knows the application (from direct classification, or from an external source such as a VM manager), that application can be carried as metadata in an SFC-specific header. For example, the classifier imposes a value that indicates that the packet belong to "Oracle." The firewall now no longer has to try to figure out if packets are "Oracle" or not, and can permit/deny based on the preclassified context. This model gets even more powerful when extended to services: they can update contexts as well and share it amongst themselves.
- External information about a flow: for example, the policy and charging rules function (PCRF) subscriber information can be encoded in the data plane. The services can use this context to apply subscriber-aware policy without having to participate in the policy/ control planes.

Metadata may be "imputed"—derived from the flow itself. A ready example would be performance data, wherein the functions can compute elapsed time in transit from function to function as well as across function (detailed, in-band performance).[14]

Metadata can be carried both inline and out-of-band. Inline carriage will require the addition, in some form, to the packet format—which the IETF is struggling with in its SFC work group (and we cover in Chapter 4: IETF Related Standards: NETMOD, NETCONF, SFC and SPRING).

Out-of-band models are present in the security and mobility spaces via PCRF (Radius/Diameter) and IF-MAP. These schemes generally provide relief from the need to extend the packet header with metadata fields, but come with their own challenges.

- Out-of-band systems place a tax on the service function developer—the inclusion of a metadata exchange client.
- An out-of-band system design has to worry about the transaction rate (scale) on both client and server and the transaction RTT (delay). This can lead into an excursion into placement algorithms for the MAP servers and the use of caching on the client functions (with the associated problems of caching metadata—eg, staleness).

Even though mobility solutions use out-of-band today, some applications like mobile traffic acceleration (payments, fraud detection, and so forth) require interactions outside the data plane that are problematic as the flows are short lived and by the time the policy/metadata is fetched, the flow has already ended. For such an application, operators and vendors alike are looking to inline metadata.

If inline metadata is useful in environments that already have out-of-band models, it might be extended in a way that subsumes the role of the PCRF and charging interface interactions (trading space for metadata in a packet header for a decrease in the number of interactions).

To accommodate inline metadata, a number of service header modifications have been proposed at the IETF that impose inline changes to packet formats to include what is in essence, a unique identifier for a service flow. This approach has a few issues of its own.

The primary issue is the global uniqueness of a metadata identifier. How is this configured, implemented and more importantly, coordinated between multivendor devices?

A secondary issue is more philosophical; mainly that one of the potential advantages to SFC is to take an approach that mimics how VMs are implemented in environments where they are unaware that they are virtual. The need to understand metadata could break this illusion.

Metadata can be signaled/imposed by the application, imposed by a proxy (like a media services proxy that does lightweight DPI by snooping signaling protocols, or implicitly by network based application recognition (DPI). It can also be associated a priori with the classifier at the ingress of the SFC by a management and orchestration system.

To implement out-of-band metadata, a methodology (client, server, and protocol) and design will need to be determined and either an association of a metadata key with some preexisting packet header identifier such as an MPLS ingress label or a GRE tunnel cookie made. Presignaling is required to establish and connect service chains, as mappings between the functions need to be established with something that maintains the cookie-to-flow mapping (a map/policy/metadata server system). The obvious downsides to this scheme are seen in its maintenance and management (eg, session scale on the metadata server, transaction loop timing limits between server and client, local caching to abate the loop with subsequent cache coherency maintenance, and imbedding the selected client[15]).

WHAT CAN YOU DO WITH SFC?

The network edge environment may ultimately evolve to a distributed data center paradigm for services when the aforementioned problems are solved.

SFC enables the disaggregation of the service offering to span a larger, more loosely arranged topology. This topology might include explicitly dedicated devices, combined or "compound" units, or even be decomposed into smaller units that can create the service. The point is to better match operational needs through flexibility, while at the same time optimizing for cost.

Many operators are moving from highly integrated BNG/BRAS functions within dedicated and proprietary hardware-based edge routers in the Metro to virtualized deployments in a Regional Data Center. This sometimes exists within the Metro Point of Presence as a small rack of compute and storage. Some came to the realization of efficiencies of such solutions when they first explored the virtualization of Layer 3 Customer Premise Equipment (CPE) functions. These deployments had their own set of economic and agility related incentives for the operator (Fig. 2.13), but still lent themselves to other types of operations. This is the beauty of new technologies: sometimes we discover new uses for them only after we start playing with them.

For example, Telefonica has proposed a Proof of Concept that has a software based Broadband Residential Access Server (BRAS) in the ETSI NFV WG. This soft BRAS is described with a limited set of functions: QinQ termination, Longest Prefix Match routing, GRE tunnel support (to enable wholesale services), and MPLS tunnel support that allows for optimized forwarding within their network.[16]

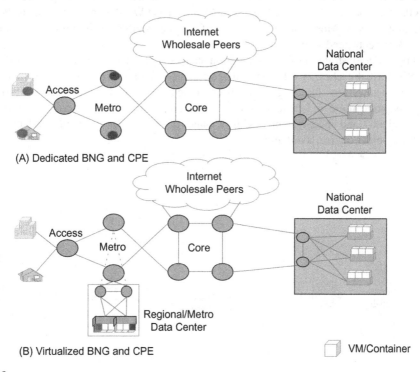

FIGURE 2.13

Dedicated BNG functionality (A) is virtualized in a regional DC (B), eliminating highly integrated devices in Metro. Similarly, CPE functionality migrates to the same COTS base.

Practical and working examples of a vVPN function exist as well. These vVPN offers are described as a cloud-based VPN services and were first described in places like the early TeraStream[17,18] project (Fig. 2.14) before any forum or standards body had studied NFV. This use case was driven by many of the same economic and operational motivations we described earlier.

It should be pointed out that while both services contain NFV and service chains, both utilize fundamentally different approaches to achieve what are ultimately similar goals.

This may be an indication that (at least for the early period of NFV/SFC) that the potential of any solution applied to one use case may or may not apply within the context of another, or the fact that one approach may not be "best" for all of NFV.

Service function reuse, and flexibility of service definition is critical to developing a common set of technologies that can apply broadly to problems we will encounter in this space.

The CloudVPN project provides the more traditional view of the migration of business services using virtualized functions. Since it evolved before any standardization of SFC, the first implementation relies on orchestrated VLAN stitching to create the service function chain. This allowed the firewall service to remain separate from the vRouter/vPE service.

The positioning of the vRouter in the CloudVPN service at a regional data center requires the service be tunneled across the infrastructure using L2TPv3 tunnels. Here a simple service offering requires a vPE termination (VPN) with a virtual firewall (vFW) that provides NAT, Policy and IPSec/SSL remote access. More complex service offerings add vISE for BYOD service authentication and vWSA for enhanced web access.

This example demonstrates how virtualization can be exploited in new service offerings by injecting vFWs, virtual caches, or other virtualized functions into the service path (virtual managed services). It also shows how building more differentiated services on a common platform can be achieved by snapping these independent services functions together. Further, these services will scale more elastically and independently with demand, at least to the limit of available compute, network and to a lesser degree, available storage.

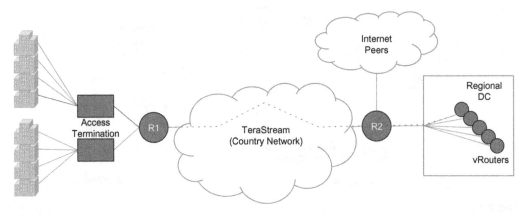

FIGURE 2.14

TeraStream CloudVPN.

For "grandfathered" or declining services (eg, Fig. 2.15 IPv4aaS—an IPv6 migration strategy that consolidates the IPv4-to-v6 translation services), the virtualized function (NAT and various application gateway technologies) can be further concentrated by creating a service overlay. Note that this also illustrates dynamic service injection by appending an additional service element (address translation) to the end of the existing broadband connectivity service chain.

In the mobile network (a growing component of overall network usage), researchers have identified that the dominant component of traffic is data/video, and represents almost 70% of traffic in the LTE Evolved Packet Core network. The interesting observation they have made is that this traffic may not require the protections of GTP tunnels that provide circuit-like behaviors with QoS guarantees because the clients of such services do local application-layer buffering of content.[19]

Proposals are surfacing that reimagine solutions where this traffic is treated differently, reducing the signaling burden of the solution as well. This includes tunnel setup/teardown, which can be quite costly in terms of overall user experience impact.

In the mobile internet service environment, an offering for the GiLAN that uses an early form of service chaining to allow the connectivity illustrated earlier (in Fig. 2.5) to be realized in arbitrary topologies has been shown as a Proof of Concept.

The solution distributes the flow classification function (to eliminate this step as a bottleneck). Once classified, the flow subsequently follows a logical overlay using an imbedded service header (akin to the NSH proposal in the IETF SFC WG) by virtue of capabilities in the software forwarder (Cisco Systems' VPP product, a version of which is open-sourced in fd.io (http://fd.io)) traversing a variety of scenario driven (treatment of HTTP depends on access technology as well as policy enforcement) service chains comprised of multivendor applications (including video optimization, firewall, self-service kiosk diversion to increase rating and NATP).

For some service offerings, NFV/SFC will allow a step-wise deployment scenario potentially starting with remote, virtualized functions, but ultimately leading to the placement of dedicated, integrated equipment or a regional/co-located compute pod. Also in terms of legacy service

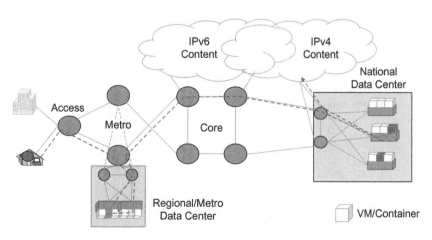

FIGURE 2.15

Providing NAT for legacy IPv4 devices in an IPv6 network (IPv4aaS).

migration, or "cap and grow" strategies where existing equipment must be capped, and virtualized versions of the services those devices provided, NFV/SFC will be capable of coexisting in these scenarios. This is shown in Fig. 2.16.

In Fig. 2.16A, the new service (eg, expansion of a VPN service offering) could originally be realized in a new market from a virtual function or (service chain of functions) in an existing on-net facility (eg, National or Regional DC). The provider could lease circuits to a colocation facility in-market and could optionally colocate the virtualized functions there if delay was an issue, in addition to basic network equipment. Service up-take and corresponding increases in revenue could justify Fig. 2.16B. Here the network circuits and other resources become dedicated, and colocation of the service might be required and even potentially dedicated. In this case, integrated high-throughput service devices might be deployed but depend on the overall strategy an operator wishes to take here. For examples, from an operational perspective, this could be driven solely by a cost/space/power equation. However, other factors such as regulatory restrictions, might result in different choices.

Though these fledgling deployments are not all directly illustrative of SFC (more so, NFV orchestration, OSS integration and elasticity), the architectural shift to move compute and storage closer to the customer can be exploited in new service offerings by injecting vFWs, virtual caches, or other virtualized functions into the service path (building more differentiated services on a common platform—Fig. 2.15). Further, these services will scale more easily (and independently) with demand (at least to the limit of available compute).

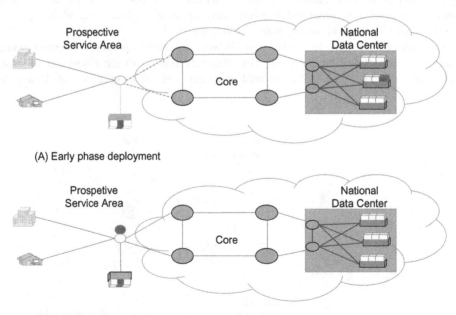

(A) Early phase deployment

(B) Advanced phase deployment

FIGURE 2.16

Step-wise deployment/expansion of service offering into a new market.

The larger savings from this operating paradigm come with changes in the operational model. These come in the near term via a shift towards DevOps-driven automation and self-service service provisioning in conjunction with NFV (reducing the cycle time to realize or alter a service), and in the long term via changes in the OSS and its cost structures.[20]

The dynamic and elastic nature of SFC is aided by evolving the use of embedded analytics in the services, virtual service platforms, and OSS/Orchestration. We will visit this in more detail in a later chapter.

Aside from this, one of the big opportunities in service creation via NFV/SFC is the ability to reimagine and simplify services. Many operators are looking at the plethora of features that vendors have provided at their and other operator's behest in existing equipment, to create new differentiated services.

Many realized that on average, they used a small portion of the overall software feature set in tightly integrated equipment, and saw the larger feature set as a potentially larger surface for security problems and general software defects (the reality of this fear depends on the vendor implementation).

Some have discovered that their more specialized service offerings, which required a high degree of feature were an economic and operational drag, did not generate enough revenue to justify the specialization (and created a barrier of entry to new vendors). This introspection allows for simplification.

Similarly, opportunities exist for many vendors who are in their "first-generation" of service function virtualization, where they simply replicate their hardware-centric models in software.

In most cases, this generation is implemented as one-service-per-VM, and performance is, as one would expect: far less than it was on the dedicated hardware.

For example, a new security service offering today might envision separate VMs for a vFW plus a vIDS and perhaps other modules as well. Going forward, these separate VMs may be homogenized in a next-generation security appliance as dynamically loadable modules within the same product—optimized for a virtual environment.

It may be that current industry virtual product delivery methodologies are driven by customer consumption capabilities (the existing operation requires that the virtual service functions replacing the integrated solution conform to their existing tooling).

In this case, until the customer's operations and management systems can accommodate these "re-imaginings," they could be stuck in this "first-generation" or "emulation" mode.

Most vendors are moving quickly to support second-generation functions, spurred both by the customer demand for new paradigms and the entrance of new competitors (who target the market with initially lower feature but higher performance variants). The future is interesting and bright in this space.

LOGICAL LIMITS

The speed of light

There are some practical bounds on SFC, even if the point is to remove topology constraints and other physical dependencies.

The three biggest limits will be the complexity of troubleshooting a very topologically diverse deployment of functions that compose a chain, achieving the overall Service Level Agreement

(SLA) requirements for the service itself, and finally the fact that the underlying infrastructure may have resource/capacity limits.

It is possible that High Availability strategies for NFV/SFC might incorporate the use of service function elements in far-flung geographies, but transport latency (eg, the speed of light in a glass fiber) ultimately might bind how far afield an operator might realistically allow a service path to wander.[21]

There may be mitigating factors in either the nature of the service or where traffic may ultimately be exiting/sinking in the network and then return. These can be due to existing equipment or other resource availability, or even regulatory requirements.

For our example, in Fig. 2.17 if an operator created a service chain ("foo") with functions ("bar" and "baz") that should be optimized geographically, but not constrained geographically, we would expect that the functions originally would all be coresident in Washington to serve traffic originating in Washington.

If there were no constraints, it "might" be possible to meet reasonable delay SLA using HA scenarios wherein the "foo" service can either be moved as a whole (via path redundancy, where the "bar" and "baz" functions are relocated to another service center/PoP) or in part (where traffic for a single function "bar" loops to and returns from an another service center/PoP.

But, in general, the delays due to propagation assuming a best case transmission, appreciate quickly and so the options in these cases can be rather limited (Fig. 2.18):

- If there were a "bar" function failure and the operator allowed atomic replacement "bar" in Washington with "bar" in Philadelphia, the overall impact to delay in the service will be almost 3 ms (round-trip).
- If the provider allowed similar "bar" substitution with an instance of "bar" in Chicago, direct access would add almost 14.5 ms of delay, and indirect access (Washington to Philadelphia to Cleveland to Chicago) would add almost 20 ms of round-trip delay.[22]
- The West Coast (eg, Seattle) delay is obviously much worse.

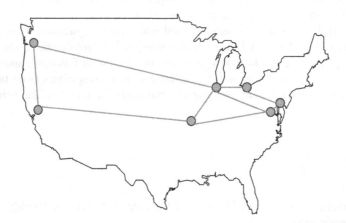

FIGURE 2.17

A subset of the fiber map of the United States with associated best-case distance versus delay measurements.

Even if the eligible functions to fit a service chain were restricted to a "regional" scope, the variability in delay depending on the specific network path taken would have to be accommodated.

These examples make it clear, at least to us, that between the dynamics of service element instantiation (NFV) and SFC chain/path updates, the paradigm of "fail fast and fail hard" may make for the most manageable future services.

Granularity and extra vSwitch or network transitions

It may also be attractive to speculate on further reusability or economy in decomposing service functions into subcomponents that may be shared between service functions.

For instance, consider the abstraction of a compute routine that is highly specialized in doing encryption, hashing or other generic service.

The immediate trade-off in Fig. 2.19 is that both functions, broken into subfunctions so that they may share one of those subfunctions, will have to do at least one[23] additional hypervisor hop. This could be worse if an additional network hop or hops results. Subsequent chains that included all three functions could also quickly become a multiplier of the effect. Consider that ultimately there is a practical limit to the decomposition of the functions imposed by the extra network

A	B	Distance (km)	Delay (ms)
Washington	Philadelphia	300	1.47
Washington	Chicago	1500	7.20
Philadelphia	Cleveland	800	3.77
Cleveland	Chicago	1000	4.55
Chicago	Seattle	4500	17.03

FIGURE 2.18

Anonymized propagation delay of a real network.

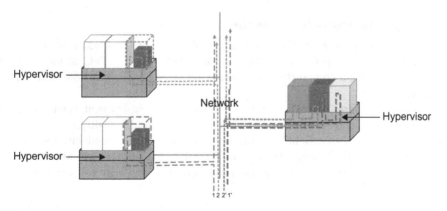

FIGURE 2.19

Two service chains, each with a subcomponent that could (theoretically) be mutually shared.

transition(s) that is governed by the limits of the hypervisor, dock/container, network and storage technologies that are in use.

Standardization above the network layer

Some operators have environments where a very tight proximity of application and service function (eg, financial applications and firewall/IDS services) is desirable. These interactions are potentially conducive to inter-process communication or other optimizations that eliminate the network hop between containers/instances.

Switching between VMs above the hypervisor is being explored in both the netmap/vale and vhost-user projects (Chapter 7: The Virtualization Layer—Performance, Packaging, and NFV)— offering both common exploitable methodologies and performance impact mitigation (certainly performing better than the loop through a hypervisor/vSwitch).

Additionally, there are some "service functions" that might naturally evolve and connect at the application layer.

For example, a Platform as a Service (PaaS) development environment might contain some services—what some might term "endpoint services"—that are treated differently from the current notion in NFV/SFC. In this environment, the specifics of what we might refer to as the "currency" of the type or types of operations a service provides might be at the packet level or the application request level. The action or actions performed might be an application-level callback. In this environment, proximity is paramount (request transaction service examples include dependency monitoring or circuit-breaker services[24]).

Once the connection between functions moves above the network layer, it becomes transparent to the current concept of "network" service path. Inter-process communication or API/callback methodologies are further from standardization and potentially harder to monitor. As these become more common scenarios, the concept of NFV and SFC is likely to expand. While some of this behavior might be developed through proposed metadata extensions to the packet header in SFC (eg, a triggered callback by the presence of metadata), this is a fundamentally different type of "pipe" with potentially higher performance requirements than just simple network-level relay.

The capabilities of old stuff—The "brownfield" of dreams

Finally, any evolving technology might lead to hybrid deployments in which some of the elements are potentially more capable participants. This is particularly true for SFC in the case where an operator wants to leverage a combination of newer, virtualized service functions with legacy, integrated hardware elements.

This is sometimes referred to as a hybrid, or "brownfield" deployment versus a "greenfield" where everything is new. (Fig. 2.20 illustrates a potential "brownfield" reality.)

In our experience, the "greenfield" is quite rare and often left to academic research environments. For the more canonical case, a business might, for depreciation requirements and/or technical reasons such as throughput or power footprint optimization, wish to create such a hybrid environment.

In other more obvious cases, the operator simply wishes to "cap and grow" legacy, integrated hardware systems and instead deploy only virtualized versions of those elements—or a subset of their specific functions.

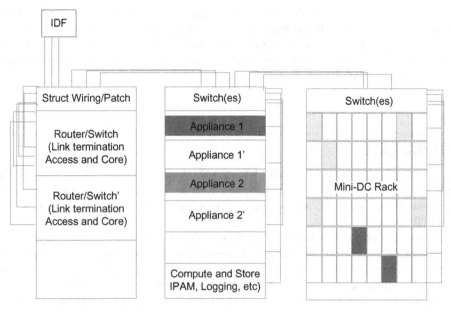

FIGURE 2.20

Service chaining at the network edge as it might look with NFV/SFC in a "brownfield."[25] (Note the access Point of Presence may already contain some compute/storage for "ancillary" services. New compute/storage are leveraged to add functions or scale out the capabilities of already existing, integrated devices.)

As we continue on, we will need to be able to describe these legacy elements as composite services in the management and planning of chains and paths so that better, and simpler planning and designs will be capable.

Because these hybrid systems may lack the capabilities and agility of pure-software solutions, it may make them incapable of fully participating in the evolving SFC without a proxy, but this is simply a design trade-off.

Such a proxy can have a varying level of complexity, depending on how much of the service overlay functionality it attempts to relay to the legacy service function. And over time, this hybrid approach will grow into one that does enjoy a majority of virtualized NFV/SFCs.

Common sense

It should go without saying, that not all network function applications backhaul or "burst" into any given cloud well. This goes hand-in-hand with the opportunity NFV/SFC presents to reimagine a service. For example, the current approach to DDoS mitigation service works well for distributed attacks, since the current concept of backhauling traffic to a virtualized "scrubber" can handle modest scale. However, backhaul of volumetric attacks that comprise data flows totaling in the 100s of Gbps, stress not only the scale out of the "scrubber" but also beg network efficiency questions such as if it was going to be dropped, then it was a waste to backhaul it.

This is an example of where NFV/SFV can be taken only so far. When you push any application towards physical/resource limits, things can break down. Keeping in mind that this example took today's model of DDoS mitigation and basically virtualized it, a reimagination of the solution, perhaps distributing more functionality might be an appropriate and workable solution. NFV/SFC give a network operator the tools to do this.

NFV WITHOUT SFC

We have already glanced at the potential of PaaS and application level connectivity as a potential future architecture for NFV. In Chapter 7, The Virtualization Layer—Performance, Packaging, and NFV, we will explore the fact that more than one architectural solution is possible for NFV.

We will look at a container/VM hybrid vCPE solution that bypasses the host hypervisor for at least the networking component, and directly terminates pseudowires from the (largely residential) service access devices (CPE) to an environment built on UML[26] containers (eg, micro-VMs), the solution provides a glimpse into a different take on the necessity of service chaining.

Designed to offload or augment a traditional BNG, this is an example where service chaining is perhaps unnecessary.

In this case, services were built out as per-customer "kernel as NFV." One interesting side note on this is that it also created and exposed a programmable API that allowed its own developers to expand the environment quickly and easily.

The challenge of this model to both SFC and the ETSI NFV model (our next chapter) is that it provides a scalable, working solution without poll-mode drivers (which potentially makes the solution more energy efficient) and minimizes the traversal of the network boundary—based on the principle that once you have the packet in memory, it is most efficient to do as many operations (on it) as possible. By chaining VMs (or containers) to implement individual services, the packet has to be copied in and out of memory several times, regardless of the acceleration philosophy applied to minimize the delay this causes.

Services within the container may still use metadata, but its allocation and use is proprietary to the service designer/architect (much like the highly integrated devices that preceded the virtualization revolution).

In some ways these approaches may seem like less-tightly integrated models that provides an open API for service developers as well as the benefits from the elasticity of NFV and is more of a step toward the "micro-services" future.

CONCLUSION

At its very core, NFV/SFC is being pursued to address the service creation problems of the past. By virtualizing services, creating service overlays and passing metadata we are enabling the conversion away from integrated service solutions.

When combined with NFV, SFC allows a network operator to properly resource a service, function-by-function, exploiting the orchestration tooling and elasticity concepts maturing in Data Center operations today.

In pursuing NFV service solutions, the operator may benefit by simply deploying a service traditionally implemented on proprietary hardware but in a virtualized environment. However, further benefits may accrue from a reimagining of such a service so that it needs fewer features in its virtualized incarnation and in doing so, allow the vendor to implement the same functionality with a much smaller software set. This reimagination might result in better scale and improved operation of solutions, which may only be possible with an NFV/SFC-type solution.

To provide benefit, the SFC architecture must compensate for the advantages of a highly integrated service, including the ability to pass a context between the service functions in a service chain and surmount the configuration complexity that might arise from the use of disparate components.

While the examples we can cite of SFC do not yet incorporate the passing of a context or clue (as they were attempted prior to standardization of metadata passing within a service chain) we feel that over time, new applications will emerge that take advantage of this evolving feature.

SFC frees the operator from topology constraints, allowing them to leverage a logical overlay to instantiate services in remote markets without having to preplace dedicated equipment. This newfound agility is important and should not be underestimated. There are, however, potential limits to those freedoms, such as meeting existing SLAs.

The world is rarely a "greenfield" deployment for a network operator, and NFV/SFC efficacy may be limited by the capabilities of existing systems in "brownfield" deployments.

With variability and freedom comes complexity. To limit operational complexity, many operators may still construct service chains by deploying service functions in localized, "logical" line-ups rather than the physical pipelines of the past. These new solutions will take advantage of the function elasticity afforded by NFV.

Finally, some deployments are emerging that provide high performance NFV services by creating a service creation environment *within* a single virtual element—obviating the need for external chaining. Other services are also evolving that might require some sort connectivity *above* the network layer or be expressed as a de-composition that needs to be managed as a single function.

END NOTES

1. To be able to express such a chain in linear text, we borrow the lambda concept (programs that program) and represent the optional outcomes as a set.
2. This is a running theme of both the programmability offered via SDN and the orchestration dynamics of NFV—that the management interfaces for traditional (highly integrated and/or loosely coupled) services. FCAPS, billing, and other operations and support functions also need to be re-invented to create an agile/cost-effective operating environment.
3. Note that elements like the PGW in this figure can also be examples of highly integrated service elements, given the range of functions above the Data Plane that they provide.
4. SDG is a term used by certain vendors to designate service steering functionality that evolved to become the 3GPP functionality of a Traffic Detection Function (TDF) to provide subscriber-aware services for both fixed and mobile access.

5. Flow Caching for High Entropy Packet Fields, Shelly, Jackson, Koponen, McKeown, Rajahalme (Stanford University, VMware) SIGCOMM HotSDN 2014. This paper contains a number of other references to studies in this space.
6. While it is possible to use a management scheme to control VLAN wastage, this too adds complexity. For example, we could maintain bridging relationships throughout and use common VLANs (for most, a non-starter), or we could localize the bridges on the ingress and egress to so that the links can use common VLAN numbers (still a lot of bridging) or we could maintain a mapping of internal VLAN numbers on the edge switches to external VLAN numbers such that the VLANs 100, 101, and 102 are common on both ingress and egress.
7. The latter are heavily leveraged within DC, while MPLS overlays are still maturing in DC but more leveraged in the SP access and core networks (the two meet at Data Center Interconnect).
8. This is addressable through MANO solutions like Tail-f NCS.
9. Without the concerns of state persistence (and VM migration), these service function instances have a simple life cycle: spawn, bind-to-path, un-bind-from-path, and death.
10. http://www.cs.berkeley.edu/~justine/ftmb-final.pdf. This is a great paper for understanding the nuances of HA for stateful applications through its numerous references to other academic work, whether you ascribe to its conclusions or not.
11. Shared session state is the first hurdle in realizing the model, remapping the sessions without session failure to a new application server is very complex.
12. Cloudified IP Multimedia Subsystem (IMS) for Network Function Virtualization (NFV)-based architectures Carella, G.; Tech. Univ. Berlin, Berlin, Germany; Corici, M.; Crosta, P.; Comi, P.
13. These examples come courtesy of Jim Guichard (Cisco Systems) as part of a group discussion on the value of metadata in the IETF SFC header.
14. Note that imputed metadata would require a push from the client in an out-of-band metadata scheme.
15. "Which" client to standardize on is also an issue, as integrating multiple clients would be painful and expensive for function developers.
16. "Making NFV Work PoCs and Trials" (Telefonica Webcast).
17. http://blog.ipspace.net/2013/11/deutsche-telekom-terastream-designed.html
18. Peter Lothberg's NANOG talk on TeraStream, TeraStream is ambitious on many fronts: conversion of a national network to IPv6 transport, conversion of the optical infrastructure to an easier to operate "drop and waste" system, real-time OSS, customer self-service provisioning and NFV for services.
19. ProCel: Smart Traffic Handling for a Scalable Software EPC, Nagaraj and Katti SIGCOM HotSDN 2014.
20. For example, changes might include the deployment of open source-based approaches that may reduce these costs.
21. Research around highly available transactions and database partition tolerance can be fairly instructive in summarizing the frequency and length of network outages. This paper also provides some interesting measurements of AWS latency in a number of scenarios: http://www.bailis.org/papers/hat-vldb2014.pdf.
22. Neither example includes the additional delay that may accumulate in handling the flow through multiple network elements—this is just the delay of light in fiber.
23. Assuming that the functions are restructured so that the component is not used in a re-entrant manner.
24. Don't Call Them Middleboxes, Call Them Middlepipes, Jamjoom, Williams and Sharma (IBM) SIGCOMM HotSDN 2014.
25. While NFV/SFC applies equally to all network environments, the Service Provider access/edge is used to dramatically illustrate the difference in paradigm.
26. Developers have contributed performance updates and patches to UML open source.

ETSI NFV ISG

INTRODUCTION

In October 2012, a group of engineers from 13 network operators published an NFV white paper that outlined the need for, and proposal to form, a work effort regarding the issues of NFV.

A second version of this white paper was published a year later, in 2013 with 25 (mostly telco) operator co-signers.[1] A third was published in October 2014 as their work wound down.[2]

In between the first and last publications, the group found a home for their work in a European Telecommunications Standards Institute (ETSI)[3] Industry Study Group (ISG).

In this chapter, we consider the contribution of the ETSI NFV ISG group's work (for the charter period ending in December 2014—which we will refer to as Phase 1) as it pertains to NFV and the potential future of the ISG. The main focus of this work is around decoupling software from hardware, creating flexible deployments and dynamic operations—the stated benefits of NFV in their architecture framework.

This contribution is found largely in their published white papers and Proof-of-Concept (PoC) exercises, which by their own admission (and subsequent recharter for a Phase 2) leave much more work to be done.

Let's now explore these efforts in more detail.

GETTING CHARTERED
EUROPEAN TELECOMMUNICATIONS INSTITUTE

The ETSI is an interesting Standards body. It was formed in 1988, with the original charter of providing "harmonized" standards in support of a single telecommunications services market within Europe originally under the auspices of the European Commission/European Free Trade Association, later within the European Union.

In support of this mission, ETSI has several levels of standard, ranging from the Group Specification (GS) to the European Standard (EN). The latter requires approval by European National Standards Organizations, whereas other standards produced (such as the ETSI Standard), require a majority of the entire organization to vote in favor of the proposal in order to ratify it as a Standard.

ETSI has wide-reaching interests that it calls "clusters," including Home and Office, Networks, Better Living with ICT, Content Delivery, Networks, Wireless Systems, Transportation, Connecting Things, Interoperability, Public Safety, and Security.

The NFV ISG falls under the Networks cluster.

The Third Generation Partnership Project (3GPP) is another contributor to this cluster, and because of this (to most readers of this book) ETSI might be known more for wireless telecom standards to those that follow networking.

NFV AT ETSI

So, why would the organizers of the NFV effort locate this work in ETSI?

The answer is primarily in expediency and structure. ETSI has a reasonable governance process, well-established Intellectual Property Rights (IPR) policies, and open membership. Non-ETSI members may pay a small fee to cover the costs of administrative overhead and are thereafter allowed to participate. Membership/participation is not limited to Europe, but is a good deal more involved in terms of paperwork and fees. In short, the organizational framework and structure are very much set up to support the proposed study and the distribution of its outputs.

The ISG structure is designed to be supplemental to the existing standardization process within ETSI, operating more as an industry forum than a Standards organization. It does have its challenges when interaction with other standards forums are considered.

In early presentations the mission of the NFV ISG was described as having two key drivers:

- To recommend consensus-based approaches which address the challenges outlined in the original white paper.
- Not to develop any new standards, but instead to produce white papers that describe and illustrate the problem space or requirements for solutions in that space, reference existing standards where they are applicable and point at them as possible solutions to the aforementioned identified requirements, and make inputs to Standards bodies to address gaps where standards might not yet exist to address the requirements.

As originally scoped, the outputs were not considered "normative" documents.[4] Early discussions around forming the ISG curtailed their mandate to delivering a Gap Analysis (described as a gap analysis and solution approach). The ETSI NFV ISG published documents appear as GS level documents—which if ratified, would empower the ISG to "provide technical requirements or explanatory material or both." Effectively, the ISG could produce proper standards solutions, but never get beyond requirements and problem space definitions.

The original work was scoped to take two years and conclude at the end of 2014. However, with the increased focus on the SDN and networking industries over the last year of their first charter, the group voted to recharter its efforts in order to facilitate another two years of operation. To this end, the group's portal was showing proposed meetings into Spring/Summer 2017 (at the time this book was written).

Although the stated original intent (during formation) was that a consensus-based approach was preferred[5] and that voting was not anticipated for issue resolution, the drafting operators were given extraordinary rights in the first three meetings as part of a founding block of network operators, referred to as the Network Operators Council (NOC).

Should a vote be called, this block of founding members would have enough "weighted" votes to outvote any reasonable opposition (assuming they all voted the same way).

This council was moderated by the ISG Chairman and originally consisting of representatives from AT&T, BT, Deutsche Telekom, Orange, Telecom Italia, Telefonica, CenturyLink, China Mobile, Colt, KDDI, NTT, Telstra, Vodafone, and Verizon.

The ISG Chairman appoints a Technical Manager who chairs the Technical Steering Committee (TSC).

ORGANIZATION

Underneath the umbrella of the TSC are several Working Groups (Fig. 3.1). At a layer below the Working Groups are Expert Task Groups, which can work with more than one Working Group in order to accomplish their goals and tasks.

The Working Groups are:

- NFV INF (Infrastructure)—work on NFV issues and recommendations in the Compute, Hypervisor, and Network Infrastructure (the "underlay") domains. These are commonly referred to as "network underlay" domains. Late in the process, they expanded their scope to include Service Quality Metrics.
- NFV MAN (Management and Orchestration)—was chartered to work on NFV issues and recommendations around Management and Orchestration.
- NFV SWA (Software Architecture)—was enlisted to produce software architecture for virtual network functions (VNFs).
- NFV PER (Performance)—identify NFV issues and recommendations in the area of performance and portability. This group also created the PoC Framework.
- NFV REL (Reliability)—work on reliability and resiliency issues and produce related recommendations.
- NFV SEC (Security)—work on security issues that pertain to NFV, both for the virtual functions and their management systems.

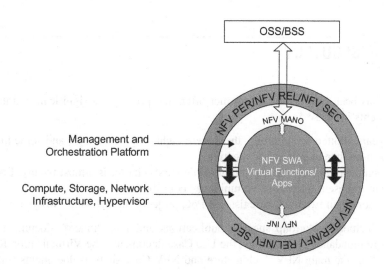

FIGURE 3.1

ETSI NFV ISG organizational structure.

The Performance, Reliability, and Security groups were chartered with overarching responsibilities across multiple areas. To that end, these groups had relationships with all other working groups and help connect the different areas together. The remaining group interactions can be implied from the interfaces in the NFV architecture.

While these groups produced their own outputs, they also rolled-up and contributed to the high-level outputs of the ISG. There is evidence that views on their topics continued to evolve after publication of the original high-level documents (as expressed in their own subsequent workgroup publications). Because of this evolution, there is a need for normalization through subsequent revision of either the WG or ISG-level documents.

IMPACT ON 3GPP

It is only natural that NFV work items might spill over into the 3GPP, as some operators see the architecture of both the 3GPP core and radio access network (RAN) for mobile networks changing due to NFV. A reimagining of these architectures would target the movement of a lot of the state management between the logical entities of those architectures into VNFs as a starting simplification. At a minimum, such changes would result in the Operations and Management (OAM—SA5) interfaces of 3GPP evolving for virtualized infrastructure. This is not surprising, given that the 3GPP architecture was envisioned prior to NFV and its related concepts and architectural implications. However, changes due to virtualization will probably be minor (at first) within the core protocols. We will not see any real impacts to these architectures until Release 14 (or later) of 3GPP standards.

The bigger impacts of NFV on 3GPP will probably be seen in discussions of the new 5G mobile architecture and, like all SDOs, the pace of innovation in virtual elements may require ETSI and 3GPP to speed up their standards process to keep pace with the demand for such changes.

DIGESTING ETSI OUTPUT
OUTPUT

The NFV ISG has been busy as the group met often and produced a significant number of papers and PoC documents in Phase 1.

- In the two years allotted to the group, there were eight major meetings, and some individual groups held more than eighty online meetings.
- The final document count at the expiration of the (first) charter is almost twenty. Each document can represent numerous, voluminous "contributions."
- There were more than twenty-five registered PoC projects[6] in that same two-year period.

The papers include workgroup specific publications and four "macro" documents. The latter include the (more mundane) Terminology, the Use Case document,[7] the Virtualization Requirements work and as well as the main NFV Architecture and NFV Gap Analysis documents (inline with the original mandate).

TERMINOLOGY

With a goal of not duplicating the Terminology for Main Concepts in NFV as identified in GS NFV 003, there are still some fundamental terms that were uniquely coined by the NFV ISG that we will use in this chapter[8] that have to be introduced here. Let's define them now:

VNF—A VNF is an implementation of a new Network Function or a Network Function that was previously implemented as a tightly integrated software/hardware appliance or network element. This is referred to in other chapters as a service component or service function to imply one of many that might make up a service offering deployable on a Network Function Virtualization Infrastructure (NFVI). For instance, a firewall function that once existed as a fixed-function, physical device is now virtualized to create a VNF called "firewall."

VNFC—A Virtual Network Function Component is requisite to discussing the concept of "composite" service functions. A composite is composed of more than one discernable/separable component function. The documentary example of a composite is the combining of PGW and SGW network functions in the mobile network core to make a theoretical virtual Evolved Packet Core (vEPC) offering.

NFVI—The NFVI is the hardware and software infrastructure that create the environment for VNF deployments, including the connectivity between VNFs.

ARCHITECTURE—GENERAL

The NFV Architectural Framework as described in GS NFV 002 tries to describe and align functional blocks and their eight reference points (interfaces) with an operator's overall needs (in the view of the membership).

Keep in mind that this architecture and the perspective of the operator is in the context of the ETSI member operators, which may not comprise the totality of worldwide network operators.

The reader should note that this document predates many of the final workgroup documents, thus requiring subsequent searches into the documents published for clarifications and greater detail to make the ISG view whole and cohesive.

We recommend reading the Virtualization Requirements document as a good companion document to the Architectural Framework. We also advise that reading some of the individual workgroup documents can be useful in filling gaps left by those main documents.

The high level architecture (Fig. 3.2) focuses on VNFs (the VNF Domain), the NFVI and NFV Management and Orchestration. These components and their relationships with one another arguably outline the core of NFV.

The large blocks in Fig. 3.2 include:

- NFVI (defined earlier)—virtualized compute, storage, and network and its corresponding physical compute, storage, and network resources. The execution environment for the VNFs.
- VNF domain—the virtualized network functions and their management interface(s).
- NFV Management and Orchestration—lifecycle management of the physical and virtual resources that comprise the NFV environment.

The connectivity between VNFs in the Architecture Framework document is described as a VNF Forwarding Graph and is relevant to the Service Function Chain of Chapter 2 or a group

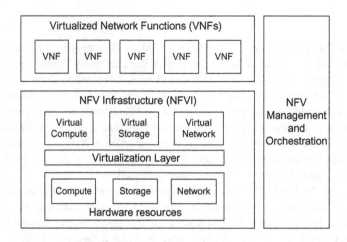

FIGURE 3.2

High level ETSI NFV architecture.

where the connectivity is not specified called a VNF Set. This latter concept is described later in the use case referring to residential networking virtualization.

In the discussion of forwarding graphs, the concept of nesting forwarding graphs transparently to the end-to-end service is described. This level of decomposition does seem practical in that reusable subchains might make the overall orchestration of service chains easier to define, as well as operate.

In the description of a VNF the architecture document states that a VNF can be decomposed into multiple virtual machines (VMs), where each VM hosts a component of the VNF.[9] This is comprehensible from the starting point of a composite network function (eg, a conjoined PGW/SGW as a vEPC is decomposed to PGW and SGW). Such a procedure may need no standardization given that the decomposition is rather obvious.

Other applications may have backend components that may reside in a separate VM—like an IMS application with a separate Cassandra database. Here the challenge is more in the lifecycle management of the composite than its connectivity. The ability of a third party (other than the original "composed" function creator) performing this separation (or joining) seems unlikely.

To get more depth, the SWA (GS NFV-SWA) document provides more guidance around these "composite" functions.

- It introduces the VNFC.
- It superimposes its own reference points on the architecture (SWA-x).
- It describes VNF design patterns and properties: internal structure, instantiation, state models, and load balancing. To some degree, these can be seen in the Virtualization Requirements document.
- It describes scaling methodologies and reuse rules—including one that states that the only acceptable reusable component is one that is promoted to a full VNF (from VNFC).

In the example case of the composite vEPC, the document describes how the components might connect logically above the hypervisor (SWA-2 reference point) and stipulates that this could be vendor-specific, but seems to imply that they connect over the SWA-defined SWA-5 interface. In turn, the SWA-5 is defined as the VNF-VNFI interface with the functionality of accessing resources that provide a "special function" (eg, video processing card), "storage" and "network I/O."

Thus the NFV Architecture (and supporting documents) establishes a general deployment model where individual components always talk through the NFVI. The granularity of a "composite" is not sub-atomic as described, for example, it does not contemplate breaking the SGW functionality into further components, some of which may be reusable (although the potential exists).

The Virtualization Layer description of the NFVI appears to be written prior to the explosion of interest in containers (eg, UML, LXC, Docker) and thus is very hypervisor-centric in its view of virtualization. The document makes note of the fact that it is written in a certain time or place, with a nod to bare metal deployment of software-based VNFs.

While it is understandable that the goal was to be nonspecific to any specific virtualization "layer," the observation here is that technology in this space has and is rapidly evolving and these standards need to keep pace. Anyone implementing the technology described therein should be sure to look around at what is happening in the state of the art before making any firm decisions for a deployment.

The SWA document published later in the timeline of ISG publications recognizes an entire spectrum of virtualization, including containers, as does an INF document (The Architecture of the Hypervisor Domain—GS NFV INF 003). The latter states that the hypervisor requirements are similar to those of containers, but more research is needed to define that ecosystem.

In their latest white paper, the ISG provides this summary of the SWA document:

*In summary, the **NFV Virtual Network Functions Architecture** document defines the functions, requirements, and interfaces of VNFs with respect to the more general NFV Architectural Framework. It sets the stage for future work to bring software engineering best practices to the design of VNFs.*[10]

These variations could point to (minor) problems with any document in a traditional standard development organization keeping up with the current pace of innovation.

ARCHITECTURE—BIG BLOCKS AND REFERENCE POINTS

The big blocks in the high-level architecture framework (Fig. 3.3) include a further breakdown of NFV Management and Orchestration (and some external components), which we will visit again in Chapter 5, The NFV Infrastructure Management and Chapter 6, MANO: Management, Orchestration, OSS, and Service Assurance:

- OSS/BSS (Operations Support System/Business Support Systems) are traditionally involved in creating service (service catalog), maintaining it (FCAPS) and providing business support services (eg, billing). This remains outside of the scope of the architecture except for the Os-Ma interface.
- Service, VNF, and Infrastructure Description—an interface for Orchestration to ingest Forwarding Graph information and information/data models (or templates) for a Network Service catalog, a VNF catalog, the NFV instances and NFVI resources. This block insinuates the need for standard information/data models that is expanded on in the Virtualization Requirements document.

- NFV Orchestrator (NFVO) provides network-wide orchestration and management of both the VNFs and the NFVI. While this can be a proprietary software entity, it's commonly drawn associated with OpenStack.
- The Virtual Network Function Manager (VNFM) provides lifecycle management for the VNF. There are suggestions (eg, in vendor white papers) that the Orchestrator provides a superset of this functionality (advocating a plug-in VNFM architecture to bring in vendor-specific VNFMs or providing the service if the VNF does not have one of its own) as depicted in Fig. 3.4.
- The Virtual Infrastructure Manager (VIM) provides resource allocation notifications for resource management and is responsible for CRUD operations on the VM (host or container) level, including creating and destroying connections between the VMs. It will also track configuration, image, and usage information. Its interface to NFVI is where the mapping of physical and virtual resources occurs. Particularly in the area of network provisioning, especially where complex (above the provisioning of VLAN chains) topologies (eg, overlays) are involved, this is often associated with a network (SDN) controller (also depicted in Fig. 3.4).

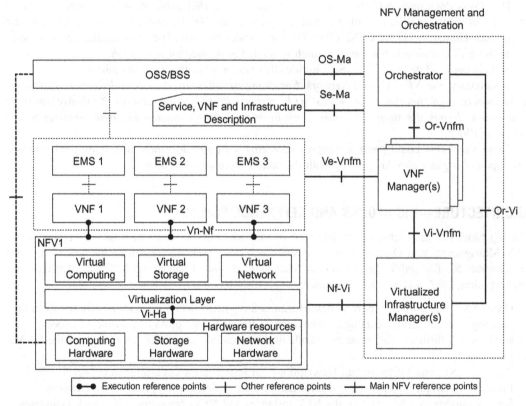

FIGURE 3.3

NFV Architectural function blocks and reference points.

The reference points shown in the figure describe and support service creation flows and their portability across infrastructure components.

The architecture illustration shows three types of reference points: execution, main and "other" (with the first two being in-scope and standardization targets).

The model often works as logical flows across the architectural elements via these well-defined interconnections.

The portability chain can be seen in:

- The Vl-Ha interface between the Virtualization Layer and the Hardware Layer is described to provide hardware independent execution and operation environment for the VNF.
- The Vn-Nf interface is supposed to provide an independent execution environment, portability, and performance requirements between the VNF Domain and NFVI in a similarly hardware-independent (and nonspecific of a control protocol) manner.

This might imply that a standard needs to evolve around how a VM (eg, an application or applications representing an NFV executing in a guest OS) connects to a hypervisor, which may attach the connectivity to an external software or hardware forwarder within or outside of the hypervisor with a simple virtualization support interface. The latter may be container definition, host resource

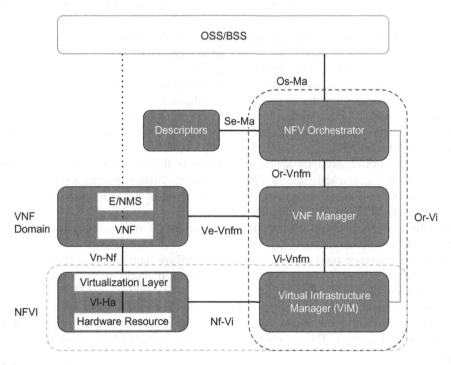

FIGURE 3.4

How the current domains of Orchestration (red, dark gray dashed line in print version) and SDN controller products (green, light gray dashed line in print version) might overlap NFV Architecture.

allocation, etc. Or perhaps this should simply be an exercise to document the de facto standards in this space such as VMware, HyperV, or KVM.

The flow of information that provides generic resource management, configuration, and state exchange in support of service creation traverses multiple reference points:

- Or-Vnfm interface between Orchestration and VNFM, which configures the VNF and collects service specific data to pass upstream.
- Vi-Vnfm interface between the VNFM and VNF Domain, which does additional work in *virtualized* hardware configuration.
- Or-Vi interface between the Orchestration and VIM, which also provides a *virtualized* hardware configuration information pathway.
- Nf-Vi interface between the NFVI and VIM, which performs *physical* hardware configuration (mapped to virtual resources).

The architecture suggests two levels of resource allocation, service-specific and VNF-specific.

There are two potential camps emerging around the implementation of this aspect of the architecture. As mentioned previously, there is a view that suggests that the NFVO takes on total responsibility for simplicity, consistency, and pragmatism, as this is how systems such as OpenStack currently function. Others may see the NFVO dividing up its responsibility with the VNFM where the NFVO is responsible only for service-level resources and the VNFM responsible solely for VNF resources.

There are pros and cons to either approach, which devolve into a classic complexity-versus-control argument in which the advocates of the latter view would hope to achieve some higher degree of control in return for a greater cost in complexity.

From a service management perspective, the OSS/BSS has just a single new interface described (Os-Ma) in the architecture and that is to the NFV Orchestrator. This interface supports the interface between back-end "business process" systems to the orchestrator. In the reality of today's systems, this represents an interface between a business process system and OpenStack, VMware, or Hyper-V's[11] north-bound APIs.

The rest of the OSS connectivity appears unchanged in this document. This is represented by the NMS to EMS connection and EMS to VNF connections. There is no mention of any change in the protocols involved in these interactions. The SWA document describes the EMS to VNF connectivity "as defined in ITU-T TMN recommendations."

Because there is only one new interface here, the bulk of the responsibility for this innovation seems shifted to NFV Orchestration.

The Ve-Vnfm reference point between EMS and VNF overlaps with the OS-Ma interface in respect to VNF lifecycle management and network service lifecycle management with the only discernable difference being in configuration.[12]

The Se-Ma reference point is more of an "ingestion" interface used by the Management and Orchestration system to consume information models related to the Forwarding Graph, services, and NFVI resources. This information can be manifested/understood as service and VM "catalogs."

The conclusion of the Architectural Framework points to a number of study items that will be fleshed out in the working groups and be returned in the form of their recommendations and gap analysis.

USE CASES

The use case document (GS NFV 001) describes nine use cases, and functions well as a standalone document. While it predates some workgroup document publications, it still provides a decent and still applicable set of use cases. The reader should keep in mind that the use cases include problem statements and requirements that were to be refined/addressed in the individual WGs. Given this, the use cases are due for an update. Whether these are done in ETSI or the new OP-NFV group is still to be determined.

The work starts with a statement of potential benefits that includes three notable items: improved operational efficiencies from common automation, improved power and cooling efficiency through the shedding, migration and consolidation of workloads and the resulting powering down of idle equipment, as well as improved capital efficiencies compared to dedicated equipment (as was the traditional operational model for workloads—one function per physical device/box).

The table below summarizes each use case:

1. NFV Infrastructure as a Service (NFVIaaS)
2. Virtual Network Functions as a Service (VNFaaS)
3. VNF Platform as a Service (VNFPaaS)
4. VNF Forwarding Graph
5. Virtualization of the Mobile Core Network and IMS (vEPC)
6. Virtualization of the Mobile Base Station
7. Virtualizing residential service CPE
8. Virtual Cache Service
9. Fixed Access Network Virtualization

In Fig. 3.5, NFVIaaS (Case 1—NFV Infrastructure as a Service) envisions an environment where one service provider (Administrative Domain #2) runs NFV services on the (cloud) NFVI of another (Administrative Domain #1), creating an offering across NFVIs that have separate administration. The incentives to do so could include (but are not limited to) the superior connectivity (and thus proximity to service clients) or resources (physical or operational) in Domain #1.

This mechanism could potentially address the scenario in Chapter 2, Service Creation and Service Function Chaining, where a Service Provider might want to offer a new service (expand) into another's territory without the capital outlay of building a large Point of Presence. However, the greater applicability is probably in the extension of an Enterprise domain service into the Service Provider network.

There is an assumption that appropriate authorization, authentication, resource delegation, visibility, and isolation are provided to the client provider by the offering provider's orchestration and management systems.[13]

The VNFaaS use case (Case 2—Virtual Network Functions as a Service) proposes a service provider offering an enterprise the ability to run services on their NFVI, with the manifest example being the vCPE for Enterprise customers. The target virtualized service list includes a Firewall, NG-Firewall (although no distinction between the two is given), PE, WAN optimization, Intrusion Detection, performance monitoring, and Deep Packet Inspection. Note here, the distinction from the former (NFVIaaS) is that the function is more of a managed service as well as infrastructure (the operator provides not only the infrastructure but the service function itself) and there can be

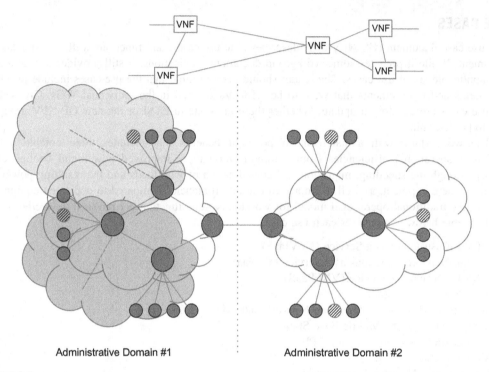

Administrative Domain #1   Administrative Domain #2

FIGURE 3.5

NFVIaaS allows one domain to extend its NFVI to another domain to create a virtual service overlay comprised of components in both domains.

subtle differences in the location of the hosted virtual services (where some providers see this as "in my cloud" and others want to offer "managed X86" on customer premise).

There is a VNFPaaS case (Case 3—VNF Platform as a Service), is a variant in which the primary operator offers the infrastructure and ancillary services required for the main service function and the subscriber provides the VNF. Examples of the ancillary functions include external/complimentary service functions like load balancing (providing elasticity) or more closely coupled functions like service monitoring/debugging environments and tools.

Similarly, there is a VNF Forwarding Graph use case (Case 4) description that appears to be a macro/generic description of NFV itself.

The use case surrounding virtualization of the Mobile Core Network and IMS (vEPC—Case 5) is interesting in that it echoes the recommendation of prudence (in Chapter 2: Service Creation and Service Function Chaining) around the relocation of services and describes a potential for full or partial virtualization of the services (there is a long list of components with potential to be virtualized)—given that there are varying functional characteristics across the set that at least in some cases, seem to contradict this. The challenges described for this service show a more realistic view of the complications of NFV rather than it being a simple exercise of repackaging an existing service into a VM (or container). In this vein, the use case does attempt to exhaustively list components with potential to be virtualized in this scenario, although it is unclear if this indicates the group's thinking on future components. Most importantly, the authors stress transparency within the context of network control and management, service awareness, and operational concerns like debugging, monitoring, and recovery of virtualized components.

The suggested virtualization of the Mobile Base Station (Case 6) has some of the same justifications as the vCPE example in the VNFaaS case in that the widely dispersed, generally bespoke implementation of the fixed eNodeB is a likely bottleneck to innovation. The virtualization targets described for both the "traditional" RAN and C-RAN include the baseband radio-processing unit (BBU)—which introduces (for the first time within the context of the use cases) a potential need for real-time signal processing![14]

Both use case 5 and use case 6 (Fig. 3.6) illustrate the potential intersection and impact of NFV on 3GPP.

Use case 7 describes how a service provider might virtualize a residential service CPE device commonly deployed as either the cable TV or Fiber to the Home (FTTH) set top box (STB) or RGW (Residential Gateway) and relocate some of its more sophisticated functionality into the service provider's cloud infrastructure (eg, NFVI). Like the vEPC, this service and its virtualization targets are well described, most likely as a result of these cases being some of the most obvious (and thus attractive) to service providers today.

Disappointingly, the virtualized residential service CPE (vCPE) use case does not segue into the potential to virtualize (or offload) the BNG, nor does the latter use case for access technologies (use case 9).

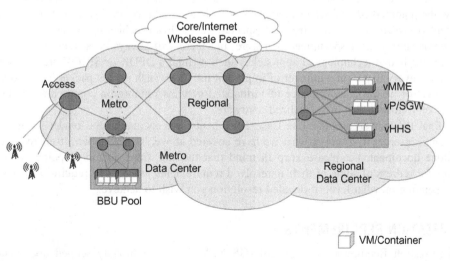

FIGURE 3.6

Various aspects of virtualization in mobility applications, including: BBU pool (RAN) and vPGW, vSGW, vMME, vHHS (core).

The virtual Cache use case (Case 8) brings out some of the fundamental issues with virtualization—the trade-off between operational efficiency via virtualization and performance loss due to virtualization (as opposed to bare metal performance[15]). There is a potential business problem this use case may address in abating the need to host a CDN provider's proprietary cache inside of a service provider—which is very specific example of the NFVIaaS use case.

The final use case, Fixed Access Network Virtualization (Case 9), targets the components of hybrid fiber/DSL environments such as fiber-to-the-cabinet (FTTC), which is used to facilitate most high-speed DSL these days, or FTTH. The proposal centers on the separation of the compute intensive parts of the element control plane, but not to the level of centralizing Layer 1 functions such as signal processing, FEC, or pair-bonding. The most interesting issue that NFV raised in this use case is the management of QoS when virtualization is employed.[16] In particular, bandwidth management (which is almost always instrumented in the form of packet buffer queues) is particularly tricky to manage in a virtualized environment so that it actually works as specified and as well as it did in a nonvirtualized configuration.

This use case also mentions the interesting challenge in managing the traffic backhaul insofar as the placement of the virtual resource used to implement the service. Specifically, when one considers the classic centralized versus distributed cloud model that was referenced in Chapter 2, Service Creation and Service Function Chaining. It is interesting and instructive to consider the particular relationship of these design choices as compared to the overall projected power utilization savings and economic benefits in NFV configuration (as they are not always what they might appear at first glance).

A notable omission from all of this work is some sort of concrete model that documents and validates the assumed cost savings in both power reduction and total cost of ownership that takes into account both the Opex and Capex expense swing expected in the use case.

In fairness, it may be some time before the platform requirements for I/O performance in virtualization for a use case like vCDN can achieve the same performance targets as dedicated hardware. Similarly, the potential cost of designs requiring real-time signal processing can be balanced against the concept of greater economics from nonspecialized hardware achieving some level of performance approaching that of specialized hardware, but there will always be a trade-off to consider. The good news is that technological approaches such as Intel's DPDK or SRIOV are making these choices easier every day as in a number of important use cases such as raw packet forwarding, they raise the level of network performance of virtualized systems running on commodity hardware to one that is very close to that of specialized hardware.

As a final thought around the Use Case Documents, we encourage the reader to go through them in detail in order to discover what we have covered above. The document itself reads well as a standalone document, but please keep in mind that the Use Case document points to the WG documents for redress of some of their unresolved requirements, which will require further investigation, depending on what level of detailed resolution you wish to achieve.

VIRTUALIZATION REQUIREMENTS

The Virtualization Requirements document (GS NFV 004) is a broadly scoped document with 11 high-level sections, each of which covers numerous aspects of virtualization relevant to every work group.

We think the reader will find that the document consistently reintroduces the requirement for information models pertaining to almost every aspect of virtualization. This particularly is a welcome addition to the work as we feel it is critical to the further advancement of this work. The document is divided into a number of sections that focus on key aspects of NFV including performance, elasticity, resiliency, stability, management, and orchestration and management.

The first section looks at *performance* focus and considers the allocation and management of resources for a VNF as they might fit into the performance requirements set in the VNF information model. This is expressed throughout the remaining sections in both the ability to both share and isolate resources. The performance monitoring requirements might actually be addressable through open source software offerings (eg, Ganglia[17] or customized derivatives).

The *portability* requirements (particularly the challenges around binary compatibility) might actually be addressed through the use of container environments (eg, Docker[18]).

From an ISG perspective, these requirements bubble up from the work of two work groups (MANO and PER). Commenting on performance in their most recent publication, they state:

... corresponding shortcomings of processors, hypervisors, and VIM environments were identified early in the work and have triggered recent developments in Linux kernel, KVM, libvirt, and OpenStack to accommodate NFV scenarios in IT-centric environments.

*The **NFV Performance & Portability Best Practises** document explains how to put these principles into practice with a generic VNF deployment and should be studied in conjunction with the **NFV Management and Orchestration** document.*[19]

The *elasticity* section defines this area as a common advantage of and requirement for most NFV deployment. Here again, an information model is suggested to describe the degree of parallelism of the components, the number of instances supported as well as resource requirements for each component.

Elasticity itself is described as either driven by the VNF itself on demand, as the result of a user command or even programmatically via external input. The former can potentially support of the case where the VNF is a composite and is deployed with an integrated load balancing function. This was described in the SWA document in the area of design.

There is a requirement for VM mobility in the elasticity section that details the need for the ability to move some or all of the service/VNF components from one compute resource to another. This is reiterated in the OAM requirements later in the document in much the same light.

It does remain to be seen if this is a requirement for a wide array of operational environments or just a corner case. While it is true that many types of VNFs should theoretically be movable, there are many operational and practical caveats to surmount, such as the required bandwidth to move a VNF, locality to other service chain functions on reassignment and/or the feasibility of splitting components in a composite. However, this requirement may drive the realization of some of the claimed power efficiencies of NFV.

The *resiliency* requirements have obvious aspects for maintaining connectivity between the functions and their management/orchestration systems. There are management facets, like the ability to express resiliency requirements and grouping (of functions) within those requirements. And, the resiliency section suggests the use of standards based, high performance state replication, and preservation of data/state integrity.

The ISG REL WG published a subsequent, separate paper on resiliency that the ISG summarizes:

*the **NFV Resiliency Requirements** document describes the resiliency problem, use case analysis, resiliency principles, requirements, and deployment and engineering guidelines relating to NFV. It sets the stage for future work to bring software engineering best practices to the design of resilient NFV-based systems.*[20]

There is a recommendation to establish and measure some metric that defines "stability" (and its variance) in the context of maintaining a SLA for a particular VNF. It yet remains to be seen if this is at all practical to implement, or if vendors can implement it in any consistent way across different VNFs. A number of what we consider difficult measurements are also suggested to measure adherence to an SLA, including: unintentional packet loss due to oversubscription, maximum flow delay variation and latency, and the maximum failure rate of valid transactions (other than invalidation by another transaction).

Beyond those issues covered in the resiliency section, management aspects are further underscored in the requirements for *service continuity* and *service assurance*. These might serve to flesh out the weaker OSS/BSS presence in the general architecture document and further shine a light on the need for often-overlooked capabilities such as consistent service quality and performance measurements.

In this regard, the document interestingly includes the requirement to be able to copy time-stamped packet copies of some to-be-determined precision to a configurable destination for monitoring. The mechanism relies on the time stamping capabilities of hardware for precision and performance. Because these are not universal capabilities, this further requires a capability discovery for these functions.

The *orchestration and management* section lays out fourteen requirements.[21] The most interesting of these are potentially in the ability to manage and enforce policies and constraints regarding placement and resource conflicts (which ties into some of the more practical constraints cited in the prior discussion of NSC/SFC).

These requirements all serve to underline both the potential fragility and difficulty of managing the performance of an ensemble of virtual functions that might come from one or more vendors.

The other broad area of requirements is in the *security* and *maintenance* sections.[22] Here, nine requirements are presented under the area of security (many to address risks introduced by virtualization and the numerous interfaces to be verified within the framework) and 16 under maintenance.

The depth and breadth of the requirements underscore how the virtual environment might sacrifice the things commonly found in a telco environment (eg, predictable security and maintenance procedures) in exchange for its massive scale and flexibility.

It is puzzling at best to imagine how the requirements can be mapped onto the rigid expectations of a telco environment. In short, it is like trying to map a "three nines" reality (for the equipment used in NFV) onto a "five nines" expectation (for service availability).

The sections, *energy efficiency* and *coexistence/transition* address issues more directly at the heart of NFV deployment decision-making.

The energy requirements start with a statement that NFV *could* reduce energy consumption up to 50% when compared to traditional appliances. These claims are according to studies that are not cited in the document. It would be interesting to have the document augmented with these references in the future.

Despite the lack of references, these claims generally rely on the ability of an operator in a virtualized environment to consolidate workloads in response to or anticipation of idle periods.

It also assumes that the compute infrastructure supports energy saving modes of operation such as stepped power consumption modes, idle or sleep modes, or even lower power using components.[23] The claim does not appear to be one of power efficiency over other methodologies during normal/peak operation. However, an assumption of certain peak to mean workload distribution or diurnal behavior may not translate to all services or all network operations.

It seems reasonable that if all these dependencies can be satisfied, there is a potential for savings (with a degree of variance between network designs and operations).

Outlining the need for coexistence with existing networks and a transition plan distinguish the ETSI NFV ISG from organizations like the ONF, which started with the premise that the network is a greenfield and have only later in their lifecycle begun to address "migration." In this section, the ISG states that the framework shall support a truly heterogeneous environment, both multivendor and mixed physical/virtual appliances, meaning that in actuality, your mileage will vary with regard to actual power savings and *should* only get better as an environment moves to a larger and larger percentage of virtualized assets over time. This claim will be highly dependent on the development of a number of standard interfaces and information models across the spectrum of appliance implementations to be realized.

Finally, the document returns to the theme of models, by discussing deployment, service, and maintenance models. The *service models* have a focus on the requirements to enable inter-provider overlay applications (eg, NFVIaaS), which seems to indicate that this is a desired use case (at least for some providers).

GAP ANALYSIS

Gap Analysis (NFV-013) consolidates gaps identified by the individual WGs and gives a hint as to where future work in NFV might be located, given the number of gaps and the number of impacted/targeted SDOs.

Drafted later in the Phase 1 document creation cycle, the document functions well as a standalone synopsis of the workgroup(s) findings.

More than one work group can identify gaps for an interface.

Referring to Fig. 3.7:

The INF WG pointed out two notable gaps. First, they identify the fact that there is no minimum performance requirement or target identified for *Nf-Vi* or *Vi-HA* interfaces and there is no common API for hardware accelerators. Another notable gap was the lack of a common interface for VIMs (eg, CloudStack, OpenStack, vSphere, or hyperV). This may be addressed via a plug-in facade around VIM selection in the future, but at present none exists. Despite these gaps, the primary focus for this work appears to be in OpenStack.

The MANO WG focused on gaps in resource management (for *Vi-Vnfm* and *Nfvo-Vi* interfaces). For starters, they identified the need for resource reservation via a common interface and the need for a common, aggregated resource catalog interface for cases where resource catalogs might be managed by multiple entities. The primary focus for this work was the TM Forum[24] and their Framework API and information models. However, the WG also cites necessary work in both the DMTF[25] (Distributed Management Task Force) OVF (Open Virtualization Format) specification and OASIS[26] TOSCA (Topology and Orchestration Specification for Cloud Applications) modeling technology. Both OpenStack and OpenDaylight Project may play a role here as well.

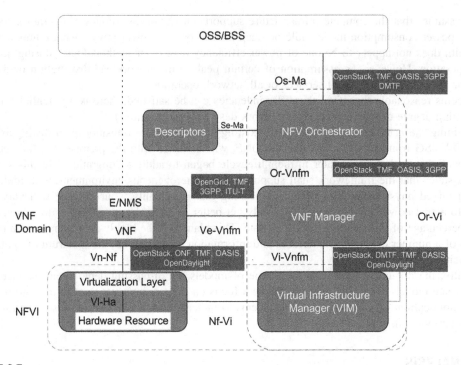

FIGURE 3.7

NFV Architecture mapping to SDOs, Open Source Software projects, and other forums. In general, OpenStack and OpenDaylight are applicable in the perceived areas of overlapping functionality (see also Fig. 3.4).

The PER WG pointed to a number of technologies aimed at boosting performance in processors. These are the *Vi-HA* and *Nf-Vi* interfaces in the NFV architecture. Specific performance improvements noted include hypervisor-bypass in CPU access to virtual memory, large page use in VMs, hypervisor-bypass for I/O access to virtual memory, large page use for I/O access, I/O interrupt remapping to VM, and the direct I/O access from NIC to CPU cache. Most of this work points to gaps in Libvirt[27] as well as vendor uptake of these technologies. Additional work in these areas for the *Vi Vnfm* and *Service VNF and Infrastructure Descriptor (Se-Ma)* are proposed as a series of OpenStack Blueprints that can potentially trigger future work if accepted by the corresponding OpenStack group.

The REL WG took a more generalized approach and pointed to both the IETF (RSerPool) and OpenStack as organizations to push for "carrier grade" solutions for NFV. In the former, they are pushing (however, unsuccessfully) for the creation of a new WG called VNFPool, and in the latter they cite a list of recommendations.

Fortunately, the SEC WG has a very comprehensive gap analysis (they have an overarching role in the architecture) that is in line with their white paper (GS NFV-SEC 001).[28] Gaps were identified in the following areas: Topology Validation and Enforcement, Availability of Management Support Infra, Secured Boot, Secured Crash, Performance Isolation,

User/Tenant AAA, Authenticated Time Service, Private Keys with Cloned Images, Backdoors via Virtualized Test and Monitoring and Multi-Administrator Isolation. At least two WGs in the IETF have been identified for inputs (ConEx and SFC), as well as the ITU-T (MPLS topology validation), TMF (TM Forum[29]), ONF, IEEE (time authentication), DMTF, and TCG.

The ISG white paper 3 notes these gaps and sums their work to date:

*The **NFV Security and Trust Guidance** document [4] identifies areas where evolution to NFV will require different technologies, practices, and processes for security and trust. It also gives security guidance on the environment that supports and interfaces with NFV systems and operations.*[30]

The SWA WG provided a gap analysis for VNF, EMS, and VNFC (largely around the *Vn-Nf* and *Ve-Vnfm* interfaces).

This work was disappointingly left incomplete in Phase 1. In the period between the publication of the draft of NVF-013 and the recharter at the end of 2014, many documents were finalized.

Unfortunately, the consolidated Gap Analysis (one of the prime promised outcomes of Phase 1) was not and its draft form was deleted from the ETSI NFV Phase 1 WG documents.

POC OBSERVATIONS

From a process perspective, the PER Expert Group is tasked with reviewing proposals based on their PoC Framework (GS NFV-PER 002).

It is important to note that the PoC sponsor is responsible for the technical correctness of the PoC.

The PoC Framework and Architecture Framework were published at the same time and the intent was for the PoC to adhere to and explore the different components and reference points of the architecture.

Given the large number of PoCs,[31] it is hard to cover each individual PoC here in detail, but there are interesting high-level trends amongst them.

Most PoCs are multivendor and demonstrate interoperable orchestration and management of services either as a vendor ecosystem consisting of both orchestration vendor and partners, or via open source (eg, using OpenStack to provide multivendor orchestration interoperability).

PoC #1 works around the lack of strict definitions, protocols, or examples of the reference points in the architecture framework by using a service integration framework (eg, the CloudNFV Open NFV Framework) that did not require the exposure of APIs.

The vendors involved in that first PoC also put forward their own viewpoints on how service "acceleration" or service optimization should be architected. There were some commonalities but these were far from a majority, nor were they necessarily consistently implemented implying some sort of uniform standard approach.

This revealed an early and later repeated/enduring focus on the potential weakness of network I/O centric applications in a virtualized environment.

As we stated earlier, in theory performance of virtualized network functions should be easily mapped onto virtualized hardware; in reality, it is not that straightforward. While PoCs based around Intel architectures and their associated specialized execution environments (eg, WindRiver or 6Wind) tend to dominate, there are other PoCs from competitors (eg, AMD or ARM) that proved worth investigating. Notably, PoC #21 focused on a mixture of CPU acceleration and the use of specialized coprocessing on programmable NICs to implement what the PoC labeled "Protocol Oblivious Forwarding." This represented what effectively was the Next Generation iteration of the OpenFlow architecture. Specifically, the output of the PoC suggested work was required in the Hardware Abstraction Layer.

Many of the PoCs champion a particular SDN technology for creating the Forwarding Graph (otherwise known as the Service Function Chain from Chapter 2), with the greatest emphasis on OpenFlow. Because OpenFlow is readily adaptable to simple PoCs, it was often used. PoC #14 tests the applicability of the IETF FoRCES architecture framework as a means of realizing NFV. Unfortunately, there has been little market momentum to date for FoRCES and so traction resulting from this PoC was limited.

As discussed as a topic earlier in Chapter 2, Service Creation and Service Function Chaining, a few PoCs concentrated on stateful VNF HA as being achievable through a variety of mechanisms.

PoC #12 investigated and demonstrated how a stateful VNF redundancy (potentially georedundancy for a site) is achieved using custom middleware by creating a SIP proxy from a load balancer, a group of SIP servers and "purpose-built" middleware for synchronizing state between these elements across each geographic site. PoC #3 shows a slight twist on the theme of stateful VNF HA, where state is migrated in a vEPC function from one vEPC to another. While not synchronized across sites to form a "live/live" configuration, it showed how live state migrations could be an important operational tool for stateful NFV. Finally, PoC #22 explores VNF elasticity management and resiliency through a number of scenarios using an external monitor as implemented using a WindRiver product.

PoC #3 focused on Virtual Function State Migration and Interoperability and brought some focus to the tooling behind portability. It also demonstrated tool-chain and operating system independence across ISAs while introducing the concept of a Low Level VM compiler. In some respects, this aspect of NFV is now also being addressed by the Linux containerization effort led by companies like Docker (as mentioned in the Virtualization Requirements comments).

To close on the PoCs, we note that the dominant PoC use cases are in the area of mobility and included detailed subcases such as vIMS, vEPC, LTE, RAN optimization, and SGi/Gi-LAN virtualization. Many of the VNFaaS scenarios hint at a carrier view that Enterprise services offload to their cloud may also be an early target.

Like the Use Case document, the PoCs do not expose much of the business/cost models around the solutions, which we feel is a very important driver to any adoption around the NFV technologies. After all, if the business drivers for this technology are not explored in detail, the actual motivation here will only be technological lust.

Finally, while a PoC can test interoperability aspects of the NFV technologies, it must also test their interoperability with the fixed network functions that are being replaced by NFV, despite existing for decades. While their functionality has been extensively tested, NFV introduces new ways in which to deploy these existing functions. In some cases, older code bases are completely rewritten when offered as an VNF in order to optimize their performance on Intel (or other) hardware. There is no mention of the burden, cost of integration and testing or even a testing methodology for these use cases.

A LOOK BACK—WHITE PAPER 3

Between the beginning of Open Platform for NFV (OPNFV) and before the final voting was completed on Phase 2, the ETSI NFV ISG published a third white paper (in October 2014). The paper introduction includes a brief justification of continued work (in Phase 2) to "address barriers to interoperability."

To the credit of the participants, the paper shows that they have realized some of the fundamental points covered in the chapter—particularly concerning the large role OSS will play in an NFV future, the importance of new thinking regarding OSS/BSS and the need for more focus on operator-desired service models like NFVFaas, NFVIaaS, and NFVPaaS (the focus of early Use Cases).

The document also clarifies, in their view, what the ISG thinks the important contributions of the work groups have been (these have been quoted in *italics* in the chapter) and provides some clarifications on the original premise(s) of ETSI NFV architecture.

To balance this self-retrospective look, it's interesting to look at the ETSI log of contributions for its first two years.

The log shows over one thousand four hundred (1400!) contributions. After eliminating administrative sources (workgroup, chair, etc.), the number is still over five hundred company-specific source contributions. Further, accounting for multiple source entries yields the graph in Fig. 3.8. The graph moves contributors of less than 1% of the total into a summary pool (Other) to maintain readability.

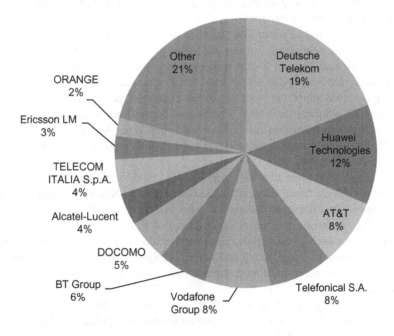

FIGURE 3.8

Who was ETSI Phase 1: contributions by company. "Other" is the collection of participants making contributions less than 2% of the total.

While it says nothing about quality of the contributions, the raw numbers shed interesting light on what voices controlled the dialog and the role of vendors. These can be compared against the original goal of provider control of the forum and the expressed limits on vendor participation. There was an expectation that vendors would contribute, but perhaps not to the extent that any of them would contribute more than the operator principals.

FUTURE DIRECTIONS
OPEN PLATFORM FOR NFV

At NFV#5 (February 2013), a document was circulated proposing the formation of an open source community as the basis for vendors to implement an open source NFV platform/forum. Given that the NFV output documents available at the time of the proposal were relatively high level, the ETSI NFV impact on other SDOs was (to that point) somewhat limited, and the Gap Analysis was not yet complete there was some expectation that this work (OPNFV) would influence the architecture, protocols, and APIs that needed to evolve for interoperability via a reference implementation.

The forum finally named OPNFV[32] was launched in September 2014 under the Linux Foundation, from which the new organization will derive its governance and administrative structure. It has been proposed that any intellectual property generated would be covered by an Apache 2.0 license[33] or an Eclipse Public license.[34]

Similar to the OpenDaylight Project that preceded it, OPNFV has a formal board and TSC hierarchy. However, like any organization under the wing of the Linux foundation, it is focused on open source code contributions, and is thus truly governed by code committers who form a subset of coders that produce the majority of source code for the project.

Since the organization starts out with no initial codebase, participants provide or create the pieces of the reference platform for VNFs, VNFM, and orchestrator as defined by ETSI NFV ISG. Products could be brought to market on that reference platform. As part of that work, the forum would further define/validate, implement, and test some of the common interfaces that were alluded to in the ETSI NFV architecture.

The platform is expected to be hardware agnostic (eg, Intel vs ARM), and amenable to VMs or bare metal implementations. Since containerization is likely to become a dominant strategy in the near future, container-based implementations are expected to be included.

The reality of the organization is that it is comprised of members from the service provider and vendor communities. As such, service providers generally do not bring traditional software developers to the party, and instead bring testing and interoperability facilities, test plans and documentation as well as a steady stream of guiding requirements and architectural points. In general, vendors will contribute traditional code.

The OPNFV platform's initial scope for the first release encompasses a subset of the ETSI defined VIM and NFVI as well as their associated reference points (Vi-Vnfm, Vi-HA, Nf-Vi, Vn-Nf, and Or-Vi) as illustrated in Fig. 3.9.

First ouputs were seen in the Arno release (June 2015) and the subsequent Brahmaputra (February 2016).

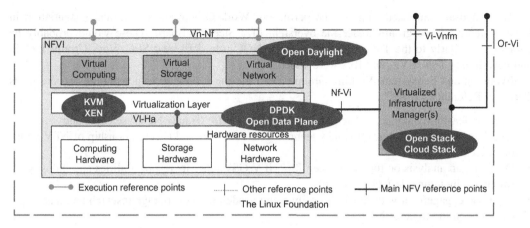

FIGURE 3.9

OP-NFV focus areas (The Linux Foundation).

At this time, the organization has formed requirements, documentation, testing integration, and a software platform integration projects.

Much of the community comprising the organization has also taken what appears to be a more pragmatic approach to its first deliverable, and has begun work on an integration project that has some very simple goals: to integrate KVM, OpenStack, and OpenDaylight.

The premise behind this approach is to first build up the infrastructure around the integration project that will support future work. In doing so, it brings the community together to work on a worthwhile project.

It also will run the integrated project through the software integration testing labs provided by the service providers, and finally produce documentation pertaining to the combined project.

The project seems to not need any custom (ie, branched) code changes initially, which is again a pragmatic approach as maintaining separate code bases is not something for the faint of heart or those without a lot of experience. Instead, the project will strive to use "off the shelf" builds of OpenDaylight and OpenStack and simply integrate them together. When changes are needed, attempts will be made to commit patches upstream.

REPATRIATION/ISG2.0 (AND 3.0)

It should be noted that here is no formal linkage between OPNFV and the attempt to reboot the ETSI NFV ISG, although they could be complimentary.[35]

At the same time that the concept of an OPNFV project was being broached, the participants in ETSI NFV were circulating a strawman proposal seeking to extend the charter of the ISG past its early 2015 remit. This proposed repatriation with ETSI NFV as an ISG v2.0, thus extending the life of the group. This proposal ultimately (and perhaps not surprisingly) passed, and Phase 2 of the ETSI NFV workgroup began in January 2015 (and continues to meet quarterly through 2016).

The proposal eliminated some of the permanent Work Groups of the original instantiation in favor of more ad-hoc groups under the oversight of a Steering Board. These would probably be composed similarly to the TSC, with a continuing NOC role. REL and SEC Work Groups remain and new groups TST, EVE, and IFA were added.

Evolution and Ecosystem Working Group (EVE) has the following responsibilities accord to its Terms of Reference (ToR)[36]:

- Develop feasibility studies and requirements in relation to: (i) new NFV use cases and associated technical features, (ii) new technologies for NFV, and (iii) relationship of NFV with other technologies.
- Develop gap analysis on topics between ISG NFV GSs under its responsibilities and industry standards, including de facto standards.
- Facilitate engagement with research institute and academia to encourage research and teaching curricula on the topic of NFV.

The Testing, Experimentation, and Open Source Working Group (TST) has the following responsibility according to its ToR[37]:

- Maintaining and evolving the PoC Framework and extending the testing activities to cover interoperability based on ISG NFV specifications.
- Developing specification on testing and test methodologies.
- Coordinating experimentation and showcasing of NFV solutions (eg, PoC Zone).
- Producing PoC case studies (eg, VNF lifecycle), and documenting/reporting the results in various forms (eg, white papers, wikis).
- Feeding feature requests to open source projects and implementation experience results to open source communities, and developing reports (eg, guidelines, best practices) from implementation experience.
- Transferring results to other ISG NFV working groups to ensure consistent delivery of specification through real implementation and testing.

Interfaces and Architecture (IFA) ToR[38] gives them the following responsibilities:

- Delivering a consistent consolidated set of information models and information flows (and data models and protocols when necessary) to support interoperability at reference points.
- Refinement of the architecture (including architectural requirements) and interfaces leading to the production of the set of detailed specifications.
- Maintenance of specifications related to architecture and interfaces within the scope of this WG.
- Cooperate with other external bodies to lead to the production of the set of detailed specifications and/or open source code development of the reference points or interfaces to meet the requirements.
- Collaborate with other external bodies as necessary related to the WG activities.

Between them, these groups share almost 30 work items.

The stated main goal of the ETSI NFV ISG reboot is simply to steer the industry toward implementations of NFV as described by the NFV documents, and to make future work "normative" and informative, with the possibility of refining/redefining existing documents into the "normative" category or deriving "normative" specifications from them. As previously mentioned, the IPR prospects would have to be re-evaluated by potential participants.

This may also lead to questions about the relationship of ETSI to other SDOs that are also working on standards or "normative" work in these areas.

The reboot effort may have some undesirable connotations:

Some may see a recharter for another two years with normative documents as a slight devaluation of the outputs of its preceding work.[39] This is natural in a move from "study" mode to "implementation" mode.

There may also be a temptation to further refine the work of Phase 1. For example, early proposals from a new Working Group (IFA) consider further decomposition of the NFVO, the VIM, and the VNFM.

Additionally, some observers may also see the rechartered ISG goal of developing an NFV ecosystem and a potential reference implementation as being a significant overlap with the newly-formed OPNFV organization, who fully intend to function in an agile and accelerated way. The slow-moving and sometimes political nature of the original NFV ISG have been cited by some as a reason for preferring to operate within the OPNFV organization.

By the end of 2015, the groups had considered more than two hundred (200) new documents,[40] almost half of which were originated by the IFA WG. Participation followed a similar pattern to the prior ISG, with even stronger vendor participation relative to service providers.

Much of the work was centered on modeling (to further define the component interfaces), including a special workshop on Information Modeling which lead to an announcement of further collaboration with other SDOs to get necessary work done (vs imposing a centralized information model)[41] with more potential workshops.

Going into 2016, the future of the ISG is again unclear, as the ISG may now be aware of how embarrassing it would be to recharter a third time at the end of 2016. Once again, the longevity and necessity of the specifications may be called into question, unless a smooth handover to some other entity occurs.

CONCLUSION

At the highest level, the ETSI NFV experiment is a good illustration of the pros and cons of "forum-seeking" (a relatively new behavior) by a user group. Lacking an SDO willing to standardize anything related to NFV, the result of Phase 1 was a "study."

The proposed marriage between traditional telco-like standards development, the desires of traditional network operators and the realities of agile, open source implementation (as a means to achieve timely and up-to-date Standards creation) is interesting and challenging. More importantly, the combination could potentially have overcome some of the traditional standards creation hurdles by rapidly creating a single, reference open source framework that could become a *de facto* standard. At least in Phase 1 of the ETSI NFV WG, this did not happen.

Outside of their generated white papers, the contribution of the ETSI NFV ISG to ongoing work in NFV and related standards is still unclear.

The resulting ETSI NFV ISG work is to date, instructive. They have created a lexicon for discussing NFV.

The PoC work has been an early peek at what may be possible with NFV and (importantly) where the interests of operators and vendors may lie (mobility and enterprise managed services).

However, a number of relevant, nontechnical items are left unfinished by the ISG for the operators and the reader to figure out, including the business cases and cost models of the prime use cases. Even the proposed energy savings rely on specific models of operation that may not fit all operator networks. As we have said earlier, the devil is in the details. Unfortunately important details such as economic impact have been overlooked, which could prove important.

The failure to publish the Gap Analysis (including the erasure of the draft) was also disappointing.

Certainly, the ETSI NFV ISG (v1) outputs will shape some vendor/operator transactions, potentially manifesting as requirements or references in the operator/vendor RFP/RFQ process (particularly for the founding operators).

But, after two years of study, the result appears to have been the recommendation of a great deal of additional work. The number of interfaces still needing specification in their ITU-T-like approach to standardization as described in their documents will take a much longer time, and require interaction with many other independent forums and open source projects to reach their goals. ETSI 2.0 seems to be approaching these as a modeling exercise.

As this work moves to other forums, participants in the newly-minted OPNFV forum may see an overlap with the proposed reinstantiation of the ETSI ISG. The success of either is not yet assured, but if OPNFV can move at the same rapid pace as The OpenDaylight organization has, it may render the new ISG effort moot.

There are already working NFV implementations that obscure the many yet-to-be-specified interfaces described in the ETSI ISG architecture (ie, blurring the lines between the functional blocks by providing multiple parts of the recommended architecture without the formal adoption of these reference points) on the market (and in early trials).

The advent of open source implementations and their associated rapid iteration may also prove the ETSI architecture moot, at least in part.

This is not the end of the world, as many view the ETSI architecture as a guide, and not a specification for implementation. The architecture has become, as a colleague described it, "a hole into which your jigsaw piece has to fit, but my concern is that it's a hole into which nothing that works will ever truly fit."

Consumers may ultimately decide that the level of granularity described in the architecture is not necessary before the targeted contributions required of (and in) other forums are accepted and codified.

Early offerings of service virtualization are not all choosing the chain-of-VMs model behind the original architecture, indicating that there may be room for more than one architectural view (depending on the service offered and the operator environment).

If compelling, these offerings, ongoing (and new) open source efforts and other standards bodies may ultimately decide the level of standardization required for interoperable NFV and how much of the ETSI NFV ISG architecture is relevant.

END NOTES

1. NFV_White_Paper2.
2. https://portal.etsi.org/Portals/0/TBpages/NFV/Docs/NFV_White_Paper3.pdf. This document is quoted in several places (italicized) to add the ISG's own perspective on their contributions.
3. http://www.etsi.org. Note, ETSI NFV uses a specific "portal" to access its work group work-in-progress.
4. Linguistically, the implication is the change between a "recommendation" and a prescriptive part of a Standard (ie, becoming "the" Standard). With this understanding, the IPR policies of ETSI are less significant to the overall effort under its current charter. However, once the documents move to normative (a potential outcome of rechartering), the IPR policies are more relevant to participants. These are that participants cannot declare broad IPR, but should cite specific patents and sections these apply to. Further, this IPR must be provided either Royalty Free or FRAND (Fair Reasonable and Non-Discriminatory—not "free")—owners cannot refuse to license.
5. Consensus was originally defined/described as no ISG member company objecting to an ISG position. Consensus was envisioned as giving nonmembers a feeling of equal participation.
6. http://www.etsi.org/technologies-clusters/technologies/nfv/nfv-poc. Note that "registered" does not necessarily imply "endorsed."
7. The ETSI NFV ISG does not suffer from a lack of Use Cases. The INF WG produced a Use Case document after the ISG-level document was published (and thus it was "held").
8. In other SDOs (eg, IETF) NFV members have pushed hard for common terminology and thus the adoption of these terms. This has not been universally agreed upon (yet).
9. The ideas in the architecture behind the granularity of decomposition and the compartmentalization of functions (packaging multiple functions as a composite, how they communicate and which methodologies are more efficient) are the grist of the "non-ETSI" implementation architecture discussed in Chapter 2, Service Creation and Service Function Chaining—which is why they are worth exploring. They resurface again in Chapter 8, NFV Infrastructure—Hardware Evolution and Testing, with the "rise of containers."
10. *Network Functions Virtualisation—White Paper #3* ETSI NFV ISG (October 2014).
11. Insert your favorite vendor's or open source orchestration product here.
12. See earlier reference in Chapter 2, Service Creation and Service Function Chaining, about the standardization of configuration process. This is particularly problematic in a multivendor environment.
13. ATIS NFV Forum (http://www.atis.org/NFV/index.asp) provides some musings on the detailed architectures and relationships for Inter-Admin Domain Virtualization.
14. The split of functionality in this use case is being revisited after early trials of CPRI-based proposals (a PHY-based split) required huge bandwidth and minimal delay characteristics that were not prevalent for the "front haul" network. In the interim, new RAN designs with a preponderance of small cells and WiFi emerged.
15. Bare metal server provisioning frameworks exist from many sources (eg, Cisco Systems, Puppet Labs, OpenStack).
16. The implementation proposed by ONOS CORD project addresses the problem through a split VNF/PNF, where the PON operation is managed by a container/VM based control entity (vOLT) but the dataplane remains on a nonvirtualized platform (OLT).
17. Ganglia, http://ganglia.sourceforge.net/.
18. Docker, https://www.docker.com/.
19. *Network Functions Virtualisation—White Paper #3* ETSI NFV ISG (October 2014).
20. *Network Functions Virtualisation—White Paper #3* ETSI NFV ISG (October 2014).
21. In this area there has been discussion of a potential "discovery" piece—a method of identifying a function. The difficulty here might be that (like the use of IANA numbers in other SDO specifications) you need a clearinghouse for these identities. This could be achievable through standardized models.

22. The referenced challenges from use cases like VNPaas and VNFaaS make the prospects of success in hosting VNxaaS (period) seem less likely (the security challenges in a home environment are not a surprise).
23. These are all an important distinction from complete shutdown of resources.
24. http://www.tmforum.org.
25. http://www.dmtf.org/standards/ovf.
26. http://www.oasis-open.org.
27. http://www.libvirt.org.
28. Security white paper can be downloaded from the published documents, http://docbox.etsi.org/ISG/NFV/Open/Published/.
29. http://www.tmforum.org.
30. *Network Functions Virtualisation—White Paper #3* ETSI NFV ISG (October 2014).
31. http://www.etsi.org/technologies-clusters/technologies/nfv/nfv-poc. Twenty-five PoCs in progress or completed at the end of Phase 1.
32. http://www.opnfv.org.
33. Apache 2.0 License.
34. Eclipse Pubic License, http://www.eclipse.org.
35. At least in the early stages, it does appear that ETSI members are "hand carrying" work items from the ETSI Phase 2 work into OPNFV.
36. http://docbox.etsi.org/ISG/NFV/05-CONTRIBUTIONS/2014/NFV(14)000323r3_Revised_ToR_EVE_WG.doc.
37. http://docbox.etsi.org/ISG/NFV/05-CONTRIBUTIONS/2014/NFV(14)000331r1_TST_WG_proposed_Terms_of_Reference.docx.
38. http://docbox.etsi.org/ISG/NFV/05-CONTRIBUTIONS/2014/NFV(14)000322r1_Architecture___Interfaces_WG_-_Proposed_ToR_and_Organization.docx.
39. For example, Phase 2 PoC Framework requirements changes might be interpreted as an indictment of the older process for lack of focus.
40. A search of the 2016 submissions gives 162 documents as of February 15, 2016. Contributions dated 2015 and 2016 combined top 800. These would have to be filtered for administrative and discarded documents to come up with an accurate count.
41. http://www.etsi.org/news-events/news/1053-2016-01-news-etsi-seeks-harmonization-of-nfv-information-modelling-across-standards-bodies-and-open-source.

IETF RELATED STANDARDS: NETMOD, NETCONF, SFC AND SPRING

4

INTRODUCTION

From the prior chapter on ETSI and the related exploration of NFV, you may have come away with the impression that standardization is currently stagnant or worse, an outdated artifact of the past. However, some traditional standards are actually making some headway around NFV. In particular, The Internet Engineering Task Force (IETF) is contributing actively in a number of areas. While it is a traditional standards organization that was formed in 1986 when many of those reading this book might not have even been born, it still remains relevant in new areas including NFV.

To recap a bit, the ETSI NFV "Phase 1" study we discussed earlier viewed the IETF relationship to NFV Standards as:

- The IETF RSerPool workgroup was identified in the draft ETSI Gap Analysis document (by the ETSI Reliability WG) as potential Standards providers for NFV (around resource management).
- The SFC workgroup was mentioned in the same analysis (by the ETSI Security WG), as well as the ConEx workgroup (in the context of security needs).
- While the FoRCES (workgroup) architecture was used in a PoC, it was not mentioned in the gap analysis.[1]

Further, there was a move to create a VNFPool workgroup. A Birds of a Feather (BoF) meeting was held,[2] and was specifically driven by members of the ETSI community. Unfortunately, it did not succeed in forming a working group due to an apparently lack of a clear definition, overlap with other existing working groups and a general lack of community interest, perhaps due to a misunderstanding of what the proposed group was trying to achieve. This has unfortunately happened a number of times in the past at the IETF in areas related to SDN.[3] The eventual outcome of that effort was the creation of the I2RS working group, which has since gone off in direction that no one seems to understand.

That experience aside, at present the IETF has several workgroups that are directly applicable to NFV either by virtue of adapting their charters, or by having been created later with a more clear or understandable focus. We particularly point to the work in the SFC, and Network Modeling (NETMOD) groups.

Other workgroups that are creating standards around transport, particularly those working on network overlays, have some overlap in the NFV space by virtue of being applicable to SDN and thus part of ETSI VIM. These include Network Virtualization Overlays (NVO3), LISP, MPLS (now called BESS), and Source Packet Routing in Networking (SPRING).[4]

The output of these groups and the efficacy of that output to actual NFV deployments varies. With that in mind, we will look specifically at the SFC and NETMOD workgroups in this chapter. We will pay particular attention to YANG modeling to describe interfaces to network systems. We will also look at the particular case of Segment Routing for IPv6 from SPRING as a practical tool that is in use in production NFV networks today.

SERVICE FUNCTION CHAINING

The IETF has had a recent history of tension between providing new solutions for evolving needs around SDN and NFV and the reuse/extension of existing paradigms like MPLS forwarding within these contexts. This has created some struggle for new working groups as their charters are continually pared back and work on solutions is dispersed amongst competing work groups. A recent attempt at reorganization will hopefully allow new workgroups to make faster progress, but the jury is still out on this attempt at renewed applicability in the new and evolving worlds of SDN and NFV.

The SFC workgroup is one of these new groups and its charter[5] makes very clear that it will develop "a new approach to service delivery and operation." The charter mandates documentation of a problem statement, architecture, generic SFC encapsulation, related control plane mechanisms, and management issues. The latter work on control plane extensions may be exported to appropriate workgroups and the management aspects need to be scoped (but may not drive actual recommendations under this charter). In addition, the workgroup decided to publish use cases—two of which were domain-specific (Data Center and Mobility) and the third a catch-all document (providing the use cases illustrated new requirements that were not found in the other use case documents).

The original goal was to deliver these work items by the end of 2015.

PROBLEM STATEMENT

The problem statement[6] lists many of the challenges first covered in our more generic chapter on SFC and the problem of service creation (see Chapter 2: Service Creation and Service Function Chaining), including topological dependency, configuration complexity (there is hope that the modeling work in NETMOD and programmability of newer orchestration systems may provide abstractions that limit syntactic variation) and constrained HA of existing service deployment methodologies.

Some additional problem areas of interest include the consistent ordering of service functions (SFs) and application of service policies that are related and deal with the limited information we currently have for verification or triggering service policy.

SFC solutions are comprised of two main components: an overlay and an underlay. The *overlay* is a network virtualization scheme that can be thought of much like a network-based virtual private network from past network technologies such as MPLS layer 2 or layer 3 VPN. In these cases, an additional context demarcation is used to create a virtual context to effectively tunnel traffic across an otherwise agnostic substrate (ie, an IP/Ethernet/MPLS/ATM/Frame Relay network). The substrate can be referred to as the *underlay*.

NFV solutions all depend on the underlying transport mechanisms to deliver traffic between their endpoints. This is because the underlay must be able to encapsulate or tunnel the overlay traffic in order to transparently carry it from its source to its destination. This is the case whether the source and destination exist within the same underlay domain, or as is rapidly becoming more prevalent, overlays may span more than one type of underlay.

In all cases, this intrinsic dependency between the overlay on the underlying transport or underlay points out a key challenge:

transport-tied solutions may require sophisticated interworking and these have been shown to introduce a great deal of often unwanted, variation in implementations.

Basically the complications add difficulty in vendors interoperating with each others' implementations. It is essentially an argument for the creation of a *transport-independent* and *dynamic* service overlay!

While we have also touched previously on the need for elasticity, more fine-grained traffic selection criteria and the need for vendor-interoperable solutions, the problem statement also notes the costs of limited end-to-end service visibility and per-function classification. This happens to also reinforce the arguments just given for an independent service overlay.

The problem statement document states three fundamental components that are the basis for SFC (and goals of SFC work):

- Create a topology and transport independent service overlay that provides service-specific information that aids in troubleshooting service failures (minimally, the *preservation of path*).
- Provide a classification mechanism that reduces or *eliminates the need for per-function traffic classification*, normalizes classification capability/granularity across all functions and equipment and enables the building of classification-keyed symmetric paths (where necessary).
- Provide the ability to *pass "data plane" or inband metadata between functions* (resulting from "antecedent classification," provide by external sources or derived).

The last two components can be inter-related.

SFC ARCHITECTURE

The SFC Architecture document[7] defines The SFC as an "ordered set of abstract service functions." The definition leaves room for services that require chain branching by stating that the order implied may not be a linear progression. There is stated support for cycles as well, and to accommodate these SFC control is going to be responsible for infinite loop detection/avoidance.

Additionally, the stateful nature of some functions and the services built from them drives a need for symmetry in SFCs. This symmetry can be "full" (meaning the entire chain is symmetric), or "hybrid" (meaning that only some functions require symmetry). The document provides a nonexhaustive list of potential methodologies to achieve/enforce symmetry, and we refer you to it if you are interested in reviewing all of these possible options.

It is worth noting that the SFC Architecture document also includes its own definition of terms that may not be entirely in sync with the ETSI definitions. This occurred despite it being strongly influenced by ETSI membership. It is also important to note that the architecture leaves interdomain chaining for future study. The document cleverly frees itself in a way that avoids having to standardize individual functions or the logic behind how a chain is selected or derived. These boundaries keep it from venturing into the function itself, and the particulars of management, orchestration, and policy of those functions while still providing the mechanisms and definitions for how to chain them together. In short, this was to avoid "boiling the ocean" of NFV and having to enumerate and define every combination and permutation of service function chains.

The Service Function Path (SFP) is the rough equivalent of the ETSI "forwarding graph" that we mentioned earlier in the ETSI chapter. It is defined in some of the most important verbiage in the document as:

a level of indirection between the fully abstract notion of service chain as a sequence of abstract service functions to be delivered, and the fully specified notion of exactly which SFF/SFs the packet will visit when it actually traverses the network.

The latter is described as the Rendered Service Path (RSP), which can again be a concise set of nodes to traverse but may also be less specific. SFC is a mechanism that allows for "loose coupling" between the service and the particulars of its instantiation.

Much of this text has a history in the early failure of a contingent in the work group to understand the value of an abstraction applied to a service like loadbalancing. It is this inherent approach to elasticity—a fundamental property of SFC, that avoids an explosion of explicit paths and the management of those paths, where the load balancing state can be locally maintained as a separate or integrated SF.

In defining the SF, which is the equivalent of the VNF in ETSI, care is taken to allow for an SF that can be either SFC encapsulation- aware or not. In this case, the SFC encapsulation is not passed to the function.

This leads us to now introduce the concept of the Service Function Forwarder (SFF) as seen in Fig. 4.1. The SFF can be integrated with the function or standalone. It forwards traffic from one or

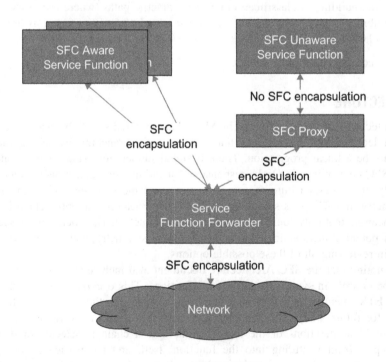

FIGURE 4.1

The Service Function Forwarder.

more attached SFs or proxies, transports packets to the next SFF on return from the SF in the SFP which is a typical overlay function, or terminating the SFP by stripping of the SFC encapsulation as its final operation.

Because the SFF can have more than one SF, the architecture has to accommodate the potential private interconnection of those SFs. The coordination of this with the SFF is out of scope. The SF can naturally belong to more than one SFP, and this is a common method of "templatizing" or reusing the function.

The document mentions that the SFF "may be stateful," creating and maintaining flow-centric information which can be leveraged in maintaining symmetry, handling proxy tasks or just ensuring uniform treatment. When we talk about creating a service overlay, the expected mechanism leverages the mapping of a service path ID (SPI) to next-hop(s), which is a construct above the normal network-level lookup.

This aligns with the second architectural principle (Section 3 of the document) that the realization of SFPs is separated from normal packet handling.

The other architectural goals outlined in the document echo some of those in the problem statement with a few additions. Most of these are around independence in the architecture:

- Independence from the SFs details—no IANA registry to catalog them.
- Independence of individual SFCs—that changing one SFC has no impact on another.
- Independence from any particular policy mechanism to resolve local policy or provide local classification criteria.

In allowing the SF to be SFC encapsulation-agnostic or unaware, the concept of the SFC Proxy is introduced (Fig. 4.2). At the lowest level, the proxy handles decapsulation/encapsulation tasks

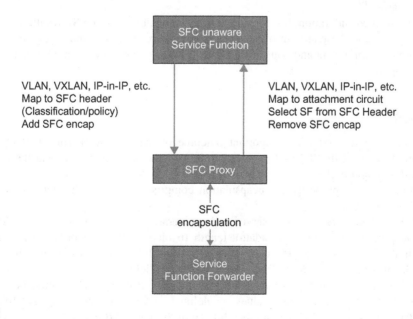

FIGURE 4.2

The SFC Proxy.

for the SF. Since a proxy can handle more than one function at a time, it would also select that function from information in the encapsulation and perform a transfer via a mapping on a more traditional local attachment circuit.

When traffic is returned, a reverse mapping enables the proxy to reapply the encapsulation. If the function has altered the packet it may need to be reclassified which the proxy can do locally or send to a default classification capable node.

In the section "Transport Derived SFF," the SFC Architecture Document does show some of the remaining tension between MPLS advocacy (by some members) and the need to create a separate service overlay. In essence, it acknowledges that some members advocate using the transport path in the form most likely of an MPLS label stack, and makes it their responsibility or that of the associated control plane, to keep forwarding aligned with the path in the SFC encapsulation.

There are a series of additional topics of interest in the architecture that require more study and we encourage the reader to look further into this by visiting the IETF's SFC Working Group page and joining its mailing list to follow ongoing discussions[8]:

- SFC Control Plane—is out of scope, but is envisioned to provide a domain-wide resource view, use policy to construct static or dynamic SFCs and propagate data plane forwarding and metadata specifications to the SFF(s).
- Operations and Management—because the scope is currently single domain, the document suggests that traditional concerns around MTU issues resulting from additional encapsulation via PMTUD[9] or by setting link MTU high enough to accommodate SFC encapsulation are sufficient. Further, the document advocates the support of end-to-end Operations and Management (OAM) in-band but declares function validation such as application-level OAM to be clearly out-of-scope. Drafts have be submitted specifically to address OAM, but are still a work in progress.[10]
- Resilience—is a consideration, but SF state is the responsibility of the SF (multiple techniques exist and these are out-of-scope) and general resilience in the case of changing load are tied to monitoring and control functions (out-of-scope) and leverage of elasticity functions (operations).

NSH HEADER[11]

Perhaps the most controversial and important outcome of the SFC workgroup will be the SFC encapsulation. Typical of the IETF, there are two drafts—one submitted early and the other later. These two different approaches may or may not merge.

The dominant draft[12] proposes an encapsulation comprised of a base header, SP header, and context headers (Fig. 4.3).

The base header includes version, reserved and enumerated flags (O to indicate an OAM packet and C for the presence of critical metadata), length (6 bits) in 4 byte words (setting maximum header length at 256 words), Next Protocol (IPv4, IPv6, and Ethernet values defined and an IANA registry will be allocated) and a Meta Data Type (MD Type) field.

The MD Type defines the type of metadata beyond the SP header. The values here will also require a new IANA register and two values are defined so far—0x1 indicating that fixed length context headers follow and 0x2 indicating the absence of these context headers.

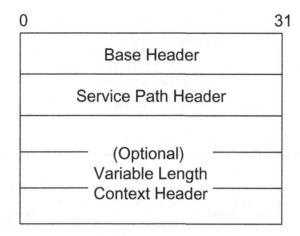

FIGURE 4.3

The NSH base, SP, and context header format.

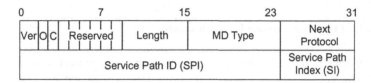

FIGURE 4.4

Base and SP Header detail.

The SP Header (Fig. 4.4) includes the SPI[13] and the Service Index (SI).

The SPI is a representative and not necessarily a canonical value (recall the separation of the idea of a "rendered" path) and the SI is an index in that path. As the packet progresses through the chain, the SI is decremented so that the SI can also be used as a loop detector/inhibitor. The idea behind the use of the fixed context headers in MD Type 0x1 comes from the desire to avoid a complex registry for metadata and its use is illustrated by examples.

The guidelines given for these headers (Fig. 4.5) is that they have four parts (each 32 bits):

- Network Platform Context—platform-specific information to be shared between network nodes (eg, ingress port, forwarding context, or encapsulation).
- Network Shared Context—metadata relevant to any network node in the chain (eg, a classification result like appID, user identity, or tenant ID(s)).
- Service Platform Context—like the Network Platform Context but for service platforms (eg, identifier used for load balancing decisions).
- Service Shared Context—like the Network Shared Context but shared between service platforms and expected to be more finely grained (eg, appID).

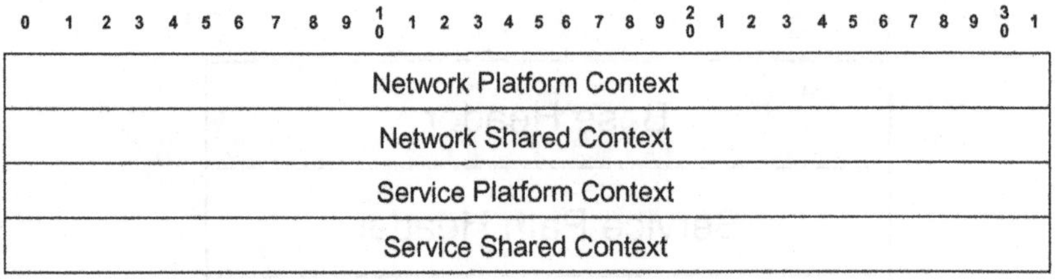

0 1 2 3 4 5 6 7 8 9 $\frac{1}{0}$ 1 2 3 4 5 6 7 8 9 $\frac{2}{0}$ 1 2 3 4 5 6 7 8 9 $\frac{3}{0}$ 1
Network Platform Context
Network Shared Context
Service Platform Context
Service Shared Context

FIGURE 4.5

Fixed Context Header block detail (these follow the Base and SP Headers for MD Type 0x1).

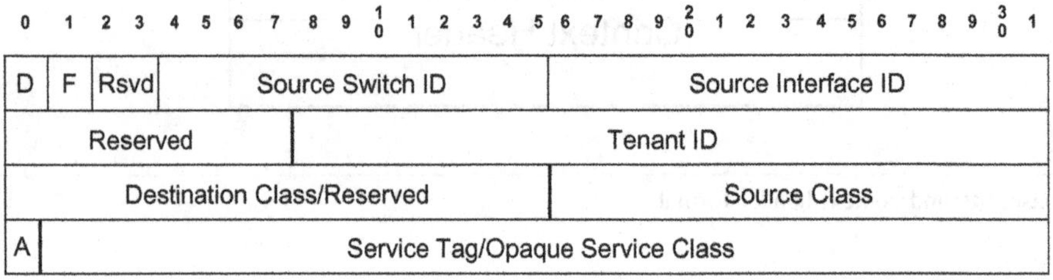

0	1	2	3 4 5 6 7 8 9 $\frac{1}{0}$ 1 2 3 4 5 6 7 8 9 $\frac{2}{0}$	1 2 3 4 5 6 7 8 9 $\frac{3}{0}$ 1
D	F	Rsvd	Source Switch ID	Source Interface ID
		Reserved		Tenant ID
		Destination Class/Reserved		Source Class
A			Service Tag/Opaque Service Class	

FIGURE 4.6

Suggested/example NSH Data Center context header allocation.

A data center-oriented draft[14] illustrates the potential use of the context headers in that environment (Fig. 4.6). The headers are designed to reflect a Data Center-specific usage and focus on application, tenant, or user identification central to DC service chains.

The suggested allocation for the Network Platform Context has a 4-bit wide Flag field with two defined flags (D bit signals whether the third word is Destination Class or Reserved and the F bit signals whether the fourth word is a Service Tag or Opaque). The Source Node ID is a domain unique identifier for the ingress node to the SFC and the Source Interface ID is the locally scoped to that node interface ID of ingress.

The Network Shared Context contains a unique Tenant ID assigned by the control plane. The enumeration of this is out-of-scope for the draft in question.

The Service Platform Context can have an optional Destination Class (signaled by the D bit), which is the result of the logical classification of the destination of the traffic. It also has a Source Class, with similar application to the source of traffic (eg, can represent an application, a group of users, a group of like endpoints). The information in these fields has many uses including Group Policy based networking enforcement.

Finally, the Service Shared Context can contain an optional Service Tag. The draft cites several uses including containing a flow ID, transaction, or application message unit. The flow ID could enable classification bypass, slow-path processing avoidance, and aid in flow programming. If the Service Tag is present, a reserved bit denoted as the A bit, enables acknowledgment of a Service Tag by a SF.

While certain aspects of the proposal are DC-specific such as tenancy, the others might have common application in other environments.

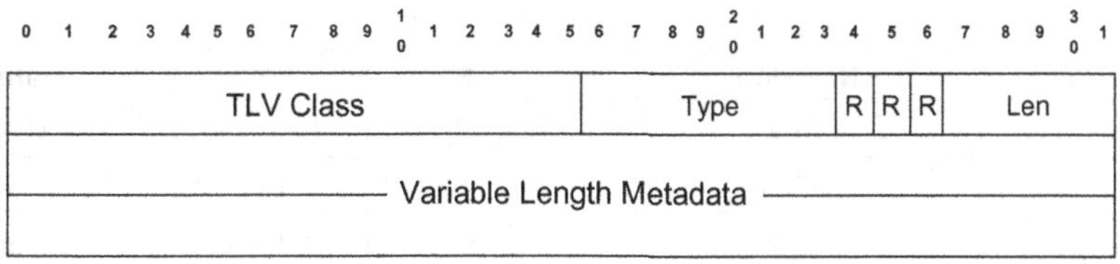

FIGURE 4.7

MD Type 2 Variable Length Context Header (these follow the Base and SP Headers for MD Type 0x2).

SPI	SI	NextHop	Transport
10	3	1.1.1.1	VXLAN-gpe
10	2	2.2.2.2	nvGRE
245	12	192.168.45.3	VXLAN-gpe
10	9	10.1.2.3	GRE
40	9	10.1.2.3	GRE
50	7	01:23:45:67:89:ab	Ethernet
15	1	Null	None

FIGURE 4.8

SFF NSH mapping example—centralized resolution (from draft).

MD Type 2 allows for optional variable length context headers and variable length TLV metadata. MD Type 0x2 can be seen as a compromise around header length in deployments that did not want to include any metadata. They can also be leveraged for private metadata that does not fit the fixed context descriptions (Fig. 4.7).

The TLV Class field allows for both vendor and SDO TLV ownership and the definition of the Type field in this header is the responsibility of the Class owner. The Type does contain a critical (C) bit, to alert the function that the TLV is mandatory to process.[15]

Both methods of carrying metadata allow augmentation of the enclosed data by intervening SFs in the path.

The Lookup

The idea behind defining a conceptual separation between the SPI and a rendered path is to allow for elasticity and HA mechanisms in the path without having to have separate paths iterated for every service instance of a function. As the draft says, "the SPI provide a level of indirection between the service path/topology and the network transport."

If the SPI/SI lookup in the SFF results in a single NextHop, then the path is "rendered." If this happens at every SI, then the SPI IS the rendered path.

The examples of the SFF lookup tables given in the draft show both a centrally administered table (Fig. 4.8) and a split or localized lookup (Fig. 4.9). The latter suggests a split in which there

(A)

SPI	SI	NextHop
10	3	SF2
254	12	SF34
40	9	SF9

(B)

SF	NH	Transport
SF2	10.1.1.1	VXLAN-gpu
SF34	192.168.1.1	UDP
SF9	1.1.1.1	GRE

FIGURE 4.9

SFF NSH mapping example—local resolution (from draft).

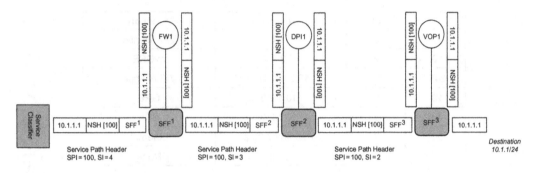

FIGURE 4.10

An SFC example using NSH.

are two tables that comprise the lookup, the SPI/SI that sets the next function SF and local resolution of the SF to an IP NextHop and encapsulation.

If the SPI/SI lookup in the SFF results in multiple NextHop(s), then the SFF can perform ECMP or weighted ECMP loading (assuming the SF is stateless).

For context-driven distribution, it is feasible that the SFF can do a secondary key lookup, integrate a more sophisticated load balancer or that the SF pointed to in the original lookup has an integrated load distribution function; this is called a composite function. In such cases, the SFF (or load distribution function, regardless of how it is integrated) can use one of the metadata/context fields as a secondary key (eg, mapping Application ID, User ID, to a path by local or centrally administered policy). This enables further load distribution that is locally transparently to the SP/chain.

Worked example

To understand how NSH is supposed to work, it may be best to follow/work an example. In Fig. 4.10, a service chain requiring the ordered traversal of Firewall, DPI, and Video Optimizer functions is depicted.

An SFC specific classifier or multi-purpose network node performs classification of a flow destined for 10.1.1.1/32 and based on that classification imposes the SFC NSH header. Though not shown, the classifier is also a SFF (SFF0). In that header the SPI is 100 and the index points to SFF1 and the Next Protocol Header would indicate IPv4 or Ethernet depending on the received encapsulation.

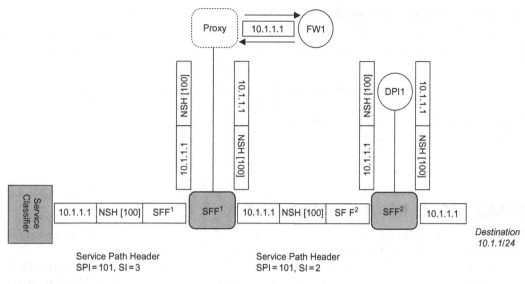

FIGURE 4.11

An SFC example using SFC with a proxy.

As an SFF, the classifier performs a SI decrement, does a lookup on the SPI index (which should now point at next SFF beyond "self"), which triggers the transport encapsulation of the frames to reach SFF1 and forwarding on that encapsulation.

The next SFF (SFF1) receives the encapsulated packet, does transport decapsulation, locates the NSH, identifies the local SF, and passes the packet with the NSH header to the function. On return, SFF1 repeats the process of SFF0—SI decrement, the lookup identifying SFF2 as the next hop for the transport encapsulation, etc.

At SFF3, on the return from the VOP function, the SI decrement operation will set the SI to "1," which will trigger the NSH removal and the resumption of native forwarding. A SI of "0" has special significance—telling the SFF to drop the packet.

If, for some reason, the SF at any step reclassified the traffic in a way that altered the path, it would need to change the NSH base header to reflect the new path.

The SF, SFF, and SC Proxy can all update context information (the latter is most likely with imputed metadata).

In the case of the proxy illustration (Fig. 4.11), we have a simple service chain consisting of a Firewall and a DPI. The Firewall is nonencapsulation aware. Typically, the proxy function would be performed by the SFF, but it can be separate and is illustrated that way for convenience.

The proxy will strip off the NSH header and forward the packet on a local attachment circuit (eg, VLAN, tunnel). Ostensibly, the "direction" of attachment can be the trigger for the restoration of the header (eg, FW1 has two VLANs known to Proxy logically as "to FW1" and "from FW1") on return.

The most significant aspects of NSH are the vendor community support for the concept[16] there are a number of planned implementations and the ability for NICs to perform header offload handling (in the longer term).

Using metadata to enhance reliability

Since the NSH draft was published, creative proposals around the use of metadata to address some of the service management tasks associated with a service overlay have emerged. Examples include:

- Imputed metadata (through timestamps applied at the SFF or VNF) can be harvested and used to infer SP performance data or even the condition of the application in the VNF.
- Metadata can be used to verify the delivery of data to a specific set of VNFs to help with higher-level compliance auditing.

SOURCE PACKET ROUTING IN NETWORKING

The SPRING workgroup focuses on the insertion of an explicit or "source routed" path into the packet transport header and the mechanics of path traversal.

Because Segment Routing for IPv4 uses MPLS label mechanics to follow the transport path, it does not satisfy the NSH goal of path preservation. Attempts to add metadata to an MPLS transport stack would also face several challenges.[17] Segment Routing for IPv6 (SRv6),[18] however, does preserve the path and has been demonstrated (in IETF90[19]) to be capable of use in SFC.

The SRv6 proposal[20] introduces a new IPv6 Routing Header type (very close to RFC2460, but with changes to make it more flexible and secure). The new header (SRH) is only inspected at each segment hop it is transparent to noncapable devices which only perform IPv6 forwarding on the frame.

The header (Fig. 4.12) consists of a number of housekeeping fields, a segment list, a policy list and the HMAC.

Next Header indicates the type of header immediately following SRH.

The Header Ext Length is an 8-bit unsigned integer that is the length of the header in 8-octet units.

Routing Type has to be assigned by IANA.

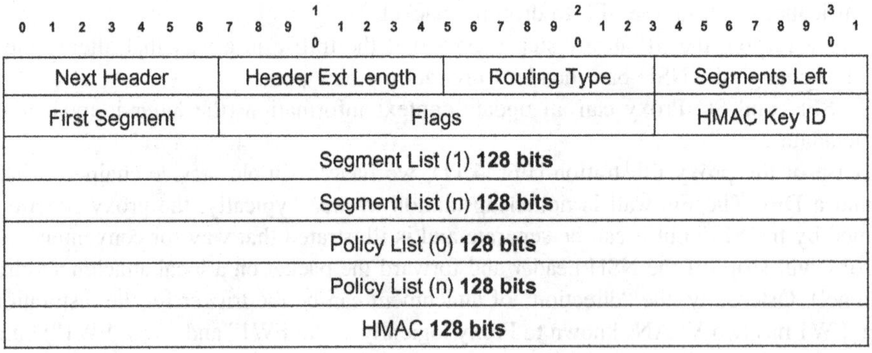

0 1 2 3 4 5 6 7 8 9	1 2 3 4 5 6 7 8 9	2 1 2 3 4 5 6 7 8 9	3 1
Next Header	Header Ext Length	Routing Type	Segments Left
First Segment	Flags		HMAC Key ID
Segment List (1) **128 bits**			
Segment List (n) **128 bits**			
Policy List (0) **128 bits**			
Policy List (n) **128 bits**			
HMAC **128 bits**			

FIGURE 4.12

The SRv6 header extension format.

Segments Left is the index into the segment list (and functions similarly to the SI in SFC), pointing at the currently active segment.

First Segment is an offset into the SRH (not including the first 8 octets) in 16-octet units pointing to the last segment in the segment list (which is actually the first segment in the path).

Flags comprise of a 16-bit field that is split into four individual flags (each 1 bit): C—cleanup, P—protected (used in conjunction with FRR), 2 bits are Reserved and the remaining bits go to Policy Flags. Policy Flags are used to indicate/define the type of IPv6 addresses preserved/encoded in the Policy List. These 12 bits are subdivided into four (4) 3-bit fields to represent the contents of Policy List segments 1 through 4. The values defined are: 0x0—Not present, 0x1—SR Ingress, 0x2—SR Egress, and 0x3—Original Source Address.

The HMAC fields are used for security and are defined in a separate draft.[21]

The Segment List is a series of 128-bit IPv6 addresses encoded in the reverse order they would be traversed in the path (eg, last is in position 0 and first is in position "n"/last).

The Policy List as seen in the Flag section above, is an optional list of 128-bit IPv6 addresses that can be used for a variety of debugging and policy related operations.

The Segment List was also envisioned as being used in conjunction with MPLS, where each segment might represent up to four 32-bit labels.

The mechanics of forwarding are illustrated in Fig. 4.13. The transactions are shown linearly, but the individual nodes can be placed arbitrarily in the network with intervening, non-SRH aware IPv6 forwarders (the draft shows a more complex topology).

In the figure, Host A is sending to Host F. Through a number of potential mechanisms, B is programmed to impose the SRH on packets in such a flow (A could have imposed the SRH as well). The segment list B is to impose is "C, D, E," which it does according to specification in reverse order.

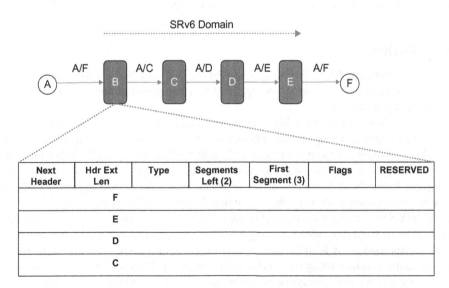

FIGURE 4.13

SRv6 forwarding example. For brevity the full IPv6 header is not shown (nor are all the SRH header fields).

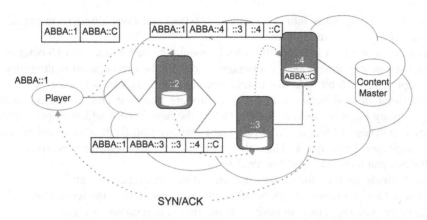

FIGURE 4.14

Hierarchical caching application using SRv6.

The Segments Left and First Segments are set "$n - 1$" (2), where N is the number of segments (3). The original Destination Address in the IPv6 header is replaced with the address of the first segment, and is place at the end of the segment list. The Flags are set to C (clean). The Policy Flags and Policy Segments could be set to reflect ingress/egress SR node (as in the draft), but this is not shown.

As the packet progresses, the SRF aware nodes will swap the address in Segments Left with the IPv6 Destination Address and decrement Segments Left. When the packet gets to E, the Next Segment will be "0." With the clean bit set, E will replace the IPv6 header Destination Address with F indicating the original destination, and strip the header.

A DEMONSTRATION

At IETF90, Cisco Systems, Ecole Polytechnique (Paris), UCL (LLN, Belgium), and Comcast collaborated on a demonstration that used interoperable SRv6 implementations for a specific application called hierarchical caching.

In the use case (illustrated in Fig. 4.14), content for an mpeg-DASH encoded video is encoded into chunks (of short duration). Those specific chunks are IPv6 addressed in the manifest of the video (where the address is usable as a consistent storage lookup mechanism, eg, hash). When the user makes a request for the content, a segment list that represents a series of anycast addresses—each representing a level in a cache hierarchy and ending with the content master—is imposed as part of a SRv6 header at the first provider upstream node from the set top box (based on a classification match).

As the TCP/SYN packet reaches each level of the cache hierarchy in the path, the cache does a lookup in its content store (using a key value based on the innermost segment value[22]). If the content existed, respond with the appropriate ACK so that the session was established, otherwise the packet would progress to the next highest cache level by the SRv6 mechanism. At the highest level of the cache system, the content master, the chunk should always be available at an offset keyed to that chunk address.

The mechanisms for priming the cache or optimizing the cache were unchanged for the trial, such that over time the lowest level cache was populated.

NEXT FOR SRv6

Although SRv6 was originally intended as a traffic engineering mechanism, the use of SRv6 in the IETF demonstration shows how SRv6 can be used for a very specific service chaining application.

The reasons for resistance to reassigning transport headers to have significance in encoding metadata for service chaining, are tied to the variable, limited amount of space per encapsulation and interoperability problems this might create in networks that mix encapsulation in their overlays (thus the need for transport independence).[23] These are still present in the use of SRv6 (even though there is arguably much more space to work with in the SRH than other encapsulations). The methodology cannot also be applied directly to IPv4 traffic, which presents a level of discontinuity that would have to be addressed for SRv6 to be seen as an SFC protocol.

As a final thought on SRv6, it is clear that it will need to coordinate closely with SFC to avoid the dissolution into transport-specific solutions. That is, to avoid the tendency toward these behaviors alluded to at the beginning of the SFC section of this chapter that could have doomed SFC to failure from the start. The authors of the SRv6 and NSH drafts are working to normalize their approaches to passing of metadata and rationalizing the transport path to the SP, which is hopefully moving things in the right direction. Only time will tell if this carries on, but we hope it does.

NETWORK MODELING

The NETMOD workgroup was not explicitly mentioned in the ETSI Gap Analysis. However, we have included a discussion about what that working group is up to because we feel that this is a fairly significant oversight considering the explosion in not only the interest but the rapid *use and deployment* of model-driven APIs based on the Yang models this group is responsible for, as well as the Yang language used to create those models.

In 2014 the ETSI architecture's numerous interfaces that were named but not defined in Phase 1 made no mention of this trend which actually began around that time, albeit slowly.[24] This is also a massive oversight given how Yang, Network Configuration Protocol (NETCONF), and most recently RESTCONF are now poised to replace *all* traditional management protocols. They are even taking a run at replacing the good old command line interface (CLI) with model generated APIs.

The basic charter of the NETMOD Working Group[25] is to define and maintain the Yang data modeling language.[26] The NETMOD Working Group also defined a number of core data models as basic building blocks for other models to build upon such as RFC7317[27] as well as guidance about how to best build network data models.[28]

The Yang language can be used to specify network element data or service models, and recently has stretched to be used as an information modeling language for other uses. Within the context of NETMOD, Yang defines the model, but this model is not carried verbatim "on the wire"; instead, it is encoded using one of various available encoding schemes, but primarily XML today. That encoding is then carried as payload in one of the two officially supported network transport protocols. These are the NETCONF and RESTCONF protocols that contain functions for manipulating the encoded models.

THE YANG DATA MODELING LANGUAGE

Yang is a data modeling language originally designed to specify network data models representing functions and features on network elements. The models also represented specific objects that could be read, changed or monitored using The NETCONF. The name Yang is actually an acronym from "Yet Another Next Generation." The Yang data modeling language was developed by the NETMOD working group in the IETF and was first published as RFC6020 in 2010. However, the language and transport protocol had been in trial or experimental development and use for a number of years prior to that. The language and first transport protocols were designed as an effort to embrace the exact management capabilities expressed in proprietary CLIs, while leveraging many of the advances in standards-based management interfaces such as the Simple Network Management Protocol (SNMP)—and avoiding the shortcomings of those previous management protocols.

The data modeling language can be used to model both configuration data as well as the values of specific data of network elements (ie, the value of an interface counter at any point in time). Furthermore, Yang can be used to define the format of event notifications emitted by network elements. One important feature that was added to Yang that had not previously existed was an allowance for data modelers to specify remote procedure calls (RPCs) and their operation. These functions can then be invoked on network elements via the NETCONF protocol to invoke certain procedures or actions that say go beyond simply fetching the value of a system variable.

Yang is a modular language representing data structures in a tree format. This is convenient because it models how the CLIs on most network devices have always been designed—as a hierarchical tree of commands. The data modeling language contains a number of intrinsic data types such as strings and integers. These basic types can be used to build more complex types forming a very rich set of capabilities. One way more complex data structures can be represented is using groupings as another means of modeling more complex entities by building upon the basic ones. Yang data models can use XPath 1.0[29] expressions to define inter-node dependencies and references on the elements of a Yang data model.

To add some historical perspective on Yang, it is an evolution of a number of previous network modeling languages including CMIP, TL1, and the SNMP. It can be argued that SNMP was at the time, the most widely deployed management protocol. The data modeling language used to define SNMP's data models is called The Structure of Management Information (SMI). SMI was based on a subset of The Abstract Syntax Notation One (ASN.1). In later versions of SNMP, the SMI Language was updated and extended and referred to as The SMIv2.

The original development of the NETCONF protocol in the IETF did not rely on models (or a modeling language to define those nonexistent models). Instead, the original protocol relied on an RPC paradigm. In this model, a client would encode an RPC using XML. These requests were sent to a server running on a network element. The server would respond with a reply encoded in XML. The contents of both the request and the response are described in an XML Document Type Definition (DTD) or an XML schema. This would allow the client or server to recognize the syntax constraints needed to complete the exchange of information between the two. However, this was not ideal, and so enhancements were made to tighten up the language insofar as to create a mechanism by which an effective programmable API could be created.

Even after these many enhancements had been made, it was clear that a data modeling language is needed to define data models manipulated by the NETCONF protocol. This created a language for defining the actual objects, their syntax, and their relationship with other objects in the system. This all could be specified prior to any exchange, which also made it easier to build the systems that were used to interact with the managed systems. Given the lineage the original authors of Yang had with the SNMP efforts, it should be unsurprising to find that the syntactic structure and the base type system of Yang was borrowed from SMIng (as are other successful elements of SNMP). When Yang was originally developed, it was tightly bound to the NETCONF protocol. That is to say, operations had to be supported by NETCONF, as well as the carriage of the data specified by the models. In this way, data model instances are *serialized* into XML and carried by NETCONF. This was recently relaxed to also include a RESTful variant of NETCONF called RESTCONF. Other attempts of late have also tried to extend an invitation to other transports such as ProtoBufs and a few others, as well as attempts to declare Yang a general information modeling language with little or no coupling to its underlying transport. These efforts have failed at the IETF to date, despite adoption in other places by network operators, as was done in the OpenConfig effort described later.

However, given the dramatic increase in model generation within multiple IETF workgroups (NETMOD, NETCONF, L3SM, LIME, I2NSF, and SUPA) and externally, the IESG moved to redistribute the Yang model workload and provide a coordination group[30] (as at December 2014). The group is to coordinate modeling within the IETF and across other SDOs and Open Source initiatives. Additionally, they will provide an inventory of existing Yang models, tooling and help with compilation, and training and education.[31]

Currently, the NETMOD working group is almost complete with an effort to update Yang to version 1.1. This work is expected to be completed and published formally in early 2016.

An example using Yang is shown in Appendix A.

THE NETCONF PROTOCOL

As we mentioned earlier, Yang models are carried by several transport protocols. Yang primarily came from an evolution in The *NETCONF*, and for a time was very tightly bound to it. Today this is much less the case. NETCONF is a protocol developed at the IETF originally to carry configuration and state information to and from management network elements and network managers, as well as to manipulate that information. It was developed in the NETCONF Working Group[32] and published in 2006 as RFC4741 and later updated to RFC6241. The NETCONF protocol is widely implemented by popular network devices such as routers and switches. Of late, it has found its way onto pretty much every other type of network element, real or virtual.

All of the operations of the NETCONF protocol are built on a series of basis RPC calls which are described below in some detail. The data carried within NETCONF is encoded using XML. As a first, the NETCONF requires that all of its protocol messages be exchanged using a secure underlying transport protocol such as Secure Sockets Layer (SSL).

The NETCONF protocol can be partitioned into four logical layers that when used together, form the basis for all of the protocol's operations including information data transportation:

1. The Content layer consists of configuration data and notification data.
2. The Operations layer defines a set of base protocol operations to retrieve and edit the configuration data.
3. The Messages layer provides a mechanism for encoding RPCs and notifications.
4. The Secure Transport layer provides a secure and reliable transport of messages between a client and a server.

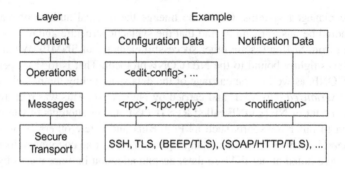

FIGURE 4.15

Conceptual layers of NETCONF protocol.

Operation	Description
<get>	Retrieve running configuration and device state information
<get-config>	Retrieve all or part of a specified configuration datastore
<edit-config>	Edit a configuration data store by creating, deleting, merging or replacing content
<copy-config>	Copy an entire configuration datastore to another configuration datastore
<delete-config>	Delete a configuration datastore
<lock>	Lock an entire configuration datastore of a device
<unlock>	Release a configuration datastore lock previously obtained with the <lock> operation
<close-session>	Request graceful termination of a NETCONF session
<kill-session>	Force the termination of a NETCONF session

FIGURE 4.16

Base NETCONF protocol defines some key operations to fetch, set, or delete a device's configuration.

Fig. 4.15 illustrates how these conceptual layers comprising the NETCONF protocol can be mapped to operations such as the modification of configuration information within a management element, or to create notifications that can be emitted by the same device and later processed by a management station.

OPERATIONS

The base NETCONF protocol defines some key operations that are used to satisfy the basic protocol requirements of fetching, setting, or deleting a device's configuration. We have detailed these operations in Fig. 4.16.

The NETCONF functionality described in Fig. 4.16 can also be extended by implementing NETCONF capabilities. These comprise a set of additional protocol features that an implementation supports. When these are defined, they are exposed by either the client or server during the capability exchange portion of a session establishment. During this exchange, only these optional items are included as the mandatory protocol features are assumed by virtue of being mandatory to implement in a compliant implementation. Some optional capabilities such as :xpath and :validate are defined in RFC6241.

A capability to support subscribing and receiving asynchronous event notifications is published in RFC 5277. This document defines the <create-subscription> operation, which enables creating real time and replay subscriptions. Notifications are then sent asynchronously using the <notification> construct. It also defines the :interleave capability, which when supported with the basic :notification capability facilitates the processing of other NETCONF operations while the subscription is active.

Some additional capabilities that are interesting are two that are defined in RFC5717 to support partial locking of the running and one defined in RFC6022 that allows for the monitoring of the NETCONF protocol itself. The former is interesting as it allows multiple sessions to edit nonoverlapping subtrees within the running configuration. This is important because multiple managers can be manipulating the configuration of a device simultaneously. Without this capability, the only lock available is for the entire configuration, which has the obvious consequences. RFC6022 contains a data model that describes data stores, sessions, locks, and statistics contained in a NETCONF server. These things can be used to monitor and manage a NETCONF server much in the way previously was available for SNMP systems. Beyond that, a very important capability it defines are methods for NETCONF clients to discover data models supported by a device using the <get-schema> operation. This capability, while optional, has rapidly become a de facto standard feature demanded by not only network operators, but also those that create network management software and network controllers. When this capability is available, a device can be "discovered" dynamically and its model and capability contents read out at run time. This is an important distinction from previous models of operation that were very static, and assumed a device was shipped with a specific firmware image whose capabilities would not change inflight. That made sense in the previous world where vendor-specific hardware was deployed to run specific services and so forth. However, this new functionality is needed in the new world of virtualized machines and services, as those things can be rapidly changed. Another important reason for this is that the software that interacts with these components can change dynamically, and it better suits this new model of software to be able to dynamically read and interact with model changes of devices.

MESSAGE LAYER

The NETCONF message layer provides a simple, transport-independent framing mechanism for encoding messages exchanged between a NETCONF client and server. There are really three types of messages described as:

1. RPC Results (ie, <rpc-reply> messages)
2. RPC Invocations (ie, <rpc> messages)
3. Event Notifications (ie, <notification> messages)

Messages are really categorized as RPC Messages[33] or as Event Notifications.[34] As mentioned above, NETCONF messages are transmitted as what are referred to as a well-formed XML document. An RPC result is matched up with an RPC invocation using a message-id attribute. This is how a message exchange is essentially tracked. One advantage that NETCONF has over previous management protocols such as SNMP is that its messages can be pipelined, effectively allowing a client to send multiple invocations in parallel and simply wait for the responses.

SECURE TRANSPORTS

NETCONF messages are exchanged using a number of available secure transport protocols. A secure transport provides end point authentication, data integrity, confidentiality, and assurances that replay of message exchanges are not possible. It is mandatory for any compliance implement to implement the SSH Protocol.[35] The Transport Layer Security (TLS) Protocol is also defined, albeit optionally, as an available secure transport.[36] RFC 5539 defines a secure transport using TLS. Other secure transports were defined in the past, but are not declared as historic and are unused, so we will not mention them here.

THE RESTCONF PROTOCOL

REST (seen also as ReST) stands for Representational State Transfer. This type of protocol relies on a stateless client-server communications protocol. In reality this usually means the HTTP protocol is used. REST itself is an architecture style for designing networked applications, and specifically how they interact with each other. Specifically, REST is a style that specifies interactions between clients and servers be accomplished using a limited but well-defined number of actions, known as *verbs*. Because these verbs are limited, but have a well-defined specific meaning, the constrain and simplify the functionality of the interface. These verbs are defined as GET (ie, read), POST (ie, create), PUT (ie, update), and DELETE (ie, delete). Flexibility of the interface is achieved by assigning resources known as *nouns or methods*, to a unique universal resource identifier (URI). This description is contained in an XML file that can be fetched by a client. This page can also include the content that the client seeks. For example, a REST-like protocol might be one that is defined as running over HTTP for accessing data defined in Yang using data stores defined in NETCONF. An example of this is the RESTCONF protocol that was standardized by the IETF. This Standard describes how to map a Yang specification to a RESTful interface. The REST-like API is not intended to replace NETCONF, but rather provide an additional yet simplified interface that follows the REST principles just described, but remains compatible with a resource-oriented device abstraction as well as the already defined Yang models.

Like NETCONF before it, the RESTCONF protocol operates on a Yang model (ie, a conceptual data store defined by the YANG data modeling language). The NETCONF server lists each YANG module it supports under "/restconf/modules" in the top-level API resource type, using a structure based on the Yang module capability URI format. In this way a client can browse the supported list of modules by simply querying this portion of the data store. The conceptual data store contents, data-model-specific operations and notification events are identified by this set of YANG module resources. Similar to NETCONF, RESTCONF defines content as one of an operation resource, an event stream resource, or a data resource. All of these are defined using the Yang language.

The classification of data as configuration or nonconfiguration data is derived from the Yang "config" statement, and is an important distinction to make on the data store's contents. Data ordering of either configuration or nonconfiguration data is stipulated through the use of the Yang "ordered-by" statement.

THE PUBLIC GITHUB YANG REPOSITORY

As we mentioned earlier in the chapter, many organizations have moved rapidly towards the adoption of Yang models as well as NETCONF and RESTCONF. To this end, many have taken on the task of development of Yang models. However, one interesting change from the past modes of development of these artifacts is the desire to build them with the collaboration and help of a wider community. To this end, many organizations including The IETF,[37] Metro Ethernet Forum (MEF),[38] Open Config,[39] OpenDaylight,[40] and The Institute of Electrical and Electronics Engineers (IEEE)[41] have adopted the use of an open area on github.com that has been created for this purpose that we refer to as the Public Yang Repository or, more colloquially, "The Public Yang Repo." In addition to those organizations, a number of vendors, including Cisco, Brocade, and Yumaworks, have elected to push their proprietary models here. One advantage to having these models all in one place is the simplicity of finding them all together. This not only encourages reuse of various components of models, but also help application builders find them without much fanfare.

The Public Yang Repo can be found by pointing your browser (or favorite github client) at https://github.com/YangModels/yang and looking through the models. A screen shot of the site's home area is shown in Fig. 4.17.

FIGURE 4.17

The landing page for The Public Yang Repo.

Most anyone is welcome and encouraged to contribute models here, as well as collaborate with the community of people using the area. The community utilizes the canonical "committer" model of administering the site and moderating the check-ins of models, especially to the "standard" area which simply keeps the quality of the models high. For example, we maintain a set of "stable" models in the repository under most circumstances. In short, this means that the models compile with the industry standard pyang compiler.[42] This at least ensures syntactic accuracy, but also does some "link" like checks on the models. We also periodically have others review the models in the repository to help improve them. Of course, those in the "standard" area are reflections of those found in some organization's official standard area.

CONCLUSIONS

The bottom line is that, without SFC (its service layer abstraction and metadata passing), creating meaningful services puts a huge burden on orchestration.

We can admittedly build service chains without SFC using traditional methodologies like VLANs or transport tunnel overlays, but any elasticity means churning the underlay/overly to keep the transport path coherent with the SP. This is an extremely important point justifying the need for a service layer separate from transport: by integrating control over a flow in the NSH header, you do not have to worry about synchronizing protocol state (synchronization is implicit).

We can optimize a single VNF (eg, a vFW) and call it a service ("Security"), but to do so is incremental OPEX/CAPEX reduction (eg, optimization of the spend on an appliance). Will that contribute meaningfully to revenue generation? Complex services (more than a single "atom" of functionality) require SFC.

Further, the ability to share data between functions makes services intelligent, manageable, and (potentially) personal/customized. Without, it the services we build may be constrained to emulating existing services instead of imagining new ones.

SFC might need to be visited again as the concept of "composable" functions proliferates (a naiive vision in the early ETSI work but rapidly evolving as container, unikernel and "microservice" concepts are considered as replacements for the early "service-per-VM" ETSI model). Equivalents or functionality mappings for inter-process communication (not traversing the vSwitch between functions) may need to be developed.

There is still some tension in the IETF between transport-based service chaining solutions and the service overlay concept. Given the size of the existing IPv6 packet header (and its extensibility) the most potential for a merger of these views exists in SRv6.

It is clear that organizations such as the IETF play an important role in the development of some of the critical protocols and API in the area of VNF control and configuration such as NETCONF and RESTCONF. The IETF also plays a significant role in defining the Yang language which has rapidly become the industry standard for data modeling languages and model-driven API generation. However, it is important to also observe that other less traditional (and often open source) organizations—or even nonorganizations per se—are playing important roles too. To this end, we examined the growing community that has formed around The Public Yang Repo on github and highlighted the IETF's own recognition of the need for interorganizational outreach and education. These organizations will continue to grow and play an important role in not only shaping how models are developed, but also in actually developing those models.

APPENDIX A
EXAMPLE OF YANG MODEL USAGE

The following example is taken from the Open Daylight Toaster tutorial and is shown here as an example of a Yang model that contains may of the important components found in any model. The toaster example is modeled after the canonical SNMP toaster MIB example found in many tutorials, and is also shipped with many of the popular toolkits. The general idea is to model a toaster that is controlled by SNMP, except in this case it is modeled with Yang and controlled with RESTCONF or NETCONF. Note that the example is slightly out-of-date in that the organizational information is not current, but it will suffice as an example. It is not our intent to create a full example of how to design and build Yang models here as many great tutorials exist online and in other places.

```
//This file contains a YANG data definition. This data model defines
 //a toaster, which is based on the SNMP MIB Toaster example
 module toaster {

    //The yang version - today only 1 version exists. If omitted defaults to 1.
    yang-version 1;

    //a unique namespace for this toaster module, to uniquely identify it from other
    modules that may have the same name.
    namespace
      "http://netconfcentral.org/ns/toaster";

    //a shorter prefix that represents the namespace for references used below
    prefix toast;

    //Defines the organization which defined / owns this .yang file.
    organization "Netconf Central";

    //defines the primary contact of this yang file.
    contact
      "Andy Bierman <andy@netconfcentral.org>";

    //provides a description of this .yang file.
    description
      "YANG version of the TOASTER-MIB.";

    //defines the dates of revisions for this yang file
    revision "2009-11-20" {
      description
        "Toaster module in progress.";
    }

    //declares a base identity, in this case a base type for different types of toast.
    identity toast-type {
      description
```

```
      "Base for all bread types supported by the toaster. New bread types not
      listed here nay be added in the future.";
}

//the below identity section is used to define globally unique identities
//Note - removed a number of different types of bread to shorten the text length.
identity white-bread {
  base toast:toast-type;    //logically extending the declared toast-type above.
  description "White bread."; //free text description of this type.
}

identity wheat-bread {
  base toast-type;
  description "Wheat bread.";
}

//defines a new "Type" string type which limits the length
typedef DisplayString {
  type string {
    length "0 .. 255";
  }
  description
    "YANG version of the SMIv2 DisplayString TEXTUAL-CONVENTION.";
  reference
    "RFC 2579, section 2.";

}

// This definition is the top-level configuration "item" that defines a toaster.
The "presence" flag connotes there
// can only be one instance of a toaster which, if present, indicates the service
is available.
container toaster {
  presence
    "Indicates the toaster service is available";
  description
    "Top-level container for all toaster database objects.";

  //Note in these three attributes that config = false. This indicates that
  they are operational attributes.
  leaf toasterManufacturer {
    type DisplayString;
    config false;
    mandatory true;
    description
      "The name of the toaster's manufacturer. For instance, Microsoft Toaster.";
  }
```

```
leaf toasterModelNumber {
  type DisplayString;
  config false;
  mandatory true;
  description
    "The name of the toaster's model. For instance, Radiant Automatic.";
}

leaf toasterStatus {
  type enumeration {
    enum "up" {
      value 1;
      description
        "The toaster knob position is up. No toast is being made now.";
    }
    enum "down" {
      value 2;
      description
        "The toaster knob position is down. Toast is being made now.";
    }
  }
  config false;
  mandatory true;
  description
    "This variable indicates the current state of the toaster.";
}
} // container toaster
} // module toaster
```

END NOTES

1. This is not surprising given the extremely limited deployment of and interest in FoRCES. As of IETF 92, FoRCES was no longer an active Work Group.
2. As part of the IETF process a BoF meeting is held to determine whether a workgroup should be chartered (two such meetings can be held, the first to gauge interest and the second to look at the refined mission statement and determine whether to charter).
3. Proposed SDN WG at the IETF 82 meeting November 13–18, 2011; Taipei, Taiwan http://www.ietf.org/proceedings/82/sdn.html.
4. I2RS is also adjacent to NFV. The push towards model-driven programmability may subsume the "router model" work (TBD), leaving standard models for topology (still useful in Orchestration, Policy, etc.) as a potentially useful outcome for NFV deployment.
5. http://datatracker.ietf.org/wg/sfc/charter/.
6. http://datatracker.ietf.org/doc/draft-ietf-sfc-problem-statement/.
7. http://datatracker.ietf.org/doc/draft-ietf-sfc-architecture/.

8. https://datatracker.ietf.org/wg/sfc/charter/.
9. Assuming that single-domain abates some of the concerns with ICMP-related security by eliminating external trust issues and enabling reasonable infrastructure ACLs to avoid abuse.
10. https://datatracker.ietf.org/wg/sfc/charter/.
11. We need to recognize the work of Paul Quinn and Jim Guichard at Cisco Systems, since the material on NSH is the direct result of their hard work in the IETF and endless attempts to explain the concept of a service overlay to the masses. Jim and Paul have written an authoritative white paper with Tom and others on the subject that you can find as http://datatracker.ietf.org/doc/draft-quinn-sfc-nsh/.
12. http://datatracker.ietf.org/doc/draft-quinn-sfc-nsh/.
13. The size of the SPI allows for over 16 million paths.
14. http://datatracker.ietf.org/doc/draft-guichard-sfc-nsh-dc-allocation/. There is also a mobility allocation draft, http://datatracker.ietf.org/doc/draft-napper-sfc-nsh-mobility-allocation/.
15. As the draft notes, the bit position (first bit position in the Type field) splits the range of values available in half between critical and noncritical types.
16. Announced at Mobile World Congress, Barcelona. 2015.
17. This problem is common to MPLS forwarding, including service chaining achieved by "chaining VRFs" (leveraging RFC 2547 VPN forwarding).
18. http://segment-routing.org/, UCL has a good SRv6 page. And, there is a trove of information at http://www.segment-routing.net/home/tutorial.
19. http://www.ietf.org/meeting/90/.
20. https://datatracker.ietf.org/doc/draft-previdi-6man-segment-routing-header/.
21. https://datatracker.ietf.org/doc/draft-vyncke-6man-segment-routing-security/.
22. The application could be designed differently using Policy Segments (the trial occurred early in the process of fleshing out SRv6 behavior).
23. Early work in the ONF for L4-L7 working group was pursuing this tack with submissions citing potential changes to VXLAN encapsulation.
24. In its second phase of operation, the ETSI NFV study has begun some modeling, using both Yang and TOSCA for some tasks.
25. https://datatracker.ietf.org/wg/netmod/charter/.
26. IETF RFC 4741, https://tools.ietf.org/html/rfc4741.
27. https://datatracker.ietf.org/doc/rfc7317/.
28. https://tools.ietf.org/html/draft-ietf-netmod-rfc6087bis-05.
29. XPath 1.0—http://www.w3.org/TR/1999/REC-xpath-19991116/.
30. http://www.ietf.org/iesg/directorate/yang-model-coordination-group.html.
31. Recent IETF meetings have featured YANG workdays for attendees. The tutorials from these meetings are available on YouTube. A good starting point can be found at https://www.youtube.com/watch?v=N7fb11dLztA.
32. IETF NETMOD Working Group—https://datatracker.ietf.org/wg/netconf/charter/.
33. RFC6241—https://tools.ietf.org/html/rfc6241.
34. RFC5277—https://tools.ietf.org/html/rfc5277.
35. https://tools.ietf.org/html/rfc6242.
36. https://tools.ietf.org/html/rfc5539.
37. http://www.ietf.org.
38. http://www.mef.net.
39. http://www.openconfig.net.
40. http://www.opendaylight.org.
41. http://www.ieee.org/index.htmlbroad.
42. https://github.com/mbj4668/pyang.

THE NFV INFRASTRUCTURE MANAGEMENT

INTRODUCTION

In this and the succeeding chapters, we will look a little bit more closely at the major building blocks of the ETSI-prescribed NFV architecture.

If we revisit our high-level architecture framework in Fig. 5.1 our focus in this chapter is indicated by the highlighted block.

The Network Functions Virtualization Infrastructure (NFVI) functional area represents the hardware (ie, storage, compute, and network) that physically supports the virtualized functions, and the software systems that adapt those virtualized functions to the hardware, and maintain the resources needed for that adaptation to function seamlessly. The latter includes the management and control of the virtualized compute, storage, and network components that together realize all virtualized functions on a given hardware platform.

Because Chapter 7, The Virtualization Layer—Performance, Packaging, and NFV, deals with the virtualization layer and Chapter 8, NFV Infrastructure—Hardware Evolution and Testing, deals with the advances in hardware to accelerate NFV as a separate topic, this chapter will focus specifically on the Virtual Infrastructure Manager (VIM).

The next chapter deals with the MANO block (Management and Orchestration). ETSI associates the VIM with that block in their model; however, we deal with the VIM separately because:

- The VIM is the axis between the physical infrastructure and service orchestration—providing a subset of the overall orchestration as it relates to compute, storage, and network. The VIM is, in our view, more closely coupled to a discussion of infrastructure management.
- Later in the book, when we talk about current organizational purchasing focus, infrastructure-centric purchasing is one of the patterns—centered around the VIM. So, some organizations are treating the VIM separately from higher-level orchestration.
- The NFVI, particularly the VIM, is the first area of focus for OPNFV.
- The VIM is a major tie backwards to the SDN movement and forwards into the open source push of ETSI NFV.

As an aside, here "network" often is used in reference to the network between hosts in a data center and not the greater network encompassing service provider access, edge and core (the "transport" network they provide). The greater "network" resource is often out-of-scope in the discussion of NFV, but becomes important in the context of "end-to-end" services

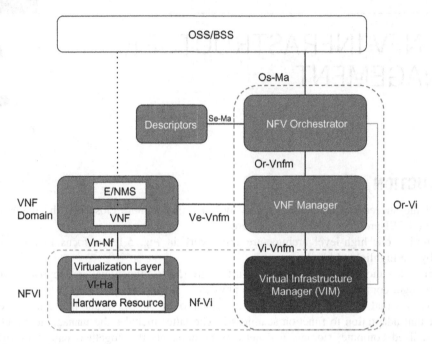

FIGURE 5.1

Architecture revisited.

and resource placement. Here, the latency and bandwidth available on different network paths can be important criteria in where and how to host a function.

Finally, we will also use this chapter to touch on the relationship between the VIM and the future potential of NFV.

NFV VIRTUAL INFRASTRUCTURE MANAGEMENT (VIM)

When we look at the VIM, we will be using the open source projects OpenStack and OpenDaylight (ODL) as exemplars of functionality applicable to this space. This is not in denial of vendor-specific products, but an acknowledgment of an open source driver in the ETSI work. These are also readily available public examples that the reader can quickly gain access to in conjunction with reading this book.

Where appropriate, we will mention proprietary efforts but will not dedicate any indepth sections to those, nor are their inclusion necessarily any sort of endorsement over any of the other options available. The reader should keep in mind that these vendor products may address functionality gaps in the open source, and may have different sets of functionality between them. Further, open source may continue to morph—adding new projects relevant to VIM.

We also do not want to give the impression that "cloud" *requires* any of these tools. To a certain scale, there has been notable success with DevOps tools like Ansible, Vagrant, Chef, Puppet, and a bit of ingenuity. While overlay networking in multi-tenant DC is a dominant part of the "cloud" conversation, operators have been networking without controllers for a quite a while.[1] However, these types of infrastructure management implementations are not normally associated with the ETSI NFV architecture.

OPENSTACK

OpenStack is a set of software tools for building and managing cloud computing systems. The project is supported by some of the biggest companies in software development and hosting, as well as a community of literally thousands of software engineers. OpenStack is managed by The OpenStack Foundation, a nonprofit organization responsible for the governance and management of the organization.

OpenStack is not limited to the VIM, but as a VIM solution, OpenStack provides controls for the NFV infrastructure; compute, storage, and networking services deployed between the virtual machines (VMs) and other physical hardware such as switches or routers. The OpenStack platform allows users to deploy, manage, reconfigure, and destroy VMs onto the resources in the platform environment.

OpenStack infrastructure can be extensive as illustrated in Fig. 5.2 and is composed of a number of server and client processes on different nodes in the infrastructure.

A collection of networks connects the redundant controllers with network elements (network, disk, and compute devices) and the outside world (Fig. 5.2). The Management Network

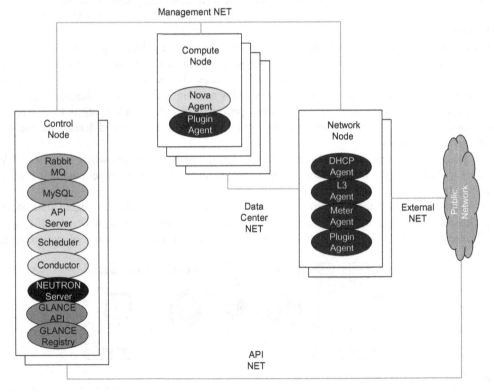

FIGURE 5.2

OpenStack infrastructure networking.

is internal and should not be externally reachable. The Data Center Network is for inter-VM data communication. Infrastructure nodes run one or more agents (here we show the Compute Node with both a NOVA and a NEUTRON agent while the Network Node has any number of NEUTRON agents depending on the service required). IP addressing depends on the plugin. The External Network provides VMs with Internet access in NFV scenarios. Access from the Public Network to the Data Center network is dependent on policies in the Network Node. Finally, the API Network offers the OpenStack APIs between tenants and operator. This interface assumes a policy-based public access. Configurations that use a common external network access for the API network and Data Center network is quite common.

OpenStack currently consists of many software projects that together form the platform: OpenStack Compute (code name Nova), OpenStack Block Storage (code names Swift and Cinder), OpenStack Networking (code name Neutron), OpenStack Image Service (code name Glance), OpenStack Identity (code name Keystone), and OpenStack Dashboard (code name Horizon) which provides a graphical dashboard through which users can use to quickly and easily control and interact with the system.

These projects deliver a pluggable and extendable framework that forms an open source operating system for public and private clouds. They are the OpenStack Infrastructure-as-a-Service (IaaS) building blocks (Fig. 5.3).

The OpenStack system has grown in popularity due to its tight integration with the most popular hypervisors in the industry. For example, support includes ESX, Hyper-V, KVM, LXC, QEMU, UML, Xen, and XenServer.

Nova is open source software designed to provision and manage large networks of VMs, creating a redundant and scalable cloud-computing platform. This project represents what most people envision when they imagine what OpenStack does. The software provides control panels and APIs required to orchestrate a cloud. This includes running VM instances, managing networks, and access control for both users and groups (ie, projects). OpenStack Compute is hardware- and hypervisor-agnostic in theory, although actual builds and support is limited largely to the most popular server platforms.

One of the main components of Nova is its scheduler, which determines where a requested VM instance should run. The scheduler has a series of filters and weights (cost functions) that it uses in selecting a target.

Swift and *Cinder* are the software components for creating redundant, scalable data storage using clusters of standard servers to store multiple blocks of accessible data. It is not a file system or real-time data system, but rather a long-term storage system for large amounts of static data that

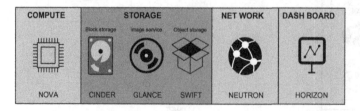

FIGURE 5.3

The OpenStack IaaS building blocks.

can be retrieved or updated. Object Storage uses a distributed architecture in order to not have a central point of failure. This also affords the user greater flexibility of deployment options, as well as the obvious scalability, redundancy, and performance.

Glance provides discovery, registration, and delivery services for virtual disk images. The Image Service API server provides a well-defined RESTful web services interface for querying information about virtual disk images. These disk images may be stored in a variety of backend stores, including OpenStack Object Storage, as well as others. Clients can register new virtual disk images with the Image Service, query for information on publicly-available disk images, and use the Image Service's client library for streaming virtual disk images. Imagines can then be referenced later much in the way a menu of dishes can be made available to a diner in a restaurant.

Nova has some primordial network capabilities. It will not configure physical network interfaces, but will automatically create all virtual network bridges (eg, br100) and VM virtual interfaces (through the nova-network subset of functions). Nova assigns a private IP address to each VM instance it deploys. This address is then attached to the Linux Bridge via the nova-network API and then (potentially) to a NAT function that allows the virtual interfaces to connect to the outside network through the physical interface. The network controller with nova-network provides virtual networks to enable compute servers to interact with each other and with the public network.

Currently, Nova (nova-network) supports three kinds of networks, implemented in three Network Manager types: Flat Network Manager, Flat DHCP Network Manager, and the VLAN Network Manager. The three kinds of networks can coexist in a cloud system.

Nova will automatically create all network bridges (ie, br100) and VM virtual interfaces. All physical machines must have a public and internal network interface.

Neutron provides the API that builds required network connectivity between OpenStack physical nodes (ie, between the vNICs managed by OpenStack Nova—providing them network as a service functionality). This makes the Neutron API most pertinent to the discussion of NFV. Though it should be noted that because of its focus on the delivery of primitives required by a single application (orchestration), the Neutron API is a subset of the capabilities that could be exposed through the northbound API of most SDN controllers/frameworks/systems.

Neutron was originally targeted at the creation of advanced virtual topologies and services like the commonly used layer 2-in-layer 3 overlays that are used in larger deployments to skirt the limits of traditional VLAN-based deployments. That is, Neutron seeks to decouple *service specification APIs (what)* from *service implementation (how)*, exploiting a capabilities-rich underlying topology consisting of virtual and physical systems.

In the Havana OpenStack release, the Modular Layer 2 core plugin was introduced in Neutron. Until then, the plugin drivers were monolithic (eg, Open vSwitch (OVS) and Linux bridge) with a lot of redundant code. The ML2 plugin allowed the installation to support a variety of Layer 2 networking scenarios for more complex networks (eg, multi-segment networks, tunnel networks without flooding, L3 service plugins) and separated the management of the network types from the mechanism to access them (Fig. 5.4).

Plugins may be distributed as part of the public Neutron release or privately. The plug-in architecture allows vendors to support the standard API in the configuration of a network service while hiding their own backend implementation specifics.

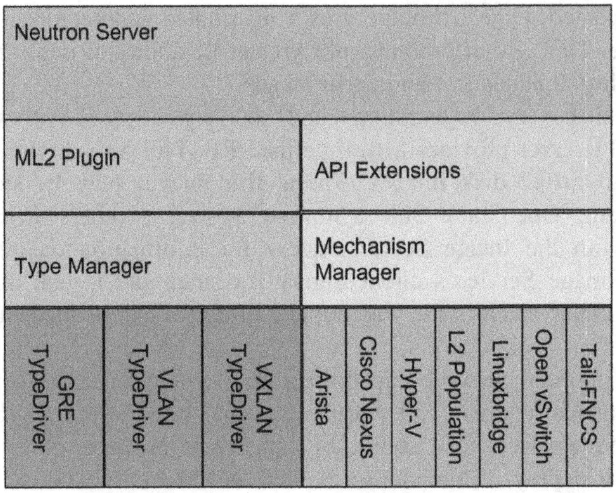

FIGURE 5.4

ML2 plugin architecture (c. Havana).

When a VM is invoked, it is typically attached to a virtual layer 2 switch, most often an OVS. However, some physical devices can be managed as well when they need to be spliced into one of the virtual network overlays (assuming the vendor provides a plugin). For example, this can be accomplished using the OVS-DB interface to program their network overlay end points (known as VTEPs when using VXLAN as an overlay). Neutron is capable of creating primarily layer 2 overlays and is most often used with this type of overlay, although one can program an OVS to do other things including creating OpenFlow paths.

In Fig. 5.5, we see Nova and Neutron interact during VM creation. Briefly, (1) the OpenStack Nova control prompts the Nova agent on a selected compute node to create a VM. In Step (2), the agent then signals Neutron server to create a port for that VM an adds that port in (3) by signaling the br-int structure that in our example, is hanging off OVS in the compute node. In (4) the OVS Neutron agent detects the port add, requests its security group association from Neutron server in (5) and binds that in the ip-tables structure in the node in (6). In (7), the OVS agent fetches port details from the Neutron server, applies these as OpenFlow rules associated with the port on the br-int structure and other associated ports in OVS (eg, the VLAN mapping on Eth0) in (8) and (if all goes well) sets the port state to active and returns this status to the Neutron server in (9). Neutron server can then signal a matching VLAN entry to the Neutron plugin element on the Network Node (a vendor switch).

The plugin architecture is how a number of vendor networking equipment and controllers are linked to OpenStack (eg, Cisco, Brocade, Nicira, Nuage Networks, Juniper's OpenContrail, HP, Big Switch).

While OpenStack is an extremely popular framework, Neutron in particular has been a bit problematic. Many of the advanced networking features supporting the networking aspect of NFV infrastructure often offloaded to a Network Controller entity, which is normally integrated with OpenStack through a Neutron plugin (often through the Modular Layer 2 framework).

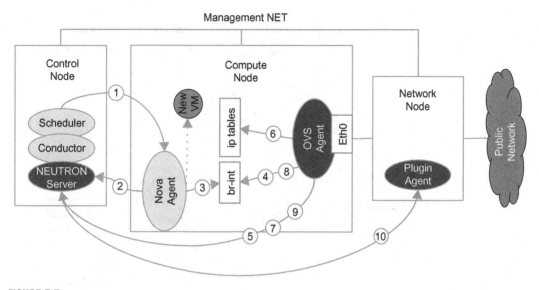

FIGURE 5.5

Nova and Neutron interaction in VM creation.

In 2015, the process of adding Neutron functionality was generally perceived as complex and slow. At the same time, the poor general performance of early OpenStack implementations was also a bit underwhelming (large VM adds were not very "agile"). As a result, there was a loss of momentum and interest in adding complex network features to OpenStack. Policy was an example of one such area. Both the concept of Group Based Policy (GBP) and early work in SFC were introduced as a combination of OpenStack and the ODL (controller) projects.

Neutron had become so fraught with projects and plugins that they have started what can be described as a master project (Neutron Stadium[2]) to help demystify the process of adding functionality and setting the rules for inclusion of a project in Neutron. Alternative proposals (e.g. Gluon—an arbiter) attempt to work around making Neutron the only provider of "ports" (networking) to Nova, but to-date have enjoyed limited traction.

The Neutron project *has* been moving some NFV-centric features forward. For example, as of the Liberty release, Neutron will support the SFC specification, including an OVS reference implementation.

Stretching OpenStack

OpenStack Foundation has their own view of how they are progressing in the support of NFV,[3] noting that they are a reference implementation of the ETSI NFV specification in OPNFV (Arno) and are actively working on a number of blueprints submitted on behalf of both ETSI and OPNFV. They also boast impressive adoption, listing support from both service provider and enterprise network operators including AT&T, Verizon, NTT Group, Deutsche Telekom, SK Telecom, China Mobile, Telus, Telecom Italia, Telefonica, and Wells Fargo.

The same document notes that a subsequent release of OPNFV (Brahmaputra) will include a focus on multisite data centers, stretching beyond the 1:1 site:VIM correlation (Fig. 5.6).

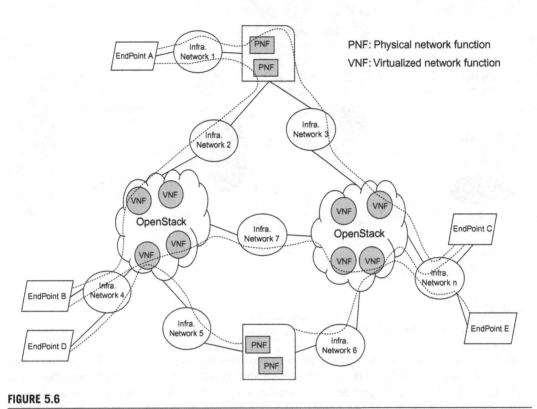

FIGURE 5.6

OPNFV picture of the OpenStack multisite use case.[4]

Because most operators envision supporting a distributed datacenter model that could include a granularity that places racks of infrastructure in more than one metro access hub or multiple small sites possibly needing a VIM instance per site, the cost and complexity of running a separate and necessarily highly available OpenStack instance per site could present a difficult hurdle to deployment.

Needless to say, service solutions that require the placement and management of infrastructure at a remote customer location will probably look to a leaner and more focused solution leveraging common DevOps tools we alluded to at the beginning of this section.

Although the original conversation around NFV infrastructure is very focused on virtualization, OpenStack has added the Ironic project (to support bare metal deployments), which could be considered a stretch of the VIM.

OpenStack is also stretching beyond the VIM. OpenStack members started Heat (an orchestration project) in 2013 and more recently added Tacker (a VNFM and orchestration project) as well as Ceilometer (Metering—which has applications in Service Assurance) which are all "interesting" to NFV. We will look at Tacker in more detail in our next chapter. The OpenStack NFV white paper also lists Astara (described as "network service orchestration" project to collapse multiple Neutron L3 related agent functions), Blazer (resource reservation), Congress (policy), Mistral (workflow), and Senlin (clustering) as NFV related projects. How well the OpenStack community delivers on these projects remains to be seen.

At the end of the chapter, we will look at another "stretch" of OpenStack that may be one of the keys to NFV in the future.

To fork or not fork open source distributions

In a broader sense, a question arose with OpenStack that is applicable to many open source projects—the question of whether a particular go-to-market packaging of OpenStack was a "fork" of the open source distribution. The drive to provide feature functionality beyond the current OpenStack distribution led some vendors to offer "advanced functionality" by forking the OpenStack distribution for their own private development. This is sometimes done because of a resistance to add functionality into the "upstream" or mainline release, or even a desire to withhold functionality as to "add value" or uniqueness to their distribution.

Generally, direct forking approaches have proven to be difficult propositions for the company maintaining the fork, and ultimately for the end users consuming and deploying them. The reason for this is simple: over time, the growing divergence from the main line code base results in more and more development and maintenance effort required on the part of the distribution vendor. Not only will they have to maintain bug fixes, but possibly larger functional patches. Given the rapid pace of change of the upstream code base of many projects including OpenStack, this may only take a few cycles to emerge as an issue in keeping up with the change. Another issue that can exacerbate this is when a vendor supports many previous releases. Having to support those past releases and their bug fixes can become a difficult burden to carry over time.

It is useful to note that there are varying shades of distribution code base purity with regard to how much they package and distribute from the upstream code base. Some vendors do not directly fork the main distribution but provide an "installer" that not only eases the installation burden of OpenStack. This, on its own, represents a true value-added service if you have tried installing any of the recent releases yourself! Other improvements that can be found in commercial distributions are patches that are "back ported" to previous releases from the most recent distribution, to bring forward particular functionality that was planned to be integrated into one or more main releases of the project in the future. Other distributions might include subsets of upstream functionality. In projects such as ODL, this is done by some of the commercial distributions due to the varying levels of stability of the upstream projects. In these cases, they may wish to only ship "stable" project components and so do not ship those marked as "unstable." This is also commonly done with Linux distributions.

The danger with a fork of the main distribution of the project is that the customer could be dependent on a single vendor due to their customizations—the vendor becomes nonsubstitutable, which is definitely counter to one of the promises of open source. A number of nonforked distributions are available commercially and include those from Canonical and RedHat.

NETWORK CONTROLLERS

Through the network controller, the worlds of SDN and NFV intersect. As previously mentioned, the OpenStack IaaS functions in networking are often augmented with a scalable and (hopefully) flexible SDN network controller. At a really high level, both components are just a layer of middleware used in ultimately achieving the goals of service orchestration.

In this section we will look at examples of open source network controllers. As with service layer orchestration (see the next chapter), there are notable proprietary offers on the market for network control. There are also controller projects that are "open in name," that is to say that project governance is such that a vendor or body controls all submissions and (in effect) are the only realistic avenue for support.

CONTROLLER ARCHITECTURE

To begin the discussion, let us start off where our previous book ended this discussion. That was roughly three years ago at the time of the writing of this book, and so it is worth updating some of the concepts discussed therein. For starters, let us begin with updating the Idealized Controller Framework as a grounded reference point for discussing other network controllers and how they have evolved in this space.

Behind every well-designed controller lies a well-thought-out framework on which it is not only based, but will continue to be built on in the future. The controller framework should act like an architectural blueprint for where the controller is and wants to be in a couple of iterations. This of course lends itself well to a quote from someone who was very important in the early days of SDN, OpenFlow, and ODL: David Meyer. He is quoted as saying, "The most important thing you can do is focus on your approach, and not on the specific artifacts that are an immediate result of the most recent iteration of that approach because those artifacts are ephemeral, and might not be useful in a short time." To this end, let us explore the important components of a sound controller framework at this point in time.

Controllers are expected to scale to very significant levels. Therefore, the usual rules of layering to achieve high scale distributed systems apply. To this end, the general design of controllers has evolved into a three-layer model: northbound interfaces, compute/data store, and southbound interfaces. At the root of this layered design is code modularity, with clear boundaries between subsystems with the ability to dynamically load or unload modules.

Also note that we indicated the northbound and southbound layers in the plural sense. This is because (as we discovered in our first survey of this space), the SDN controller should not be a mono-protocol culture. Limiting the southbound narrows the addressable market space and applicability of the controller. As a goal, this is called "protocol agnosticism."

In general, a preference for ReSTful interfaces has evolved, especially on the northbound side. As the rapid evolution of application programming has taken hold, these sorts of APIs are critical to interface with those applications. This is less so on the southbound side where protocols such as NETCONF or even the old-school SNMP, remain due to the widespread deployment of both old and new devices in most nonresearch networks of the day.

A controller needs to support "brownfield" networks, and not just "greenfield" networks. For those unfamiliar with the terminology, the former is a network that has evolved over time—or at least grown in place via the addition of new equipment, and the often-slow replacement of older pieces. In the case of greenfield networks, these are defined as being brand new or "clean slate" deployments. Even in the case of many greenfield deployments, these are simply built as facsimiles, at least architecturally, of existing networks. An example is, say, a new "pod" for a new data center. While it is technically a brand new installation in perhaps a brand new building, its equipment and design are identical (or similar enough) to existing ones. In general, true greenfield networks have been limited to academic research or the rare startup network operator. While NFV focuses a lot on the networking between the virtual service instances, they will still need to be stitched into traditional networks.

Over time the controller system has evolved to serve more like a service bus that interconnects various internal services to the northbound and southbound interfaces—effectively becoming a message routing system. This approach has proven to be very effective in facilitating horizontal scale through various clustering approaches.

A model-driven approach has also proven itself to be critical in driving rapid development and evolution of some controllers. Particularly, the use of the Yang data modeling language as the model and the literally hundreds of models available as well as tools to compile, edit, and manipulate those models.

Further, attaching the controller to an enterprise message bus is critical in both bridging the gap between existing enterprise applications—of which there is a huge mass—and the controller's functions. This also lends itself to another important element which is a large scale or "big data" collection and management interface (which recently has been evolving more toward a Kafka interface). This is critical to provide data to postfacto analytics or even machine learning backend systems that can comb over the data, and then push back changes to alter the network's behavior based on decisions made often automatically.

In an idealized framework, this can exist as part of either the northbound or southbound interfaces, or even as a bespoke plugin into the inner portion of the controller for perhaps more direct access to the data store and functions therein.

One often-overlooked element of a controller is some form of policy management and an interface that provides a clean and easy model to manage and program those rules. Much research, discussion, and coding have gone into various approaches in this area. It is too early to conclude any a particular winner, but there seem to be a momentum gaining around *intent-based* policy management. That is, policy rules are specified in terms of intended result or outcomes, and then programmed. Once programmed, they are enforced later by the system. In this way, the resulting state can be better modeled by the network operator. However, the real trick with intent-based API is whether it can flexibly render the intent into more than one southbound expression—which ties back to the modularity and dynamic nature of a controller mentioned earlier.

Finally, a high-scale, clustered data store is needed within the middle layer of the controller. This can augment or extend the just-described data collection and management framework components of the controller, but must be present to provide the controller with simple, often overlooked things such as configuration storage and migration capabilities, or data collection snapshot/caching services.

We have illustrated all of the aforementioned concepts in the three-layered illustration in Fig. 5.7.

In this picture, based on the earlier functional descriptions, the infrastructure (the layer in the middle) needs to function as the enabler of a microservice architecture—providing the data structures and message handling to flexibly connect producers and consumers—otherwise, the controller ends up being a collection of unrelated-able, protocol-specific pipelines.

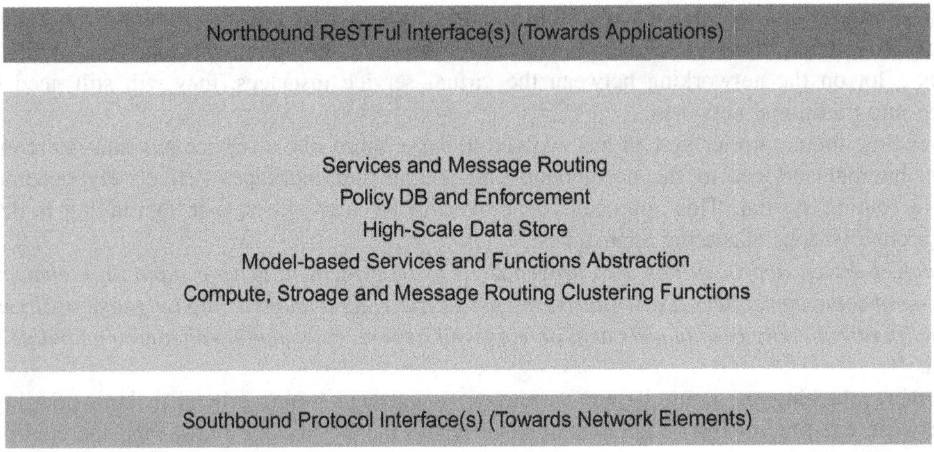

FIGURE 5.7

A layered controller model.

OPENDAYLIGHT

In March of 2013, the OpenDaylight (ODL) Project consortium[5] was formed as a Linux Foundation project.[6] The ODL project sits squarely tasked with the creation and evolution of the SDN Controller, although many other projects exist within the organization. Prior to the formation of ODL, a number of companies, including Nicera, Cisco, Big Switch, and IBM had all either investigated, or created their own proprietary, controllers. However, in 2013 it was obvious that the creation of yet another proprietary controller was going to overload the industry. The logical decision at the time was to form an open source SDN controller project whose goals would be to create a common controller infrastructure as a vehicle to overcome the market duplication the plethora of proprietary controllers had brought to the marketplace.

While the project began with the support of a modest set of prominent equipment and controller vendors, as well as a number of popular open source software vendors in the industry, its membership has grown dramatically since then. A few original members have dropped out, but by in large, the trajectory has been very positive. In 2015 AT&T and Comcast both joined ODL, the organization's first service provider members. ODL's success can be squarely attributed to its robust and relatively diverse community of some 150+ software developers, and dozens of supporting corporations.

A number of others including Ericsson, Nokia, and Ciena forked initial distributions of the controller to combine that code within some internal products (see prior comments about the forking of OpenStack). It is unclear if those projects have continued (in fact Ciena announced a switch to the ON.Labs ONOS controller in 2016). It is also worth noting that in 2015, commercial distributions of the ODL were made available from Brocade,[7] Inocybe,[8] and Cisco.[9] AT&T also publically announced its use and deployment of ODL in its Domain 2.0 network initiative,[10] proving ODL's commercial viability. It is reported that ODL is in dozens of commercial trials as of the time of this writing in early 2016.

Since the ultimate goal of this organization would be that of application portability and robustness of features, the organization was thus chartered to create a common SDN controller "core" infrastructure that possessed a well-defined (but not Standards-based) northbound API based on the IETF's RESTCONF protocol, as well as support for a variety of southbound protocols including the now prominent NETCONF protocol.

ODL continues to be at the pinnacle of OpenFlow performance numbers, and as such has grown into a very viable controller used not only in commercial applications, but also in academic and research environments.

The result of the ODL Project is a true open source controller/framework that ultimately a wide variety of SDN applications can be built upon.

For the longer term, contributions may arise that standardize the east–west interface for the exchange of network operational state between ODL and other controller solutions, as well as to enhance the interoperability of controller federation both within a single operational domain, but also across administrative domains.

The ODL framework is very modular, Java-based (ie, a pure JVM), and supports bidirectional REST and OSGi framework programming. To simplify OSGi package management, Karaf has been incorporated. This will support applications that run in the same address space as the controller application.[11]

One of the main components of ODL that differentiates it from many other offerings, but which we feel is a critical part of the ideal controller framework is its Model-Driven Service Abstraction Layer (MD-SAL).

The MD-SAL maps both internal and external service requests to the appropriate southbound plugin and provides basic service abstractions that higher-level services are built upon depending on the capabilities of the plugin(s). This is an example of enabling a microservice architecture. It specifies this to a large degree, using models that are defined using the Yang modeling language. These models are used by the core functions of the project, including the yangtools parser and compiler, to generate a large portion of the internal code of the controller. Not only are the internals of the controller generated from models, but the portions of the northbound and southbound plugins are (dynamically, at run time) as well. These are what create the actual north and southbound APIs shown in Fig. 5.8.

The project had advanced its functionality to also include an AKKA-based clustering and data store framework. This provides the system user with high availability functions, as well as an avenue to horizontally scale the system. ODL is also adding a Kafka plugin, which will make ODL capable of publishing its data to analytics engines. In addition to these key features, the project also has many subprojects that are poised at adding auxiliary functionality or integration with such things as OVS-DB, Neutron/OpenStack, Tacker, SFC, or Policy functions (ie, the NIC[12] and GBP projects).

Although still in early days, we mentioned previously that there are now commercial deployments of ODL with dozens of commercial trials underway. The future is bright for ODL as long as network operators continue to see value in its community-based development model and the quality of the project itself. Future points of integration for NFVI are also important.

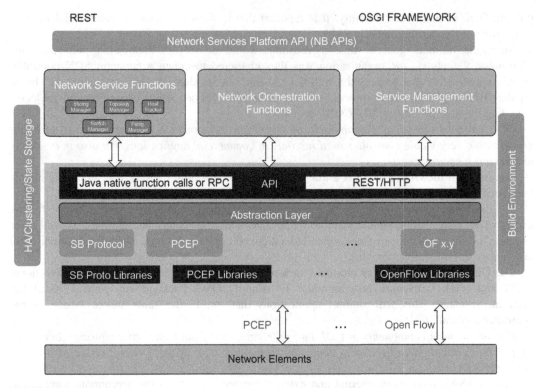

FIGURE 5.8

The architecture of the ODL project.

ODL AND OPENSTACK COLLABORATION

ODL has proven to be a great base for exhibiting NFV-related behavior that has been harder to complete in the OpenStack project. Using the ODL Neutron plugin for OpenStack, collaborators have extended the functionality of both projects to implement SFC the IETF Standard-in-progress, and GBP.

The latter, GBP,[13] shares some concepts with Promise Theory and is essentially an intent based policy system. GBP is built on the concepts of endpoints (hosts, VMs, containers, ports), endpoint grouping (a group of related things), and contracts (their relationship). The contract is a mixture of subjects, rules, classifiers, and actions—the relationships of which are used to express "intent." Using a render framework in ODL, mappings between Neutron primitives, other policy "surfaces" like existing state, and operational constraints and the expressed intent are resolved into primitives or rules for a number of southbound protocols. This essentially moves from a "core" model to a forwarding model (a network context). The first instantiation could render to OVS and OpenFlow overlays, but NETCONF or other renderings are possible.

Both the functionality of GBP and SFC renderer were considered (at the time) to be too complex to execute in OpenStack.

In Fig. 5.9, an NFV Orchestrator provisions SFCs and GBPs in ODL. Using metadata, it triggers OpenStack to place workloads. The metadata includes endpoint groups to place the workload in

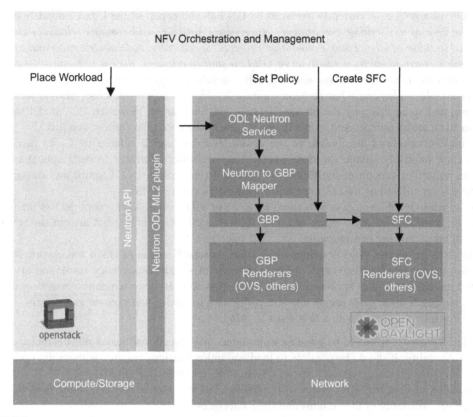

FIGURE 5.9

ODL and OpenStack cooperating to provide SFC with GBP.

and a VNF-type. The metadata passes from OpenStack to ODL via the Neutron v2.0 plugin for ODL. ODL maps the workload to a policy and that policy to a service chain, rendering and implementing the protocol appropriate ruleset/forwarding entries to instantiate both.

Like most ODL capabilities, the rendering infrastructure makes GBP/SFC available across heterogeneous network types, regardless of the northbound, domain-specific language the devices might speak (if the proper rendering module in the rendering framework is available).

OPEN NETWORK OPERATING SYSTEM (ONOS)

ONOS is also an open source SDN controller comprised of multiple modules in a tiered architecture. While this architecture should now be familiar, it has a few twists. ONOS has generated interest through its CORD (Central Office Re-architected as Datacenter) project—with a first use case to implement PON access networking.[14]

ONOS, as a project, is currently managed by ON.Lab and is part of the Linux Foundation.

At the time of this writing, the project's governance structure still remains relatively closed as compared to those of other Linux Foundation projects. Specifically, code contribution and architectural decisions are made by a small set of ON.Lab staff developers. Recent agreement to re-home ONOS under the Linux Foundation umbrella will hopefully change and improve these processes.

Source code, builds and other resources are made available to outside observers via an Apache 2 license, and so in this way the project is open and transparent. However, this model makes it difficult to create an independent, commercial release of the controller (unless you fork).

A single commercial distribution of the controller exists and is offered by Ciena in order to implement a relatively simple use case wherein the controller interfaces to their optical switches using an unratified version of the OpenFlow protocol (ie, version 1.4). Control and management applications are offered as well as integration with their existing EMSs.

The overall ONOS project is structured as a set of subprojects. Each subproject is maintained as its own compartmentalized entity not only for development purposes, but also in the reality of loading it into a running configuration.

Like ODL before it, ONOS is written to leverage Apache Karaf as its OSGi framework. In doing so, it also enjoys similar advantages to ODL in terms of startup dependency resolution at startup, dynamic module loading (and unloading) at runtime, as well as strict semantic versioning of code bundles making it safer, more secure and straightforward to invoke and execute as a system.

ONOS itself is designed with a few goals in mind:

- Code Modularity: It should be possible to introduce new functionalities as self-contained units.
- Configurability: It should be possible to load and unload various features without disrupting the system, although some may require the system to be restarted in reality.
- Separation of Concern: The system will maintain clear boundaries between subsystems to facilitate modularity of the systems and their interfaces.

Fig. 5.10 shows the ONOS multilevel architecture.

ONOS labels the top layer, *consumer interface*, the Application Intent Framework layer. This layer is also where a variety of controller services such as topology management reside.

The northbound API provides applications with abstractions that describe network components and properties, so that they may define their desired actions in terms of *intended policy*. The intent framework provides a system by which intended policy gets translated into OpenFlow rules that can then be programmed on the network devices (ie, switches) using the southbound plugin. Unlike GBP's rendering framework in ODL, this intent framework appears to be a static mapping.

The edge of the intent framework provides ReSTful interfaces to network applications built around the controller framework. These applications can reside within the controller, or exist externally.[15] This is the growing canonical model of applications build around a controller framework.

The distributed core layer is responsible for tracking, routing, and serving information about network state, and applications that consume and act upon the information provided by the core upwards into the northbound interface of the controller (the consumer interface).

In many ways, the ONOS architecture is like ODL when it only had the AD-SAL, a manually supported API. It lacks the plug-in, model-driven, run-time loaded API expansion that ODL demonstrates.

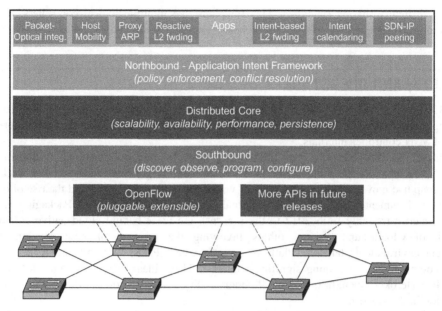

FIGURE 5.10

ONOS architecture.

At the lowest layer, the *provider interface* to the system is OpenFlow. Although the ONOS architecture claims to strive for protocol agnosticism the northbound API is bound to the southbound instantiation—OpenFlow, and it appears to be difficult to add any other functionality to the existing infrastructure. There have been many statements made about future support for items such as NETCONF. However, the realization of any NETCONF model currently will likely be limited to functionality that fits expression in a Layer-2/Ethernet model (eg, access control lists).

In its core, ONOS has a single producer and a single consumer model. In combination with the governance (core code control by a single entity), this inhibits the ability to add functionality to the controller. A developer who wants to exploit new capability has to wait for the core team to provide an API. That capability normally has to be representable as an Ethernet/Layer 2 function.

While all the right words are in the description of the ONOS architecture design principles, it is hard to work around the fact that it is a static, single-protocol design. As long as a solution required can be hammered into this model, it is realizable with ONOS. The question is whether all solutions can be made to conform to that model—either through the native support of OpenFlow or some abstraction by an entity agent—and if that abstraction is "lossless" when it comes to functionality and data transparency.

There have been other single-protocol design controllers (proprietary) that have expanded their claims over time to include "other southbound protocols" (some of those claims ironically included the addition of OpenFlow support!). These too theoretically had policy "compilers" that could accommodate these new protocols. Over time they have failed to deliver this functionality because the proper framework is not in the core.[16]

Without the proper framework, such designs CAN implement vertical stacks within the controller that are hidden on the surface by a broad API. Such a design is compromised because the stacks have great difficulty sharing state/data. This functions like multiple logical controllers, where the task of resolving the state/data sharing and orchestration coordination is pushed to "a higher level."

PaaS, NFV, AND OPENSTACK

Both in Chapter 3, ETSI NFV ISG and later in Chapter 7, The Virtualization Layer—Performance, Packaging, and NFV, the concept of microservices is raised. We have even seen them here in the context of SDN controller internals.

In Chapter 3, ETSI NFV ISG, the ETSI early work focused on functional decomposition of complex VNFs into multiple components (VNFC), but did not go much further. Later work by the Phase 2 group had moved from the VM basis of virtualization to containers—and the rise of container networking is documented in Chapter 7, The Virtualization Layer—Performance, Packaging, and NFV.

In the interim (roughly from 2012 to the present), the ideas behind cloud native computing,[17] the work of CloudFoundry[18] and others involving the creation of new development-and-deployment environments labeled "Platform as a Service" (PaaS) were advancing in developer-oriented communities and gaining significant interest. These ideas were an evolution from earlier projects like Heroku, OpenShift, to CloudFoundry, CliQr, and Kubernetes/Marathon, with a great acceleration in 2014/2015.

The frameworks that support these concepts made the rapid shift to applications based on cooperative small functions using container runtimes in a continuous delivery environment.[19] These cooperative small functions were called "microservices."

The idea of "microservices" has trickled down to NFV, but it generally terminates with a smaller vision—"does your function run in a container?" Yet there is no reason to limit the vision.

The real issue here might be (again) cultural, because the target of the cloud native environment is the developer—NOT the IT professional or the traditional network operator. Of course, these are the dominant sources of input into the ETSI architecture.

Many of these frameworks are open source projects.

For example, a CloudFoundry "foundry" itself provides a number of enabling services. You will note that many of them have parallels in what we currently conceive of as service chaining: traffic routing, authentication, lifecycle management, state and elasticity management and reconciliation, a code repository (blob store), execution agents, logging and statistics services, and perhaps the most interesting—service brokers and a message bus. More specifically, the PaaS approach takes care of the Middleware and runtime so that we can focus on the application and data.

True to the open source business model, others build value-add features around the framework—enterprise features, documentation, support, certification, and other services.

Each of the frameworks listed would be a separate picture, all slightly different, and longer descriptions would take a separate book. Our purpose is to point you in this direction so you can explore the idea yourself.

The point is, a PaaS framework will efficiently deliver a microservices development and deployment environment. Thinking IaaS alone for NFV is not going to make it hard to deliver the benefits of microservice architectures as efficiently and transparently.

Although some frameworks have their own deployment and optimization services (eg, cloud controller), they can work in combination with IaaS tools like OpenStack, Kubernetes, etc.[20]

OPENSTACK CUE[21]

Fortunately, the OpenStack community has already anticipated this potential synergy. Cue provides a service for OpenStack to provision, manage, and administer message brokers.

The use case they describe is integration with the CloudFoundry service broker.

The great benefit here is that OpenStack is extended to understand and manage the messaging service infrastructure the PaaS framework requires. Authentication is also passed through so that the worker in the PaaS environment does not need to know OpenStack.

THE IMPACT OF PaaS ON NFV

The impact of PaaS on how network operators deploy NFV can be difficult to estimate—but when deployed using this approach it could be potentially revolutionary because:

- It can allow for an environment where there is not so much duplication between the functions, thereby optimizing the resource footprint of the service. By their very definition, microservices are relatively atomic, so there is no need to have multiple similar "microservices" unless of course its done to scale-out/scale-up growth of total resource power for that service. This is a clear step forward in efficiency.
- It can be used to create "complete offers" from vendors that overlay the IaaS below it and work beside the MANO pieces to create a new view of how a service is constructed. When based on an open framework, this environment has the potential to be extensible to include an operator's custom microservices or those of additional partners. Examples of how this works might be found in commercial PaaS offers today such as Amazon Web Services' media services offer. This service includes their own tools as well as integrated set of tools from Elemental. An OTT service such as Netflix can then build their customizations *on top of* those services by extending them or adding to them—adding value to the environment.
- Once we are working at the *microservice* level, we now have the license and freedom to change our view of service creation and how to build new services that are not built around traditional functional boundaries. We illustrate this in an example below.
- It may change the way we think about "chaining" in service creation in that not every microservice needs to see the original packet in order to render the overall service![22]

The latter points are demonstrated in Fig. 5.11. In the figure, several microservices each denoted by a series of similarly colored boxes, each a container.

The container clusters for each microservice do not all have to be in the packet path. What they do have to be is the most optimized containers possible. That is, in order to maximize the underlying resources, the containers should only contain the minimum functions and processes needed to achieve their goal. This also promotes maximum reuse down the road, as well as scale of the entire system.

Service A can scale via external load balancing or internal routing to handle the incoming/outgoing packet events—dissembling the packet into multiple data fields (and reassembly on egress).

A majority of the work could be done in A, with exceptions in that code set spawning further work that is handled by the other services, which can all scale to handle demand and all have their

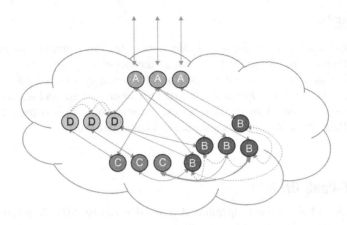

FIGURE 5.11

NFV services realized through microservices and PaaS.

own interrelationships. A-B, A-C, A-D, A-B-C, A-B-D, etc. are all potential interactions of microservices that make a complete service (or subsets of total service functionality).

Each of the services may have their own interconnectivity to provide cooperative state management as well as associated data repositories. Microservices B and D exhibit this behavior.

In the underlay network, their containers may be on separate hosts (this is a question of the algorithms involved in resource placement, lifecycle management, and other interactions between PaaS framework elements) so that there is a potential network transaction to service the request.

The big difference as it applies to our present understanding of NFV is that those microservices are actually linked at the application layer via a message bus. They are often working on a "unit of work"—a transaction, and not necessarily the original packet.[23] Their relationships are managed by the service broker and connected by a message bus.

We do not need to worry about the internal, underlying network transitions from a service chaining perspective as much as we did in the IaaS focused approach to "service."

Both IaaS and PaaS paradigms for NFV rely on a resource optimization or packing algorithm that can maintain certain SLAs while at the same time maximize resource "bin packing." For example, in order to maximize the CPU/memory resources of a particular physical server, this resource optimizer might place as many containers on the same host as possible without overdriving its resources so as to not violate the overall service SLA.

With the PaaS approach an NFV service can appear to the consumer as a single somewhat amorphous network element—much like a web service.

Ironically, the explanation of the network versus application level differences in approach completely ignores the strengths of the environment as a continuous develop/deploy platform—which is part of the cultural shift we have to make. This includes the reusability of the microservices as components of multiple services.

Perhaps a simple way to think of a PaaS approach might be to look at how a cloud-driven business might look at one of the services network operators offer today.

For example, think about how a new competitor might approach a security service. Would they chain together a series of physical or virtual devices labeled "firewall," "intrusion detection," "web security" in some virtual pipeline that mimics taking the physical equivalents of these services and physically wiring them together, or instead to completely reinvent the concept of security with a collaborative set of functions that used a message bus to communicate instead of a fixed pipeline and were used deployed in a manner that was more "situation aware" than "topologically bound." Of course, underlying their approach, they would have the same elasticity and resource efficiency goals as the current goals of NFV prescribe.

When it comes to NFV, a PaaS orientation is complimentary to the IaaS focus we exist in today. The additional layer of abstraction, if embraced, could remove some of the expertise burden around IaaS noted earlier in our major section on OpenStack—for the subset of the network operator that will be service function developer. These frameworks provide a layer of abstraction that handles the resource management and placement problems for them.

CONCLUSIONS

This chapter focused on presenting the reader with the first big architectural block in the NFV conceptualization of the ETSI NFV work: VIM. The discussion honors two recurring themes in NFV—open source (though proprietary solutions for the VIM functionality exist and may have some value-added capability) and programmability.

OpenStack projects enjoy a great degree of interest and adoption for resource orchestration in the VIM. OpenStack is the open source framework for the VIM. However, shortcomings in Neutron and the potential complexity of evolving network requirements have led to the use of network controllers in the VIM.

The fact that OpenStack has flaws is not a surprise and certainly not unique to an open source framework. At a high level, OpenStack is working on eliminating some of its shortcoming (eg, user awareness of project interdependencies that had unexpected consequences during upgrades) including the networking aspects. Of the things that may bedevil the VIM related projects, user competency in OpenStack is a difficult hill to climb and probably the biggest obstacle in its use for NFV.

The ability to move complexity from the orchestrator into the network controller has proven to be a boon for rapid prototyping around concepts like SFC and policy.

We updated our concept of an idealized controller framework (from our previous book on SDN) to reflect what have been successful framework designs available today.

For example, model-driven approaches, not only for API definition but also the frequent use of automated code generation based on these models is an important advance in the state of the art. This lends itself to rapid development and iteration of various components inside of software systems. This is important because one of the most important features of SDN and NFV is *rapid programmability*. The ability to quickly iterate on and evolve a software platform, whether it be derived from open source projects or proprietary, is now emerging as a key feature of successful software systems in this space.

We looked at two open source network controllers in this regard—one apparently bit more open and flexible than the other. Setting aside the governance issues, the question remains whether NFV solutions will be single protocol in their network (OpenFlow) or a polyglot. Whatever the answer, we have to move beyond "controller wars" if we are to make progress. In the end, controllers are middleware in the NFV process—not the focal point.

Beyond the VIM, OpenStack has a growing sprawl of projects that have spun up to expand the functionality of OpenStack. Whether these distract from core competencies and/or add value that rivals proprietary products in these new areas remains to be seen. We venture into some of these areas in the next chapter—service management and orchestration (MANO).

A PaaS approach to NFV brings a different perspective to the development and deployment of services, providing a framework required for cloud native computing using container runtimes to realize application (network services) built on microservices. The relationships between these microservices can have a profound impact on how we perceive NFV and SFC.

One of the OpenStack projects, Cue, allows for the integration of a PaaS foundry with an OpenStack IaaS-focused resource manager.

PaaS for NFV may be a hard concept to deal with while we are grappling with the existing architecture already prescribed for NFV.

The IaaS approach is much easier to understand because it is still focused on "how we wire things together," which is very consumption- and deployment-oriented and not very creation-oriented. The PaaS approach seeks to minimize the deployment problem and enable creation.

If it is any comfort, in many ways, thinking about NFV as a PaaS problem instead of an IaaS problem is compatible with the basic thinking behind NFV—it just takes it to a slightly different place.

At this point we can ask ourselves a few questions too. First, "how are we going to realize microservices for NFV?" and second, "can we achieve the goals set out by the ETSI working group, albeit using methods and architecture that likely differ from those that might have been specified?" While these are questions that may occur to you when we get to Chapter 7, The Virtualization Layer—Performance, Packaging, and NFV, at this point we offer that PaaS is a viable answer to both questions.

END NOTES

1. In many OTT data centers, "network" is still BGP-driven control.
2. http://docs.openstack.org/developer/neutron/stadium/sub_projects.html.
3. https://www.openstack.org/assets/telecoms-and-nfv/OpenStack-Foundation-NFV-Report.pdf.
4. https://wiki.opnfv.org/multisite.
5. http://www.opendaylight.org/announcements/2013/04/industry-leaders-collaborate-opendaylight-project-donate-key-technologies.
6. The announcement was immediately followed by statements from the ONF that they too would be working on a standardized northbound (application) API.
7. http://www.brocade.com/sdn.
8. https://www.inocybe.com/platform/infrastructure-controller/.
9. http://www.cisco.com/c/en/us/products/cloud-systems-management/open-sdn-controller/index.html.

10. http://www.networkworld.com/article/2936187/cloud-computing/atandt-looking-at-white-boxes-as-cpe.html.
11. http://www.osgi.org/Technology/WhatIsOSGi.
12. https://wiki.opendaylight.org/view/Network_Intent_Composition:Main.
13. https://wiki.opendaylight.org/view/Group_Based_Policy_(GBP).
14. https://wiki.onosproject.org/display/ONOS/Whitepapers. CORD is a solution comprised of applications that ride on top of the ONOS controller.
15. In the top application layer, we show the list of sample applications that are included in the current releases.
16. Perhaps they were hoping that consumers would be so enamored with the existing functionality that those promises might not be fulfilled.
17. https://cncf.io/.
18. https://www.cloudfoundry.org/.
19. Some of these frameworks are agnostic to the deployment vehicle and support bare metal, VMs, and containers.
20. In fact, the CloudFoundry BOSH project for "release engineering, deployment, and lifecycle management" boasts "multiple IaaS providers like VMware vSphere, vCloud Director, Amazon Web Services EC2, and OpenStack. There is a Cloud Provider Interface (CPI) that enables users to extend BOSH to support additional IaaS providers such as Google Compute Engine and Apache CloudStack."
21. https://wiki.openstack.org/wiki/Cue.
22. When we described decomposition in Chapter 3, ETSI NFV ISG, this was the element—the connection at the application level—that was missing from any existing NFV approach.
23. The unit of work is based on data derived from the packet by the referring service.

MANO: MANAGEMENT, ORCHESTRATION, OSS, AND SERVICE ASSURANCE

INTRODUCTION

While the preceding chapter dealt with the NFV infrastructure (including the VIM), the other new (and big) chunk of logic introduced by NFV centers on Management and Orchestration (MANO).

If we revisit our high-level architecture framework in Fig. 6.1, our focus in this chapter will include a further breakdown of NFV MANO. In particular, we will look at the Virtual Network Function Manager (VNFM) and NFV Orchestrator (NFVO) components as well as some external but related components.

While the original focus of the ETSI architecture was primarily on orchestration and lifecycle management of VNFs, we need to elevate the discussion to the orchestration of services and introduce elements that are now becoming more common in both current ETSI and open source solution dialogs. We also need to explore the practicality of doing this *en masse* across an existing network, which will introduce a number of its own challenges.

While some concepts rudimentary to the understanding of service chaining and an indicator of the discussion of more complex services in the future (eg, service graphs) were part of the original NFVO vision, familiar elements of service orchestration like the management of a service catalog were not originally emphasized.

The open source orchestration concept of that time was being borrowed from Data Center and was centered on resource orchestration tasks. However, these concepts did (and still do) exist in more integrated vendor-led service orchestration offerings. Logically, the NFVO will become part of existing higher level service orchestrators or will evolve to become a higher level service orchestrator.

Similarly, the scope of the VNFM can be seen as just an element in the larger FCAPS (Fault Management, Configuration Management, Accounting Management, Performance Management, and Security Management) approach to existing service management more common to traditional Operations Support System (OSS) thinking.

Whether by accident or on purpose, one of the outcomes from the NFV MANO perspective is a blurring of the line between service and resource orchestration.

On the other hand, one of the serious oversights of the ETSI architecture lies around its overall impact on OSS. If we ignore the history of OSS in provider service creation, we ignore the potential of NFV and virtualization to become an even worse proposition for network operators. We delve into this in more detail in Chapter 9, An NFV Future.

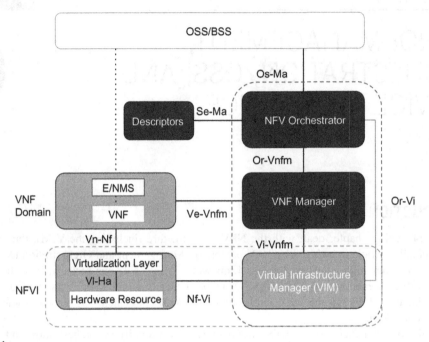

FIGURE 6.1

Architecture revisited.

Our goal in this chapter is to elevate the MANO discussion from resource orchestration and management (VNF centricity) to the service and emphasize one of the "big wins" that will propel NFV—the reimagination of OSS.

Although there is some intersection in the discussion of architectural components covered in our last chapter (eg, VIM), here we will focus more on the darkened blocks in Fig. 6.1.

For completeness, and because it is not considered part of MANO but is relevant to a discussion of OSS/Business Support System (BSS), we will start with a look at the Element Management System (EMS) in the VNF Domain.

THE VNF DOMAIN

The VNF Domain, which we will define loosely as the collection of the virtualized network functions and their management interface(s), will not be the focus of any specific chapter in this book. It is not our intention to look at specific-vendor VNFs or services unless they are used in examples.

VNF Domain also has an important functional block often overlooked in discussions around NFV: Element Management.

Element Management and the EMS, has long been a companion to physical network elements, be they servers, switches, routers, or storage arrays. The essence of their functionality is to allow operators to remotely configure, operate, and monitor these pieces of equipment that, in many cases, are located remotely to the network operators.

There are numerous examples of EMS but generally speaking, most equipment vendors offer some sort of EMS along with their products. Some are addons, and some come for free as part of the cost of the product. Most are proprietary and very specific to the product in question, although a few examples over the years of broader EMSs have existed with varying levels of success. In many cases, especially in larger networks, these systems are integrated into a larger OSS/BSS for the purposes of "end to end" monitoring, configuration, and management purposes.

Specifically, this is done to provide a more ubiquitous layer by which a network operator could view the often disparate set of devices both from a single vendor, or especially when multiple appliances were invoked from different vendors.

The OSS interfaces with EMSs primarily using what is referred to as their northbound interfaces. These interfaces are well defined, but not always standards-based. The goal here is to hide these abnormalities from the OSS, which then in turn provides a consistent look, feel, and interfaces to these devices.

Some of the most consistent feedback we have heard from operators planning NFV deployments is that they see the EMS being gradually supplanted by emerging functionality in other aspects of the NFV architecture. We tend to agree and see its inclusion as necessary for a transition period—as older systems and their management mechanisms age out of networks.

THE OSS/BSS BLOCK

An OSS/BSS is the traditional frameworks that connect the business to the services created. Example frameworks like those from TM Forum (TMF) were implemented as tightly integrated and closed solutions. Some of the component implementations relied on processes and protocols that did not scale well with an agile, virtualized, and dynamically scaled environment.

Fig. 6.2 shows a simplified OSS/BSS stack for review. There are a number of components in both the BSS and OSS blocks that provide services.

Within the OSS layer, we find the components that we are talking about throughout the chapter. As the picture depicts, the whole discussion of Orchestration overlaps just the "C" portion of FCAPS.

The BSS undertakes customer care and customer experience management. These manifest as order entry and bill delivery in the picture. Hidden inside that high-level description are functions like portal creation/management, billing (and billing mediation), a hefty bit of business analytics, and CRM. That latter function provides the most obvious linkages to OSS.

The OSS high-level accounting and monitoring description hides process engineering for order fulfillment, trouble ticketing, inventory/resource management, and service/resource catalog maintenance. And that's not an exhaustive list!

Although BSS is less likely to proliferate/duplicate for most of its functions (eg. multiple billing systems), some service offerings in the past came with custom BSS/OSS pairings. The closed nature of the OSS aspects of the solution often led to OSS silo proliferation. Integration into or across existing systems often required expensive customization (further embedding the OSS vendor).

Most service providers have many OSSs—creating a huge cost center.

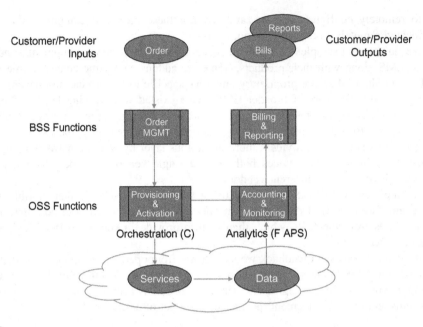

FIGURE 6.2

A simplified OSS/BSS stack.

Many operators point to the costs of integrating new services, particularly new vendors, into their legacy OSS/BSS as a great challenge to service innovation. They also cite the distinct speed or lack thereof, that legacy systems had in regard to deployment, creation, changes to, and destruction of services. The lifecycle management of VNFs alone will create additional stresses on these existing systems. The tooling required to create services through recombinant catalogs of VNFs and edge-specific glue functions, including the associated Service Assurance (SA) definitions and customer and operator portals will probably outstrip their capabilities.

The ETSI GAP analysis did mention the need to integrate NFV with legacy OSS/BSS. This is an unfortunate reality. Telcos rarely, if ever, actually shut down and decommission any existing deployed services or the systems that manage them. While it is possible to evolve to a new "real-time OSS/BSS" that supports the dynamics of NFV and agile concepts such as customer self-service, early deployments are finding that some sort of shim will be needed to the existing OSS/BSS to bridge the gap, at least for the foreseeable future. Market research indicates that early adopters are aware that they are deploying ahead of solution availability in these areas.

Here, the ETSI prescription is notoriously weak, perhaps because this area of service delivery has long remained separate from the network architecture and operations that keeps packets flowing from point A to point B.

This is unfortunate because you cannot talk about service creation unless you can address OSS integration and SA. This is simply because you have to be able to monitor, maintain, and bill for a service.

The ETSI ISG ultimately recognized the importance of changing OSS, suggesting:
"OSS architectures must evolve along the following lines:

- Taking a holistic view of operations rather than the current piece-meal approach.
- Inheriting terms and definitions from standards rather than creating a separate language.
- Flexible architectures rather than static interface definitions.
- Building blocks defined by existing software rather than architecture-specific software.
- Full automation of the capacity management, optimization and reconfiguration cycle should be done by orchestration and cloud management techniques with open and multivendor components rather than vendor-specific management solutions.
- OSS focusing on portfolio management and end-to-end service management."[1]

Several individuals can be credited for pushing the thinking forward around this relationship, in spite of the gap.

REIMAGINING THE OSS (AND BSS)—BROWNFIELD PARTNERSHIP

Earlier in the book we pointed at some of the earlier concepts coming out of the Terastream[2] project. Before NFV was a "thing" that every operator realized they had to embrace, while the ETSI architecture was nascent, the project architect Peter Lothberg was speaking publicly about the need to integrate the OSS of his project with the existing OSS/BSS as a step in the transition from "legacy OSS/BSS" to what he coined as "real time OSS/BSS."[3] This is represented as a generalization for discussion in Fig. 6.3.

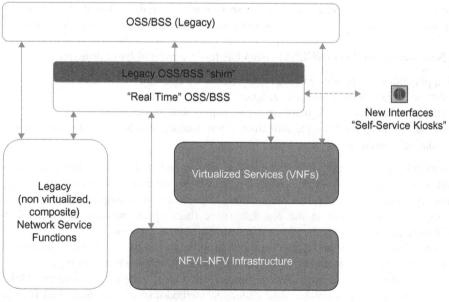

FIGURE 6.3

A much simplified brownfield real time OSS/BSS.

As part of the new architecture, many of the BSS aspects around customer care and experience management (the building of self-service kiosks and monitoring consoles driven through APIs on top of the OSS orchestration and SA pieces) are open, flexible, and modernized.

But the interesting aspect of the transitional OSS/BSS plan is the acknowledgment that the implementation of newer, virtualized services may require some interaction with existing infrastructure—that an operator may not have the luxury of a greenfield there either.

Thus, the first phase architecture has a shim to the existing OSS. This was labeled an "OSS Gateway" and was shown leveraging the billing, CRM, and process engineering of existing systems while also providing a path for resource/inventory reconciliation.

Subsequent phases created a "Fast Track" Order Management system (enabling self-care/customer order kiosks).

The final stage realized a new Real Time BSS (Billing, CRM and Analytics), a Real Time OSS (Process Engine, Service/Resource Catalog and Inventory) bracketed by API-driven Consumer Portal, Partner Portal and Service/Web Developer functionality.

This final stage is also notably prescient in that it shows the ultimate direction a new OSS can lead—to a PaaS environment for service creation.

REIMAGINING THE OSS—OPPORTUNITIES IN SA

Focusing a bit more on the SA aspects of OSS, people like John Evans[4] have been tying the idea of the modern "cloud" OSS to the evolution of analytics and the fundamental value of the massive amounts of data generated in modern service provider infrastructure in making informed network-wide service optimizations and comprehensive service impact analysis in response to fault.

John was one of the first architects to articulate that these aspects of OSS were a "big data problem."

The Next Generation OSS (NGOSS) vision has just a couple of basic principles:

- OSS applications can be viewed as arbitrary functions against an OSS data set.
- The data set is fed by many diverse streams.
- The OSS solution was more a platform for managing and querying that data.
- Current data streams for SA were inflexible, rarely shared, and the resulting analysis functions were relatively ineffective.

Through this lens, looking beyond the closed nature and cost legacy OSSs, the subtlest, but important, problem they create is the impediment to sharing (and thus exploiting) data (Fig. 6.4).

By reworking these aspects of the architecture, you can create a simple, scalable open platform that leverages the innovations in the big data space (high speed message bus technology, open source software for MapReduce, log processing, stream processing,[5] etc.).

The principles of the proposed platform enable an analytics-based approach to analysis functions (eg, combinations of streaming apps, real-time queries, and batch processing).

A related concept was proposed as a project for OpenDaylight (by Andrew McLaughlin) that changed traditional less-scalable data collection methodologies associated with traditional SA (eg, SNMP polling and event monitoring) into pub/sub-structures that utilize a similar message design.

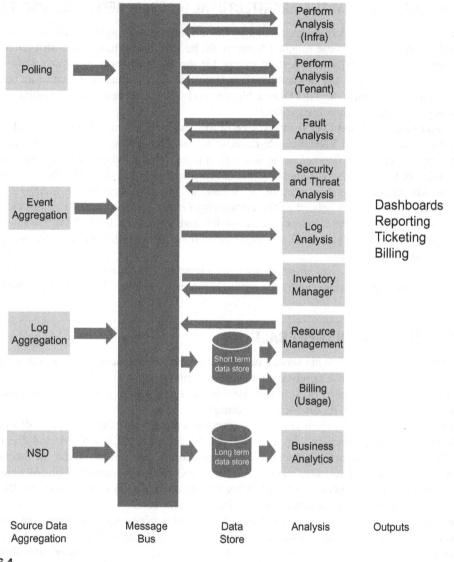

FIGURE 6.4

An imagining of a new platform for OSS SA.

All of these ideas push the realization of an NGOSS forward. The most telling and shared charac-teristics of that OSS vision are that the OSS of the future is a platform not a product (driving back toward the goal of an open framework) and that platform is an architecture that did not exist before.

INTERPRETATIONS FROM THE ARCHITECTURAL DIAGRAM REFERENCE POINTS

Backtracking to the brownfield reimagination of OSS, a definition of such an interface/gateway as described in Terastream in some standard form would be very useful here, but it still remains outside of the scope of the ETSI architecture except for the Os-Ma interface. Again, while not formally defined, this conceptually defined interface is critical in the actual operation of an operator's network many have joined the NFVO to a higher level service orchestrator or existing "legacy" OSS through interfaces of their own volition.

The other reference point (Ve-Vnfm) between EMS and VNF potentially overlaps with the OS-Ma interface with respect to VNF lifecycle management and network service lifecycle management with the only discernable difference being in configuration.[6] This overlap is a bit ambiguous in the initial version of the spec, and is something that is being considered in the ETSI phase 2 work.

The Se-Ma reference point is more of an "ingestion" interface used by the MANO system to consume information models related to the Forwarding Graph, services, and NFVI resources. This information can be manifested/understood as service and virtual machine (VM) "catalogs." This can provide a bridge to a higher level service orchestration function (through a model provider: the model consumer relationship).

Because there is only one new interface here, a common interpretation of the prescribed architecture is that the bulk of the responsibility for service creation seems shifted to NFV Orchestration.

NFV ORCHESTRATION (GENERAL)

The NFVO provides network-wide service orchestration and management. These services can comprise purely physical elements, purely virtual ones, or a mixture therein.

As we saw in the section on OSS, in the past this functionality was part of OSS and represented by traditional vendors like CA, Amdocs, or Accenture.

With the advent of NFV, there are also new vendor entrants into the evolving OSS space that provide many of these functions (eg, Cienna/Cyan Blue Planet, ALU's SAM, and Cisco/Tail-f NSO). These products sometimes include their own, proprietary pieces of the architecture, for example their own VNFM software and/or (in some cases) their own virtualization software. Some are evolving from a more modern approach (than their traditional OSS predecessors) to PNF-based service orchestration with the incorporation of virtual element control.

Note that the concept of orchestration does not stop at the infrastructure management we saw in the preceding chapter (compute, disk, and basic network underlay). Recently, the VIM-centric Openstack project started adding projects to try to move forward an open source capability in the area of service orchestration.

There are subtle constructs that expand the resources to create a service lifecycle manager. Before we look at service lifecycle orchestration, we will start by looking at some of these concepts: the service graph, service descriptor, and service catalog.

SERVICE GRAPHS

As we mentioned earlier, VNFs can be deployed as singletons (ie, an aggregated piece of software that once was running on a physical device), perhaps with explicit external networking connecting

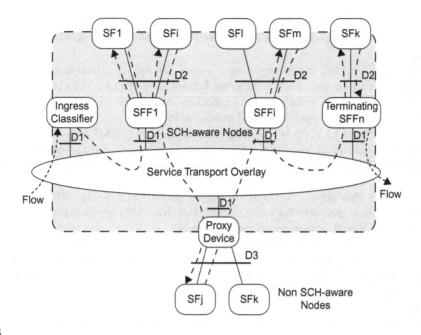

FIGURE 6.5

A Network Service graph.

the services represented by the VNFs together, or by explicitly chaining them together using mechanisms like the IETF's Network Service Header (NSH).

The connectivity between VNFs is described in ETSI terminology as a graph between the set of network paths between the VNFs. This is typically a collection of their network interfaces in some sort of forwarding graph. The graph is part of the description for a service. This is demonstrated in Fig. 6.5.

Note that this graph need not be acyclic, as the VNFs themselves maybe responsible for routing traffic. This is also why the concept of nesting forwarding graphs transparently to the end-to-end service is a capability that will be made available. This level of path decomposition is practical in that sub-chains that are copied might make the overall orchestration of service chains easier to define, as well as to deploy in a "cookie cutter" manner. Supporting these path types is important.

NETWORK SERVICE DESCRIPTORS AND MANO DESCRIPTORS

The service graph becomes part of the next element(s) in the architecture (see Fig. 6.1): the service, VNF, and infrastructure descriptions depicted in the figure by the box entitled "Descriptors." These service components are inputs to the Orchestration system, from which it will create the resulting service.

Information such as forwarding graph nodes, links or other resource constraints, data models or templates such as those depicted in the TOSCA template example below, comprise this input.

Note that this is yet another area in which the use of models like those discussed in Chapter 4, *IETF Related Standards: NETMOD, NETCONF, SFC and SPRING, overlap with NFV deployment.*

While NETCONF/YANG has emerged as a model for service description for classic Metro Ethernet Forum (MEF) services such as Ethernet Private Line (EPL),[7] TOSCA[8] has evolved as a preferred model language for virtualized service because of its ability to define application components and their relationships, capabilities, and dependencies.

The current generation of VNFs is becoming more complex (eg, vIMS and vEPC) with additional requirements like associated databases. Most service instances have supporting application dependencies with DHCP, DNS, or other processes and (depending on your philosophy for VNF-M) assurance.

In our examples that follow, we will be talking about Open Source TOSCA orchestration (because that is publicly available for examination). However, NFV provisioning and configuration is only a part of the overall service orchestration picture.

What has evolved outside of the original ETSI specification is a discussion of layered orchestration such as a case where more than one orchestrator may be involved in service realization. For example, in a multidomain configuration where each domain might be managed by different departments, each department could choose a different orchestrator based on its own, localized requirements.

Of course, one set of functionality in one system could be adapted to accommodate another modeling system functionality. Or they can be used in parallel—a best-of-breed orchestrator deployment (both TOSCA for virtual functions and YANG for physical functions). Some of the orchestration vendors in the evolving OSS space have their own viewpoints on the relative benefits of both.[9]

THE NETWORK SERVICE CATALOG

The Network Service Catalog is another important element usually found here, although not explicitly called out in the architectural diagram. Its purpose is to manage all of these bits of information including NSD, VNFFG, and VLD, which are related to a network service. It is here that this information is organized into a format in which the network operator can readily consume, deploy, and manage—as well as customize. This information is generally segmented into service profiles and service functions—the combination of which are presented as a service catalog.

A separate repository is used to document the active NFV instances, and associated NFVI resources—the state that results from the interaction between the service orchestration and resource orchestration.

The visualization of the catalog and the service state is normally done through a portal that may be service specific. The Service Repository is the state of the exchanges.

An example is shown in Fig. 6.6. Note there are many variations on this theme, but the concepts are similar across commercial products in this space, as well as the open source efforts.

It should be noted that this part of the architecture benefits from standard information/data models such as those being worked by many Standards organizations such as the IETF, MEF or IEEE, as well as those from open source communities such as Open Daylight, Open Config,[10] or the

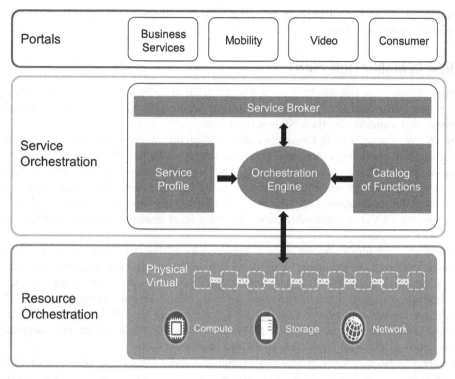

FIGURE 6.6

An abstract view of the components of the service catalog profiles and functions.

Public Yang Repo.[11] The reason is because standard templates, or components of those templates can be created once and then shared amongst the various tools available.

GENERIC RESOURCE AND POLICY MANAGEMENT FOR NETWORK SERVICES

The flow of information that is used to implement generic resource management of the underlying resources managed by the Orchestration system includes configuration and state exchange in support of service creation traversing multiple reference points. To achieve this the interface between Orchestration and VNFM, referred to as the Or-Vnfm in Fig. 6.1, constitutes the interface by which one configures the VNF and collects service specific data to pass upstream. The Vi-Vnfm also shown in that figure provides an interface between the VNFM and VNF Domain, which does additional work in *virtualized* hardware configuration.

The Or-Vi interface between the Orchestration and VIM, provides a *virtualized* hardware configuration information pathway. Finally, the Nf-Vi interface exists between the NFVI and VIM, and is used to enable *physical* hardware configuration. This also provides a mapping from the physical hardware to virtual resources thus forming an important part of the platform-independent interface towards the VNF. It is the use of these interfaces as well as the "eye in the sky" management and coordination of the overall network resources, that constitutes the resource management function of the orchestration system.

THE VNFM DEMARCATION POINT

As a subset of that view, one might observe that the ETSI architecture suggests that resource management might be divided into two pieces: resource service-specific deployment, allocation and management, and a similar one for VNF-specific tasks.

There are two potential camps emerging around implementation of this aspect of the architecture. As mentioned previously, there is a view that suggests that the NFVO take on total responsibility for simplicity, consistency, and pragmatism, as this is how systems such as Openstack currently function, although recent additions such as Tacker have divided this functionality out into its own identifiable component. Others may see the NFVO dividing up its responsibility with the VNFM where the NFVO is responsible only for service-level resources and the VNFM responsible solely for VNF resources.

How this all plays out is anyone's guess, but our take is that it is likely to be divided up into two separate sections of functionality. This guess is based on the premise that there is a significant thrust to standardize these functions, as well as the VNFs themselves—or at least the templates used to deploy and manage them within these systems. While several vendor products implement in this fashion, further evidence of this appears to be evolving through a number of open source projects and initiatives such as OPNFV, OPEN-O, or OpenMANO in which the components are being segregated to allow for clean separations and implementations.

There are a number of services that can be bundled under the general umbrella of "VNF lifecycle management"—though not all VNFMs may actually provide these services. These include:

- Manage the "scale up/down" elasticity of the VNF through a rules system or policy.
- Manage startup sequences and the affinities we mentioned previously in the discussion of TOSCA templates.
- Manage "Day 0" configuration and license management.
- Instantiate the VNF monitor.

The VNF monitor in turn can manifest through a range of functions both integrated and external to the function. These tools can often be open source (eg, Ganglia[12] or Nagios[13]), although some custom tools are also found here. The differences in approach between the various implementations of the monitor revolve around whether the monitor requires an imbedded "agent" in the function.

Though the architecture does allow for a relatively static VNFM, it is possible to have multiple VNF-specific VNFMs in a single deployment. The presence of rules, affinities, and policies in a generic VNFM implies some level of flexibility/programmability.

OPEN ORCHESTRATION

The next sections detail and describe a variety of industry efforts underway that attempt to provide open source alternatives to the readily-available proprietary solutions in the Orchestration space with some form of community effort.

These current open source efforts range in approach from the canonical open source efforts in the Linux Foundation, to those that are born of the ETSI organizations, and adopt their mannerisms and governance styles. There is even the "potential" open sourcing of AT&T's ECOMP software (the idea was shopped to the press along with a white paper describing ECOMP and seeking feedback from other operators at ONS 2016), under yet-to-be disclosed licensing and governance. This distinctive "bloom" of efforts makes it particularly difficult for anyone researching the space to determine a specific winner/direction given the multiple efforts have the potential to be counterproductive. We affectionately refer to this situation as "MANO gone wild."

In fact, at the time of the publication of this book a new organization called no-org.org (http://no-org.org) was created as a reaction to all of the formal organizations forming in this space. Its sole mission is to create an organizational-free space in which individuals can collaborate on open source software for other orchestration projects.

As you might imagine, there are also subsets or components of the wider Orchestration space being worked in some Standards organizations, and those will be called out separately throughout the text.

Where appropriate, we mention proprietary efforts but will not dedicate any indepth sections to those. The reader should keep in mind that these vendor products may address functionality gaps in the open source, and may have different sets of functionality between them. Further, open source may continue to morph—adding projects under different organizations related to NFV MANO.

From here, we will walk through the Openstack Tacker project to illustrate some of the fundamental concepts in the prior section.

TACKER

Tacker is an Openstack project for *NFV Orchestration* and *VNF Management* using The ETSI MANO Architecture. In particular, Tacker concerns itself with portions of the NFV Orchestration and VNF management components. The Tacker project kicked off to tackle the NFV Orchestration problem in early 2015. It was later announced at the Openstack Vancouver Summit in May of 2015. The project has met lots of community support and will be added to The Openstack Big Tent soon, meaning it will become a core project that is part of the mainstream distribution.

When looking at Tacker its, key features include:

- VNF Catalog
- VNF Lifecycle Management
- VNF user-data injection
- VNF configuration injection—during Instantiation and Update
  - SDN Controller using NETCONF/YANG
  - Custom management driver
- Loadable Health Monitoring Framework

As we refer back to the reference architecture we discussed above, we will observe that as expected, a subset of the overall functionality is implemented by The Tacker project. This is simply due to the point we made earlier—that the ETSI MANO architecture is a reference point, but is not meant to be taken literally. Through close engagement with the open source community and network operators that wish to use the project in their specific network situations, Tacker has only implemented those components deemed necessary.

Tacker VNF catalog

This is a repository of VNF Descriptions (VNFDs). It includes VNF definitions using TOSCA[14] templates. TOSCA templates are a templating mechanism that in the context of NFV are used to describe the VNF attributes, Openstack Glance image IDs, Performance Monitoring Policy, as well as the Auto-Healing Policy an operator wishes to invoke on the VNF. TOSCA templates also provide Openstack Nova properties and VNF requirements such as those used for the optimal placement of the VNF. As we will discuss in detail in Chapter 8, NFV Infrastructure—Hardware Evolution and Testing, and Chapter 9, An NFV Future, these are quite important and are also rather dependent on the underlying hardware's support for attributes such as CPU Pinning, NUMA policy, virtualization technology support such as SR-IOV, and so on.

The Tacker VNF catalog function supports multiple VMs per VNF Virtualization Deployment Units (VDUs), as well as the simpler single VNF per-VDU model. The VNF Catalog also includes APIs to onboard and maintain the VNF Catalog. VNFDs are stored in The Tacker Catalog data base.

An example of a Tacker VNF Catalog is shown in Fig. 6.7. Note the catalog shows a variety of choices to choose from when deploying the VNFs that are prepopulated in the catalog. Also note that an import feature for new templates is available, while editing and construction of new ones is simply a function of using a text editor and proper syntactic formatting. Further enhancements to this will allow for more detailed and easier manipulation of the forwarding graph that attaches the constituent components of a VNF (or a service chain).

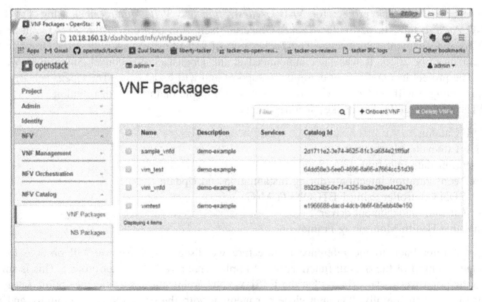

FIGURE 6.7

Tacker VNF catalog.

Tacker VNFM

As we discussed above, one of the critically important functions of the MANO system is the VNFM's Lifecycle Management function. Tacker API deploys VNFs from its VNF Catalog using a number of functions and approaches. This includes a "pluggable" infrastructure driver framework, which enables the system to scale in terms of vendor support for VNFs and their associated templates used to deploy, configure, and manage their VNFs. This plug-in system might raise questions about the ability of the project to keep up with the creation and maintenance of these templates. There might also be cases where vendors do not wish to put a plug-in driver out into the open community for consumption. In these cases, vendors could distribute the templates along with their proprietary VNFs. The Life Cycle Management feature supports Nova deployment of the VNFs. It also supports the use of HEAT templates (by default) for initial configuration of VNFs. This is achieved using a HEAT driver which uses a TOSCA to HEAT convertor. As one might expect, the TOSCA system does support the instantiation of more than one VM described in a TOSCA template. Finally while TOSCA is capable of describing creation behaviors for VNFs, it also can and does describe termination behaviors as well. If a VNF is defined as using multiple VMs, it will delete all of the VMs associated with the VNF instance.

VNF auto-configuration

In addition to the usual lifecycle management, Tacker is capable of performing bootstrapping and startup configuration of its VNFs or constituent VNFs. To achieve this, the Tacker Extensible Management Driver Framework allows vendors to plug-in their specifics in terms of HEAT or TOSCA templates. It also facilitates VNF configuration based on service selection, which is important from a service catalog perspective in that it allows users the ease and flexibility of choosing from predefined templates or customizing specific ones. Once a VNF has been deployed, its initial configuration can be injected using a variety of approaches. These include pushing initial configuration through an SDN controller such as Open Daylight using NETCONF and YANG models or a "config-drive" which is a preconfigured virtual boot disk from which the VM will boot that contains the initial configuration. Another option is to use a custom mgmt-driver and connect to the VNF using an ssh connection, or use its available REST API in order to apply the initial configuration. These same mechanisms can be used later to update the configuration of the running VNF. The pluggable nature of the framework is operator friendly, extensible, and customizable.

VNF monitoring

The VNF monitor feature of Tacker is used to track specific KPIs of a VNF to determine its health/status. Today, this amounts only to an IP ping message sent to the VNF. A failure to answer after several configurable queries results in Tacker determining that the health threshold for the VNF has been reached, and will then terminate the VNF and restart it if so configured. It should be noted that while this seems like a very simplistic approach, a host of configuration options are being added to allow a network operator to tailor this to their specific needs. Imagine options such as bandwidth usage, memory or CPU consumption, or even failed calls from a virtual call server. In the future, the project will also be adding additional functionality that allows an operator to specify a third action that upon a health threshold trigger causes a VNF "resize" operation rather than a termination and/or restart. This allows Tacker to treat VNFs as an elastic system. Specifically, when a

VNF is comprised of a system that scales horizontally, that system can be told to invoke the specific expansion or contraction of itself.

TOSCA templates and parser

Tacker includes support for TOSCA templates via a built-in parser and conversation process to and from HEAT templates. To this end, we wanted to demonstrate a basic TOSCA parser and HEAT translation. First, let us begin by showing a basic TOSCA template. This is shown in Fig. 6.8. Note that we do not want to take too much time here to explain the intricacies of defining TOSCA templates; for that please refer to the footnote reference to OASIS[15] for additional information and tutorials.

Now that we have shown a basic template, we will investigate how a basic TOSCA template is consumed by the parser.

To begin, the TOSCA-Parser and Heat-Translator are part of the Openstack Heat orchestration project. The code for these projects is worked on by the upstream open source communities that work there. The latest TOSCA features that have been integrated into the parser include Networking, Block and Object Storage. This should be obvious given its relation to the Openstack project. Other features include:

```
tosca_definitions_version: tosca_simple_profile_for_nfv_1_0_0

description: Template for deploying a single server with predefined properties.

topology_template:
  node_templates:
    VNF1:
      type: tosca.nodes.nfv.VNF
      properties:
        id: vnf1
        vendor: acmetelco
        version: 1.0

    VDU1:
      type: tosca.nodes.nfv.VDU

    CP1:
      type: tosca.nodes.nfv.CP
      properties:
        type: vPort
      requirements:
        - virtualLink: PrivateNetwork
        - virtualBinding: VDU1

    PrivateNetwork:
      type: tosca.nodes.nfv.VL
      properties:
        vendor: ACME Networks
```

FIGURE 6.8

A TOSCA template.

- The availability to use on command line and user input parameter support.
- Tacker NFV MANO integration using a TOSCA NFV Profile.
- Murano (Application catalog integration) with Openstack client.
- The TOSCA parser is now available as an independent Python library (pypi).
- TOSCA now supports policy schema and group schema constructs.
- Supported Plug-ins: HEAT Orchestration Template (HOT) Generator now supports additional plug-ins to allow translation to other DSLs besides HOT, such as Kubernetes.

With these components and features in mind, let us consider Fig. 6.9. On the left, the parser takes a TOSCA template as input. At this point the TOSCA parser derives TOSCA Types and Nodes, as well as performs validation tests on these elements using syntactic rules. If these are passed, the second phase performs a mapping, validation, generation, and test operation using the TOSCA heat-translator. The output of this phase will be a valid HOT. This can be then deployed—or passed—into a Heat processing engine that uses the template as an instruction set to orchestrate the various Openstack resources such as compute, storage, and networking.

Fig. 6.10 shows the resultant Tacker system with the parser and Openstack components broken out into their constituent pieces. Notice in the figure the workflow from start to finish. On the far left of the process Policy and data modeling are used as inputs to the system as the ETSI NFV Descriptor (as we mentioned earlier in this chapter). Those are consumed by and used as directives by Tacker in order to create, manage, or delete NFV components in the underlying Openstack system components. Those are then referred to specific TOSCA and HEAT reference components. It should be noted that Tacker is working to abstract its interfaces southbound to support other VNFMs including VMware and KVM in the near future, so you could replace either of those with the Openstack components in the figure.

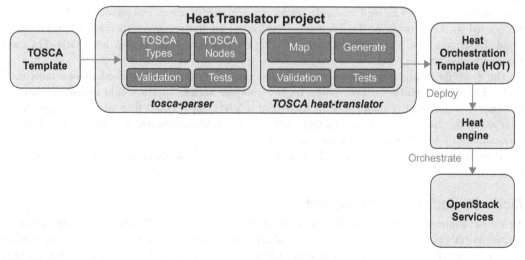

FIGURE 6.9

TOSCA/HEAT translator.

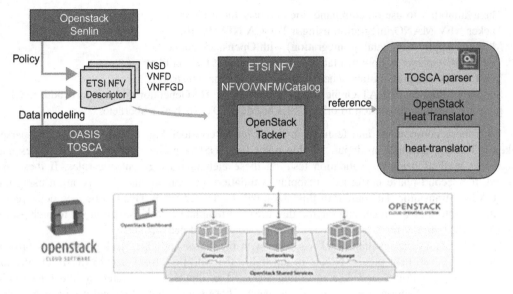

FIGURE 6.10

A Tacker/Openstack system.

Tacker and service function chaining

Recently Tacker added support for service function chains using what the project refers to as its SFC APIs. In this way, Tacker can now support VNF Forwarding Graph construction using the APIs that project has added to the ODL controller. These APIs allow a user via Tacker to define flow classification rules as well as easily render service chains across instantiated VNFs as part of the normal Tacker workflow. This functionality has added the precursor to the VNF Forwarding Graph Descriptor that we described earlier in the ETSI architecture. It also adds ODL-SFC/net-virtsfc driver support.

The example in Fig. 6.11 shows a service function chain that is comprised of two individual VNFs. These represent two virtual routers on two compute nodes. Tacker would instantiate them as it normally would deploy multiple VMs as part of a VNF, but it could then make the appropriate calls using the SFC API that would then call into the ODL controller to attach network paths between those VMs, thus creating a service graph.

At present, the SFC API supports the use of the controller's southbound NETCONF and OVS-DB interfaces.

Tacker integration with Open Daylight

As we have already seen, Tacker has been integrated with the Open Daylight controller using its normal northbound RESTCONF APIs. In addition to using the normal interfaces to invoke NETCONF or OVSDB commands southbound towards deployed VNFs, the Tacker project is also considering expanding these interfaces in order to expand connectivity for functions such as health monitoring capabilities for specific health monitoring functions (Fig. 6.12).

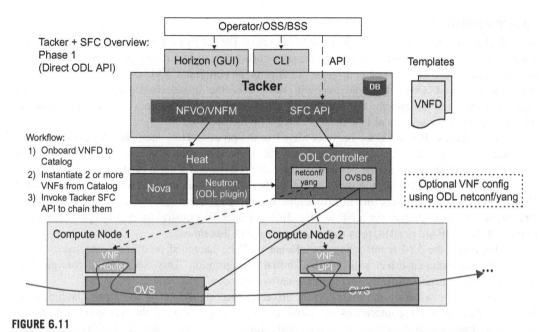

FIGURE 6.11

Tacker SFC functionality.

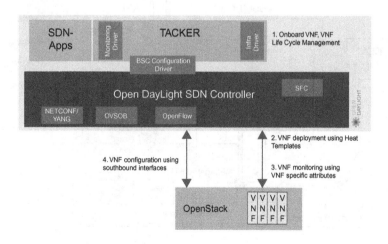

FIGURE 6.12

Tacker ODL integration.

Tacker workflow

We will demonstrate all of the just-described features of Tacker by now walking the reader through a workflow. The use case here starts with the user choosing a virtual router from the services catalog and deploying it in a router configuration. Any other compliant VM-based VNF could just as easily be deployed. Once deployed, we will show how the instance's status is monitored and reported up through the system. We should note that the process can be re-wound to extinguish the instance, or redeploy additional instances as needed by the operator.

In the workflow (Fig. 6.13) we begin at Step 1 in the process. Here the network operator selects a vRouter from the VNFD Catalog. Conceptually, we show the operator selecting this, but in reality all of the communication with the system will be achieved using Tacker's Rest API.

Step 2 has Tacker starting the deployment of the VNF. In this case, it will find its associated HEAT template via its specific infrastructure driver, and use those to push a command to Openstack NOVA to deploy the VNF in Step 3. If any specific constraints about deployment positioning of the VNF are needed, then those are specified at this time.

At this point, the VM representing the vRouter will be launched, and once detected as being booted, the management driver will install its initial configuration. This is a minimal configuration that sets up basic access policies, and the base networking configuration.

In Step 4 we now utilize the management driver connecting Tacker to the Open Daylight controller to push a more comprehensive initial configuration down to the vRouter utilizing its NETCONF interface. If the responses to the configuration are positive, the VM is fully operational.

In Step 5, we optionally invoke the SFC driver in the controller in order to connect this VM to another in order to create a service function chain.

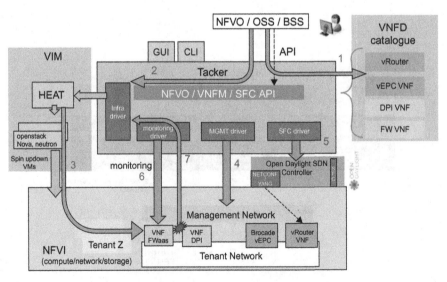

FIGURE 6.13

Tacker workflow.

Finally, in Step 6 we establish the health monitoring of the newly-deployed VNF based on the configured policy. In this case, we will simply ping the vRouter and await its replies. If the replies continue at a regular rate, Tacker does nothing except perhaps update internal counters. If the responses to the pings are not received for some preconfigured time, say 30 s, Tacker can be configured to destroy the VNF and optionally kick off a new instance, as well as sending a notification to the operator via its northbound interface to indicate that a fault was detected, and perhaps a corrective action (ie, respawn) was invoked.

OPEN-O

Formed in early 2016 under the auspices of the Linux Foundation, the primary goal of the Open Orchestration (or Open-O organization) is to develop a comprehensive open source NFVO stack. This software stack is envisioned to also support inter-DC and access or SD-WAN use cases while employing an SDN orchestrator. The project is slated to create a complete open source software solution for NFV/SDN orchestration, multiVIM and multisite use. These components will integrate with existing VIMs and possibly future ones that are not yet defined.

The project also aims at targeting VNF interoperability. While laudable, the practicality of that goal is yet to be determined.

Another important goal is ETSI MANO specification compliance, at least as much as possible within the framework proposed by the organization's founding members. The organization has support initially from a number of large service providers, and thus has stipulated a desired goal to work on information models as a key component of the project. As we mentioned earlier in the Tacker section and still earlier in the general architecture discussion, templates and their standardization either through traditional standards, or open source methods, is critical to the scale and success of any of these projects. To this end, rapid updates and maintenance of a data model translator are slated as work items.

Other goals include:

- OPNFV interfaces alignment
- Openstack modules and interfaces (select and promote standards)
- SDN services: ODL (Service Chaining)
- Decoupling VIM, VNFM, Orchestrator
- End-to-end SDN services such as Service Chaining, BGP/MPLS VPN, vDCI

Fig. 6.14 demonstrates what the organization began with as a framework or architecture. This looks very similar to what many other approaches are attempting to pull off in this space, so the stack of components and how they are arranged should not come as much of a surprise. At the top level of the architecture, service orchestration is present. This takes a page from the ETSI architecture described earlier and encompasses the same goals. Below this, resource orchestration takes commands from a service orchestrator in order to fulfill the higher level service provisioning requests. In some ways, this is already covered by functionality already present within Openstack for example.

Below this, we find the VFNM, in this case this is defined as the Tacker project we described. Tacker is present in its entirety including the template parsing capabilities.

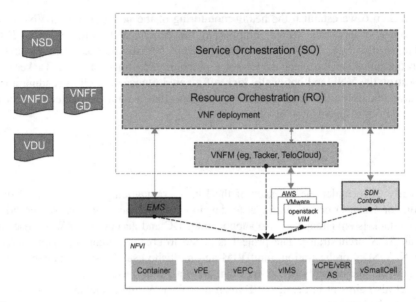

FIGURE 6.14

Proposed NFVO high-level architecture.

To the left of the figure are inputs to the system—service descriptors and templates. It is envisioned that these will be leveraged from Tacker as well. In cases where other custom parsing is needed, those functions will be added.

Below the VNFM we have EMS and SDN controller plug-ins (assuming the VIM uses a controller for the networking portion of resource orchestration). The EMS connections will be to proprietary EMSs that are used to manage the specific VNFs deployed by the VNFM.

Finally, underneath this is the NFVI which is comprised of the usual functions that we described earlier in the ETSI architecture.

OPEN MANO

The Open MANO effort was started by several engineers at Telefonica in 2015 as an attempt to consolidate the MANO open source communities that were (at the time) not well organized or formed. During that period, there was a lull in the ETSI efforts with no real open source alternatives in the industry to vendor provided solutions for orchestration. Also during that period, a number of startups were initiated at this time to solve this problem taking mostly, a proprietary or closed approach using the guidance of the ETSI framework.

The Open MANO approach was largely focused on the performance of virtualized functions that were being used to create services. Efforts here included giving more visibility to the hypervisor and underlying server capabilities such as those we describe later in Chapter 8, NFV Infrastructure—Hardware Evolution and Testing, and Chapter 9, An NFV Future. This was done in

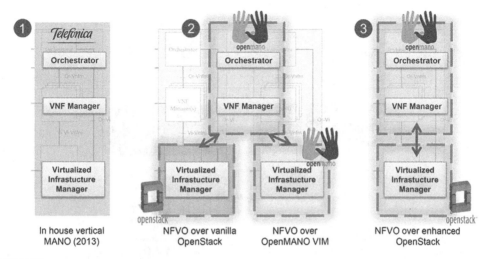

FIGURE 6.15

Open MANO approach and architecture.

an effort to maximize the performance of VNFs. In reality, what was achieved was a minimization of the possibility of suboptimal placement of VMs, but this did not always succeed.

To this end, the effort tried to minimally integrate with open source VNF Management systems such as Openstack, as well as attempt to create their own VNFM (called Open Mano VNFM). There was also an attempt to create an orchestrator called the Open MANO Orchestrator. Fig. 6.15 illustrates the Open MANO approach and architecture.

In the end, the organization did not make much progress due to a simple lack of interest by a wider community. The efforts were largely focused on solving Telefonica's use cases. The effort also faltered in that it did not attract any coders. A lack of coders usually spells certain death for any open source effort, and this happened in this case. The code repository on github is currently slim and only has contributions from a few people.

In February 2016, the Open Source MANO (OSM) project was started under ETSI auspices (https://**osm.etsi**.org/) with Telefonica as an announced co-founder.

OPENBATON

OpenBaton[16] is an open source project providing an implementation of the ETSI MANO specification. It provides a NFVO that closely follows the ETSI MANO specification described earlier in Chapter 3, ETSI NFV ISG, a generic VNFM and a generic EMS function.

The generic VNFM function is able to manage the lifecycle of VNFs based on their descriptors, and also provides a set of libraries which could be used for building your own VNFM. Extension and customization of the VNFM system to manage third party VNFs is done via a set of scripts that need to be built and integrated.

The generic architecture is illustrated in Fig. 6.16.

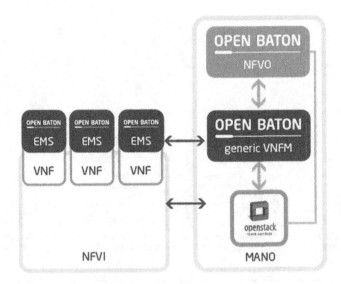

FIGURE 6.16

The OpenBaton approach and architecture.

The generic VNFM and EMS can be used that execute generic scripts that are provided, or customized ones that integrate other VNFM solutions. A generic VNFM and EMS can be used to manage such an integration.

Communication between the management system and the VNFMs is accomplished via a message bus with a pub/sub mechanism or by using a RESTFul interface. Interaction with the NFVO subsystem uses either a REST or JMS interface.

The project also supports a developer SDK that can be used to help accelerate the construction of an entirely new VNFM.

OpenBaton is integrated with OpenStack, allowing OpenBaton to reuse and leverage iOpenStack's many useful functions and features. For example, it uses the OpenStack APIs for requesting virtual compute and networking resources.

The OpenStack API is just one of the VIM interfaces possible. A plug-in mechanism allows potential extension towards the support of multiple cloud systems.

OpenBaton provides the user with a dashboard function (Fig. 6.17). The dashboard is similar to OpenStack's Horizon interface in that it enables the management of the complete environment. From the dashboard, an operator can control the infrastructure providing "at a glance" and "single pane of glass" views, modify the system's components and status and perform CRUD operations on existing services.

ARCHITECTURE ON STEROIDS

As we alluded to in the discussion of Network Service Descriptors, there is a tendency of certain providers to imagine their network resources as multiple independent domains (perpetuating

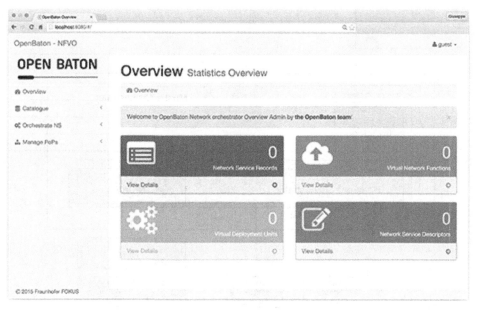

FIGURE 6.17

The OpenBaton dashboard.

existing organizational subdivision). This returns us to the discussion around a more layered or nested view of service orchestration—which leads to a more complicated picture.

Already some providers are specifying multiple, domain-specific orchestration and control (Fig. 6.18). Neither has been federated in the past.

This could be a perceived "best" solution after trying to implement early open source efforts that attempt to implement very complex architectures. Given a lack of appropriate skill sets within the provider, a scarcity of support options from established sources and a lack of immediate full functionality in the solutions, a tendency may arise to invite turnkey silo solutions to get quickly to an implementation that works at scale.

While possible to implement on the orchestration side, a federated orchestration architecture can introduce additional moving parts (eg, an Enterprise Service Bus) to do API brokerage and pacing.

These orchestrators may also need to share NFVO access and attempt to coordinate to avoid multiwriter complications in that resource pool.

Further complications can arise if policy limiting resource access between domains is necessary.

As services span domains, it may be difficult to coordinate feedback from individual lifecycle managers into a master control loop. Because SDN controllers have different internal databases and schema, it can also be difficult to create a consolidated monitoring/SA view unless the controllers can export their state into the big data repositories described earlier in NG-OSS.

Given our earlier focus on the importance of reinventing OSS, providers need to be careful that this sort of architecture does not replicate the existing "multi-OSS" silos that impede them today.

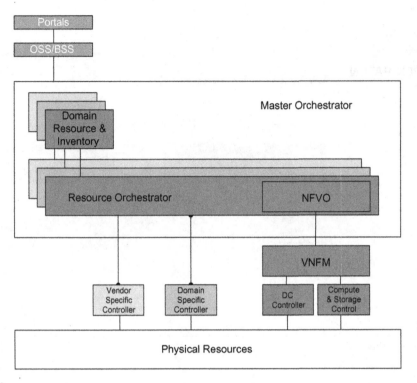

FIGURE 6.18

Multidomain silos with a master orchestrator.

CONCLUSIONS

Just like SDN, NFV rarely occurs in a "greenfield" environment.

There is a long tail of existing infrastructure and systems deployments delivering current services to which future solutions need to be grafted. Additionally, there is a cycle of integration and "sun-setting" of closed systems and services ahead, but we predict that, as in the past, it will be much longer than the enthusiasm and optimism around this technology would imply.

Interoperability with legacy systems is paramount to enable a smooth transition to NFV-driven services, full stop.

Admittedly the OSS/BSS can be fairly complex as it is currently implemented, and as such offers some of the most likely resistance to any transition. This is actually logical because this is where the rubber meets the road in terms of these new virtualized systems and services, and the existing physical ones. It is also where much of the human resistance to change exists.

It is for this very reason that users of owners of custom-built OSS/BSS should carefully consider how their existing system is defined, and what its ability is to accommodate any new protocols and interfaces that are being defined for NFV. This includes open source implementations which might not implement standard interfaces, but instead choose to build their own published interfaces.

Ultimately the ability of the combined system to create, deploy and manage services that a network operator sells to its customers will be the measuring stick by which the system lives or dies.

In theory, NFVs should be a logically similar (or the same) extension of existing OSS/BSS implementations, but in practice, observations of existing incarnations of these systems has proven them to not be.[17]

While the original ETSI work can be interpreted as a mandate for open source solutions, we cannot assume that: (i) that any particular open source organization IS open (check the governance); (ii) that it will provide the only open source solution; (iii) that it won't expand its mandate and bog down; (iv) that it is going to provide more utility than closed source; and (v) that it will be "free."

Open source will be an alternative and organizations will have to decide what combination of vendor-provided and open source will make up their architecture.

The ETSI MANO components provide a good example of some of these cautions and trade-offs. There are the multiple MANO projects noted here and maybe more in the future.

As we mentioned earlier in the review of early ETSI work, and in Chapter 5, The NFV Infrastructure Management, there is room for liberal interpretation regarding the construction of the interfaces between and separation of the functional blocks in solutions.

You will notice that, so far, the dominant dialog around MANO does not really include containers or the leap to microservices and a PaaS environment.

Finally, the meta-architecture for MANO is an open question. If operators implement multiple silos or multiple levels of orchestration and control, what manages and binds them? And, how do we avoid repeating the OSS morass of the past?

END NOTES

1. Network Functions Virtualisation—White Paper #3 ETSI NFV ISG (October 2014).
2. Deutsche Telekom Terastream Project, http://www.slideshare.net/ceobroadband/dt-tera-stream.
3. See Peter's presentation at RIPE87.
4. John Evans of Cisco Systems: https://www.linkedin.com/in/johnevansuk?authType=NAME_ SEARCH&authToken=XhmV&locale=en_US&srchid=163755471455470690987&srchindex=1& srchtotal=3417&trk=vsrp_people_res_name&trkInfo=VSRPsearchId%3A163755471455470690987% 2CVSRPtargetId%3A9643914%2CVSRPcmpt%3Aprimary%2CVSRPnm%3Atrue%2CauthType%3ANAME_ SEARCH.
5. ELK (Elastisearch, Logstash, Kibana, HBase, Spark); the tool list available is impressive.
6. See earlier reference in Chapter 2, Service Creation and Service Function Chaining, about the standardization of configuration process. This is particularly problematic in a multivendor environment.
7. EPL—Uses a point-to-point Ethernet virtual circuit between two User-to-Network Interfaces (UNIs) to provide a high degree of transparency such that service frames, headers, and most Layer 2 protocols are identical at both the source and destination UNI. It does not allow for service multiplexing; that is, a dedicated UNI (physical interface) is used for the EPL.
8. Topology and Orchestration Specification for Cloud Applications.

9.   http://www.tail-f.com/wordpress/wp-content/uploads/2015/02/HR-Cisco-ALU-TOSCA-YANG-WP-2-17-15.pdf

10. http://openconfig.org

11. The Public Yang Repository can be found at https://github.com/YangModels/yang.

12. http://ganglia.sourceforge.net/

13. https://www.nagios.org

14. Oasis TOSCA, https://www.oasis-open.org.

15. Link to OASIS.

16. http://openbaton.github.io

17. In theory, theory and practice are the same thing. In practice, they are far from the same.

THE VIRTUALIZATION LAYER—PERFORMANCE, PACKAGING, AND NFV

INTRODUCTION

Proponents of NFV see applications that stretch from the replacement of individual fixed network appliances (eg, firewall) through reimagination of whole service architectures (eg, vEPC and vIMS), to large swathes of the forwarding infrastructure (eg, vRouters). When you peel away the service state components (eg, bearer/tunnel management or subscriber management), which we can agree are well suited for processor offload, these applications are built around network I/O.

Many vendors of standalone network appliances were already moving from their dedicated chipsets to an Intel- or ARM-based architecture before NFV was in our lexicon. The fusion of datacenter orchestration methodologies (enabling elasticity and management paradigms for this transformation), more aggressive marketing by manufacturers like Intel (and the optimizations of their driver architecture and core technologies to make them more suited to network I/O applications) accelerated an existing trend and expanded the scale of potential applications to Service Provider scale (clusters of machines capable of handling hundreds of gigabits per second of throughput).

In this chapter, we will look at the evolution of virtualization techniques and software network I/O acceleration to satisfy these application requirements. We will also look at how the constant evolution in the compute component of the (ETSI-labeled) "NFVI" might affect the current aggregated, VM-centric NFV model, our concept of Service Function Chaining and the potential economic assumptions behind the NFV proposition.

The original vision of the economics behind NFV was predicated on the use of "COTS" (commercial off-the-shelf) compute—bespoke hardware (general purpose processors[1]) and operating systems found in a data center environment. The fundamental attraction of a COTS-based solution is in the simplification of supply chain, inventory management, and operations gained from the use of common equipment and software configurations.

While the current discussion of NFV and the ETSI NFV architecture are predicated around an Intel model (it is no accident that Intel is a leading contributor to and proponent of the de facto NFV architecture), through the course of this and succeeding chapters it may be fair to ask if this is just a "first phase" assumption that enables conceptual adoption of NFV.

The pursuit of network IO performance on Intel x86 can introduce the use of specialized environments and toolkits (in comparison to other data center workloads). There is an implied dependency on rapid architectural changes in the Intel Architecture (IA) that bring into question the definition of COTS and the economics of the model.

Also, in the current Intel-centric environment, a classic chase of performance bottlenecks in software has emerged.

Whenever the narrowest bottleneck is removed from a system, the next-less- narrow bottleneck will become the limiting factor.[2]

EVOLVING VIRTUALIZATION TECHNIQUES

The proposed ETSI NFV solution architecture optimizes limited, shared resources through virtualization.

There are numerous techniques to share the CPU resource, and they revolve around privilege (based on the x86 privilege four "ring" model—with Ring 0 being the most privileged and Ring 3 being the common privilege level for applications) and resource abstraction.

Virtualization started with emulation (in which all CPU instructions are translated from guest to host) and native virtualization (in which privileged commands are passed to the host kernel without translation but access to other peripherals is still emulated).

The hypervisor is the most common construct in machine virtualization today. There are two different types—Type 1 (eg, Xen, KVM, VMware ESX) in which the virtual machine manager (VMM[3]) runs on the host machine without a host OS (native), and Type 2 which runs on a host OS (hosted by, eg, VMware Virtual Workstation, VirtualBox, JVM).

Within these hypervisor types there are two techniques of virtualization: para-virtualization (or OS-assisted) and full virtualization. The mapping of a particular hypervisor to virtualization mode has gotten a bit murky with time (eg, VMware supports a para-virtual-like mode though it is commonly used in a full-virtualization mode).

Using KVM[4] as an example, with paravirtualization (Fig. 7.1), the paravirtualized network driver in the guest, shares virtual queues with QEMU[5] (a hardware emulator). A data path is created through the TAP interface to the guest VM via a virtual queue mechanism (signaling and notifications are a separate logical channel between virtio-net and KVM).

As a networking resource, virtio evolved as the cross-OS I/O device abstraction that replaced fully emulated network devices (eg, the e1000 device in Linux systems).

The original implementation of the driver (virtio[6]) placed the network stack into user space with QEMU handling the virtual queues, causing memory copies and context switches as packets traversed the kernel (KVM) to user (QEMU). Ultimately, vhost-net reduced this overhead by bypassing QEMU and pushing the stack and virtual queue system into the kernel.

While paravirtualization had some advantages, in that guest applications have the ability to make privileged calls to some hardware resources, the network I/O ran from an imbedded paravirtualized driver in the guest operating system that worked in conjunction with a host emulator (which would emulate the function of the shared NIC) via an I/O call to the hypervisor. Nonvirtualize-able instructions are replaced with "hypercalls" to the virtualization layer.

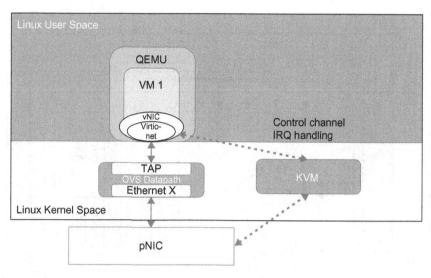

FIGURE 7.1

KVM execution and QEMU emulation.

The reduced performance and required modification of the guest OS (to imbed the driver) combination made paravirtualization less attractive. The original operator-driven NFV focus on performance and operational transparency could eliminate these techniques in favor of full virtualization.

In full virtualization, machine language codes of the guest are translated into machine language codes of the host by the VMM—full binary translation (depending on the implementation, some direct access is possible).[7] Attempts to run privileged commands (eg, accessing a device driver) trigger a trap for the event in the hypervisor. The guest runs unaltered (in Ring 1). As might be expected, translation has performance impacts.

Through its Virtual Machine Extensions (VMX)[8] for the x86 architecture, Intel enabled hardware-assisted virtualization (2005), allowing the VMM to run below Ring 0 (they extended the four "ring" privilege model to include VMX root and non-root modes). The result provides a combination of attributes from full and paravirtualization (the guest is generally unaltered and performance overhead of virtualization is minimized thanks to the hardware assist). This is the focus of NFV VM-centric operation today.

As Fig. 7.2 illustrates, the hypervisor provides abstractions between the physical NIC (pNIC) and virtual NIC (vNIC) associated with a specific virtual machine (VM). These typically connect through the virtual switch construct (vSwitch).[9] However, as we shall see with both PCI pass through and SR-IOV, the VNF can connect directly to the pNIC.

Memory is virtualized as a resource through the cooperative action of the Memory Management Unit (MMU) and Translation Look-aside Buffer[10] (TLB).

The VM is constructed[11] (in cooperation with the local host VMM) from virtual memory that maps back to host memory and virtual CPUs (vCPU) that map back to physical CPU resources (discrete cores or individual threads in a multicore socket).

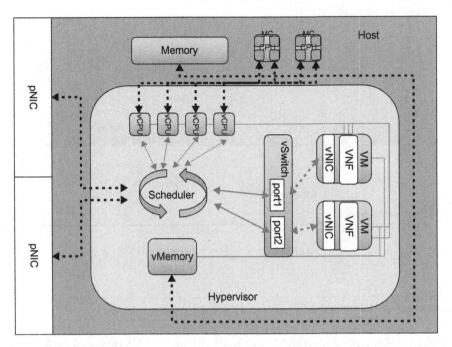

FIGURE 7.2

A hypervisor maps physical resources to virtual ones.

Abstractions of a physical resource into a shared virtual resource affect the memory/CPU overhead on the machine and the speed of orchestration. They may also impact network performance by nature of the pipelines we create between guests and these resources.

THE VM-CENTRIC MODEL

As we saw in Chapter 3, ETSI NFV ISG, the (Phase 1) ETSI model continues to evolve. While subsequent iterations of the work group have begun to discuss containers, the Phase 1 architecture is commonly modeled as "a VNF per VM."[12]

In ETSI NFV architecture it is suggested that all interfunction transfers happen through the hypervisor (through the vSwitch construct). That is, service definition implies a service chain comprised of multiple VNFs connected through the hypervisor—even if the functions are on the same host.

This model trades the ability to understand the service at a network level (providing a clean demarcation point for debugging)—for some performance and resource utilization overhead.

Several alternatives to the default vSwitch (OVS) have appeared that can satisfy this requirement. As a class, "virtual forwarders" have appeared that can run in their own container or VM (in host or guest) offering a range of functions from full stack (some VRF-aware) to simple patch panel between virtualized functions.

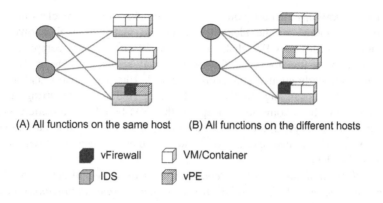

(A) All functions on the same host   (B) All functions on the different hosts

■ vFirewall   ⬜ VM/Container
▥ IDS   ▨ vPE

FIGURE 7.3

VM distribution where the VNFs comprising a service are (A) all on the same host and (B) different hosts.

Of course the need to transition through this demarcation point does incur some overhead. For example, in Fig. 7.3, given a service chain that was composed (vPE, vFirewall, vIDS), the most predictable performance scenario will be in "A"—where all the VMs are on the same host (assuming their resource usage patterns are not suboptimal in that configuration—they do not clash). This obviates the variability of network delays between the hosts in the chain and results in two pNIC to vNIC transfers of the packet (coming off the wire into vPE and returning from vIDS or vFW) and one or two transfers via the hypervisor (depending on whether the traffic was forwarded from the vFW to the vIDS).[13]

If, for some reason, the operator thought it better to separate the functions (eg, by type "Firewall," "PE," and "IDS"—as in "B"), the overhead would change to six pNIC-to-vNIC transfers—two at each host (and incur the variability of the intermediating network).

All of these transfers have costs that are part of the current performance focus in NFV studies.

The root of a recommendation that necessitates this overhead might lie in familiarity with the vNIC logic commonly used (at the time of ETSI's work) to connect to the local vSwitch (eg, the traditional tun/tap logic of Linux). Direct connection of VM-to-VM was uncommon[14] and there was an expectation that the vSwitch would connect the VM to the physical network.

The original ETSI recommendation that VM migration was necessary for NFV High Availability is also suspect. This may have been rooted in the familiarity of Telco personnel with VMware (vmotion is a common selling point) and their general lack of familiarity with massively scalable data center application designs (which have their own inherent high availability aspects without vmotion).

In reality, the application/VNF could manage its elasticity on its own or in conjunction with a VNFM.

That elasticity coupled with appropriate system and application designs that protect application state (for those functions that might be stateful) provide the availability model (examples of this approach appear in our chapter on SFC).

Further, VM migration can be unreliable, comes with many caveats, and has some additional expense (at the very least through the performance overhead or resource allocation that has to be planned for the move). And, not all applications are currently designed to work well with vmotion.

Various ETSI workgroups also did point out that the behaviors of one class of application may clash with those of another, so the idea of mixing and matching applications with dissimilar (noncomplimentary) profiles of CPU, disk or network I/O usage may complicate the ability to predict performance of a function (and thus the overall service). There is interesting support of these observations in early application-specific studies[15] (the performance and breadth of virtualization choices have been changing rapidly, quickly dating findings—a recurring theme here).

There may have also been some misconception that VM-based virtualization was required for large-scale orchestration (beyond tools like Puppet/Chef/Ansible). Work has already started in OpenStack to support orchestrated bare metal,[16] and container management environments also have solutions that integrate here.

Experience with the limitations and perceptions surrounding the VM-centric model are the keys to the ongoing evolution of NFV/SFC architectures—which for some applications may soon include containers, microVMs, or bare metal deployment.

The exploration of bare-metal compliments the original ETSI finding that a number of emerging applications for NFV do not require the "V" overhead, since they do not incorporate the per-user or per-organization customization requirements in rendering service (a driver of the ETSI NFV vision) and (due to their critical nature) are unlikely to be shared on a platform with other applications/ machines—unless the conceptual revenue streams imagined in the ETSI PoCs and use cases via subletting NFV infrastructure to OTHER carriers (much like a mobile MVNO) bears fruit.[17]

For example, in the mobility architecture, the vGiLAN may be more amenable to a virtualized environment (where a service function may have organization-specific or user-specific instantiations) while the vEPC components (vMME, vSGW, and vPGW) may see no such benefit and thus be more suited to bare metal. In these cases the "v" for virtual is misleading. Simply by moving these functions onto COTS, we are optimizing the solution (without virtualization).

CONTAINERS—DO WE NEED HYPERVISORS?

The most compelling attributes of VMs are security (isolation), compatibility (host OS and VM OS are independent), and mobility (you can move the application while it runs—with a number of caveats).

However, several issues flow from the use of the hypervisor.

Resource scale is an obvious one—every VM has the overhead of a full OS. Without rigorous tuning, nondeterministic behaviors result as well—notably in the scheduling of vCPUs and traffic shaping on vNICs.

The hypervisor is also an additional solution part, and as the solution optimizes—as the industry has moved to solve application performance predictability problems by moving toward direct access to hardware (eg, working around CPU and memory affinity, IOMMU, and interrupt handling by introducing new hypervisors, soft forwarders, and acceleration techniques amongst them) the presence of the hypervisor can create a testing permutation problem in support and validation. An organization might eventually support multiple hypervisor/soft forwarder/OS variants, with differences in performance of and compatibility with various optimizations.

The guest OS(s) also created (yet another) security surface/frontier and maintenance object—the latter creating a perception that maintaining the guest OS presented an obstacle to agile development (application support programs within the VM might require maintenance to enable new features) and portability/mobility.

These issues led some to question the value of the hypervisor abstraction and to the rising exploration of alternative virtualization packaging in containers and microVMs—starting with Linux containers and UML[18] (LXC is a common management tool for Linux containers).

An IBM study in 2014 concluded that containers generally outperform virtual machines (in almost all cases), but both require significant tuning for I/O intensive applications.[19] It further suggests that given the present NUMA (nonuniform memory access) architecture typical of today's servers, that per-socket virtualization (ostensibly, containers) would be more efficient in spreading a workload than bare-metal deployment—spreading the workload across sockets (minimizing cross traffic).

From Fig. 7.4, the key differences between containers and VMs (as they pertain to NFV) are obvious.

A container is an OS kernel abstraction in which the applications share the same kernel (and potentially the bins/services and libs—a sandbox), and the VM is a hardware abstraction in which the applications run separate kernels.

While the VM emulates hardware (leveraging extensions on existing server processor architectures like Intel's VT-x) within the VM, the container does no device emulation and has no specific CPU requirements (easily supported across multiple processor architectures). The container concept does not require a specific CPU, but any given application is compiled for one. Containers replace the x86 whole machine environment with x86 instructions (without virtual memory, trap handling, device drivers, etc.) plus the Linux kernel interface.

Containers exist in Linux[20] user space and leverage dedicated namespaces (namespace separation) for their hostname, processes, networking, user, and IPC. Though they share a kernel, they can isolate resources (CPU, memory, and storage) using cgroups.[21]

In Fig. 7.5, the applications using a network namespace shared with the host appear as applications running natively on the host (physical connections are mapped directly to containers with access through Linux system calls rather than virtio), whereas the applications using separate namespaces appear as applications reachable on a subnet from the host (multiple bridges and virtual topologies are possible).

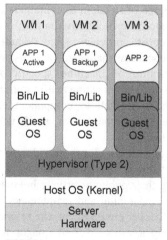
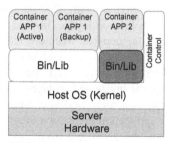

(A) VMs   (B) Containers

FIGURE 7.4

VMs and containers.

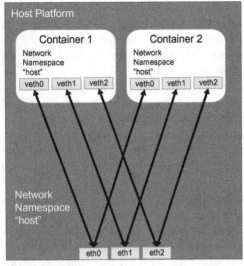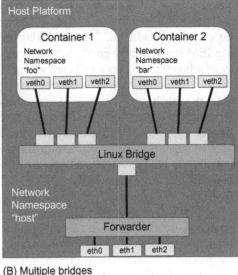

FIGURE 7.5

Linux container (LXC) networking using shared or discrete network namespaces. The host will control a (separate) management Ethernet interface (not shown).

Beyond the Linux container and UML environment, a number of new container runtimes have sprung up, led by Docker.

Docker[22] is built around either LXC or the more customizable libcontainer—so Linux containers are its root technology. It brings an even greater degree of freedom to containers in that it abstracts away host machine specific settings, provides an automatic build environment (supporting a broad range of tools, eg, rpm, make, devops—chef, puppet), provides some default kernel isolation to enhance container security, and has its own repository management tools to push, pull, and commit changes. The key benefit is the abstraction of machine specific settings enabling portable deployment (the same container can run on different machine configurations).

As a development environment, Docker lends itself well to component reuse through the definition and use of reference layers (layered filesystem images) on which the application sits. (These are shareable using copy-on-write mechanisms.)

The overall design[23] (common to Docker and Rocket) allows the developer to bundle an application crafted of these layers (all the environment variables, config, file system) into a container and manage the image and its layers using their public or private Index/Registry(s).

This extra layering/separation makes common provisioning and maintenance tasks a push of a (potentially) thinner application layer (in a largely-Docker environment, the reference layers should already be present on the host) and troubleshooting a simple diff of images to determine layer changes that might have caused problems.

The layering and accompanying automation also makes the applications within the container runtimes more agile around version dependencies between the layers that comprise critical support infrastructure within the container (moving the line for what is "shared" further into the container itself).

Docker's native container networking model uses NAT. It assigns a private range of IP addresses to the containers and maps them to an internal bridge. It uses its own ip table mechanism to manage this port mapping as well as external and intercontainer communication. General connectivity supported by libvirt is incorporated (eg, empty-network, veth, macvlan, etc.). Docker also works with Pipework,[24] a general container networking with DHCP support, external addressing, etc.

The move toward containers brings additional nuance to the orchestration (and networking) solution space, and because of this the market is still developing.

Several Docker networking startups have also sprung up—eg, Socketplane (which was acquired by Docker in 2015),[25] who are proposing an SDN integration solution for Open vSwitch and Docker, and Weaveworks[26] who offer container networking (a private shared virtual switch abstraction for all containers, regardless of location, with options for selective/controlled public connections) and service discovery.

Open source initiatives to improve container networking via OpenStack or Docker are beginning to crop up (eg, Calico which uses IPinIP tunneling for overlay construction and Bird BGP for route distribution—and does kernel based forwarding). fd.io provides a potential forwarding mechanism for containers in user space (fd.io is covered in greater depth later on in this book).

Kubernetes[27] (an open source project started by Google and recently endorsed by RedHat[28]) was an early original pairing with Docker to create an orchestration solution, but Docker had initiated its own solution (Machine/Swarm/Compose).[29] Kubernetes has a different approach to networking and a good comparison with Docker's default approach.[30]

Joyent[31] offers a provider-focused twist on Docker deployments that they claim addresses container security concerns (tenants attacking tenants) around shared Linux OS infrastructure through Linux Branded Zones (LXz). The offering markets against potentially unnecessary performance penalties in a hypervisor-based environment, and plays on some of the security concerns around running "default Linux infrastructure containers."

CoreOS[32] goes in a similar direction, offering a host OS comprised of minimal components (originally systemd, kernel, ssh, and Docker) as the basis for a container runtime environment and as an alternative to the "full Linux distribution plus containers" model. Its focus is the orchestration of Docker containers.

Perhaps spurred by the current opacity of Docker community governance, and Docker's rather monolithic structure, CoreOS (Fig. 7.6) claims that their individual components can run on other distributions than CoreOS (eg, Ubuntu) to provide their services.

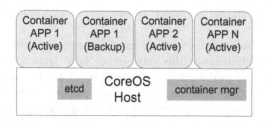

FIGURE 7.6

CoreOS. With the launch of Rocket, the container manager becomes more abstract (you could use either container runtime).

CoreOS emphasizes cluster management and a simplified "orchestration" stack built on their core components: etcd -> fleet -> (multiple) system. These supporting functions enable the containers, but are not specific to them:

- systemd provides init (initialization), resource management, ipc, cron (timer), config, logging—a very simple environment.
- etcd provides key-value store for shared configuration and service discovery. etcd also supports a VXLAN based overlay between containers (Flannel).
- Fleet enables the management of a fleet of system instances, much like Mesos (consensus algorithm is Raft, not Paxos).
- CoreOS has also announced a Kubernetes cluster management interface—Tectonic (https://coreos.com/blog/announcing-tectonic/).
- CoreUpdate provides a management dashboard.
- Flannel provides a simple overlay networking (a private mesh of directly addressed containers).

Another component, "locksmith," is the reboot manager and cluster lock manager (semaphore system) that works in coordination with the update engine to spawn/retire/update members.

Application versioning is managed automatically and includes supporting infrastructure like Java version (moved from the host OS to container) using a partition system to allow reversion.

CoreOS recently launched their own container runtime, Rocket, as a Docker alternative. With the launch of Rocket, CoreOS is attempting to standardize an "App Container Specification"—describing the container image (file assembly, image verification, and placement), container execution environment (cgroups, namespaces, and network), and image discovery behaviors (eg, name to URI mapping).

At this point, containers appear to offer some resource separation with a lower performance penalty[33] than the VM-centric approach—although larger security questions remain to be answered.

Like the early stages of the SDN movement, the container movement is currently volatile and mimics the SDN struggle between for-profit products, open source solutions and for-profit hybrids that enhance open source.

Some clarity as to what parts best remain true open source and the answers to the questions about governance around them may emerge from the opencontainer project in the Linux foundation.[34]

While it is easy to get lost in the orchestration business angle of the CoreOS/Docker entanglement, the underlying container is still a Linux variant (Debian in the case of Docker). That is to say, the surface of binaries and executables within the container, from a security perspective, is still relatively broad—even though the container is ostensibly providing a single service function (microservices).

And, while the distribution management scheme for a container runtime like Docker enables very incremental, layered maintenance, this may not be "best" from a security perspective. If the kernel is made small enough, pushing the (equivalent of a) whole container may be a security scheme easier to manage than allowing individual components to be dynamically altered via orchestration (since this may be the same mechanism an attacker might use, to load a new version of some binary). That is, treating the container as an "immutable" entity may be preferred.[35]

Intel professes to be working on a more secure Linux that leverages their VT technology.[36]

As confusing as the rise of container networking may appear, containers are one of the keys to the most reasonable vision of NFV—microservices. Microservices are collaborative, combinable atoms of functionality that can be reconfigured more nimbly into services. Think of them as the generation beyond "VNF per VM" architectural thinking and the deconstruction step beyond the faltering first step of NFV (simply virtualizing an existing physical function). There is an important tie between the orchestration of containers, the concept of microservices, and the thinking around PaaS coupling to orchestration, as discussed in Chapter 5, The NFV Infrastructure Management.

UNIKERNELS

That brings us to Unikernels, which attempt to address the concept removing any unnecessary binaries and executables—creating a very close linkage between the application and OS (in fact the application code, configuration, and OS runtime are compiled together into the Unikernel). The Unikernel created has a single virtual address space and requires no dynamic linking or initialization of user space applications.

Unikernels are a direct descendent of library operating systems (libOS) but are more feasible now that a hypervisor can provide hardware isolation and virtualization.

Unikernels are seen as a container substitute. A few of the touted benefits of using Unikernels include:

- Compiler driven performance optimizations can be driven by the presence of the configuration (your specific execution environment settings).
- Implementations use higher level language constructs for both the kernel and application that provide memory management advantages.

Unlike the microVM strategy which is focused more on the API exposure within the VM for security, the Unikernel strategy is particularly well adapted for cloud operations. The focus here is on binary size, speed (boot) enable immutable operation. Of course, there IS a potential bonus in security through a much smaller attack surface.

A nonexhaustive list of examples includes Click, OSv,[37] MirageOS,[38] and Unikernel Systems.[39]

The acquisition of Unikernel Systems by Docker implies a merging or hybridization of approach (Unikernels in containers) to realize the vision of "immutable infrastructure."[40]

HYBRID VIRTUALIZATION

In Chapter 2, Service Creation and Service Function Chaining, we also pointed to a hybrid mechanism that leverages either multilevel virtualization using containers and VMs or microVMs.

The VM and container combination allows an orchestrator to combine trusted containers within a secure trust boundary (the VM) to achieve greater scale at lower risk (enforcement extends to a harder resource allocation boundary as well).

The use of a microVM is actually a purposefully different example of this hybrid, and a great example can be found in vCPE application—using a low cost direct tunnel origination (customer site) and termination (operator site) into a microVM. This vCPE model was demonstrated by engineers at Cisco Systems in 2014.[41]

The fundamental thrust of the model is that a kernel-per-customer model of operation for the application (vCPE) underutilizes the kernel scalability. Further, the use of a microVM[42] is critical to the application as it isolates the CPE application from the host OS (the extra isolation provides additional protections against the effects of introduced malware through a form of permitted process awareness and self-regulation).

A multilevel virtualization is applied using a single Linux kernel instance as an outer level that is modified UML[43] featuring multiple subscribers/guests (up to 64 and still scaling in future releases) per kernel being run as a containers with up to 1024 network interfaces per kernel (capable of further scale as general purpose processing performance curve progresses). The inner level containers (also modified UML) run an instance of CPE firmware (eg, OpenWRT, OpenRG) in user space. This design reduces cache thrashing, decreases context switching, and improves memory footprint/efficiency.

New paravirtual network drivers published as open source for kvm/quemu and UML—particularly "raw" and "tap" bring the tunnels/vlans directly into the VM where they support direct encapsulation and decapsulation of overlays and L2VPNs on the vNIC, eliminating the need for virtual switching.[44] These connections are then passed as virtual Ethernets to the containers (the containers do not talk to each other so there is no common bridging or switching functionality required).

This is the first of two important features for NFV architecture discovered in the approach—the ability to hide the overlay network from the VM (there is no shared network state accessible from the containers via a virtual switch if they are compromised).

This architecture (Fig. 7.7) has a few noteworthy tricks including; multi-packet reads, a rewritten paravirtual interrupt controller (Edge vs Level virtual interrupts) that moves the interrupt handling for I/O from the host kernel to the VM, and multipacket transmit I/O events (decreases context switches and system calls per packet).

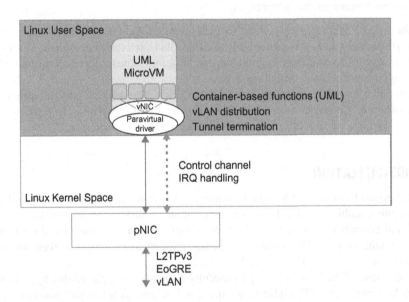

FIGURE 7.7

A UML and container hybrid.

One of the other benefits of using the UML kernel across multiple customers is realized in reusing contexts and timer events for forwarding and QoS, changing their performance/scale from linear to logarithmic.

This is the second important feature for NFV architecture discovered in the approach (and validated in other work[45])—for QoS to work, the VMM (or its equivalent) has to provide a high-performance timer (the developers also wrote and contributed a high-performance timer system using high-performance posix timers to UML).

Other enhancements improved event loop and interrupt controller behaviors that obviated the need for KVM or other alternatives for most use cases (although some of the enhancements to UML mentioned here were also submitted for KVM/qemu).

In its current instantiation, the architecture/model does not use poll-mode drivers (PMDs) (and thus does not disable power/thermal management), but it is adaptable to some of the evolving accelerators covered in the rest of the chapter; NIC or specialized hardware offloads, VM bypass, and kernel helpers like Netmap.

This sort of hybrid suggests that there may be some environments/applications, particularly in the broadband environment, where a hybrid VM/container or microVM/container approach is appropriate for performance, resource optimization, and security.

SECURITY TRADE-OFFS

The VM/hypervisor environment comes with a perception of relative security. "Relative" is used as a description because many security-minded professionals feel that all virtualization mechanisms are potentially fraught with problems—many of those concerns related to hypervisor virtualization are rooted in compliance (eg, user mounted VMs can be noncompliant with corporate security practices) and data security (eg, VMs can be copied, mistakenly orphaned leaving around information). Pervasive virtualization in cloud computing has provided more security experience and contributes to this "relative" sense of wellbeing (as does the burgeoning specialized security product and service industry around cloud and numerous best practice publications).

Hypervisors are small and relatively simple pieces of code and some see "relative" security in that simplicity. But vulnerabilities in the hypervisor can expose VM behaviors like memory use, system calls made, or disk activity that are valuable to an attacker.

Few casual users have knowledge of hypervisor compromises or bugs, yet these do occur[46] and are the potential Achilles' heel of the VM environment—a single potential point of failure that (if breached) can allow a tenant to compromise another tenant or the whole system.[47]

Hypervisors also allow machine-to-machine networking that does not go out onto the wire, creating a potential visibility problem unless instrumented.

"Relative" can also reflect the operator's knowledge of the level of trust amongst coresident virtualized applications. Unlike the typical cloud environment, the NFV environment may often have a single tenant (the provider/operator), and thus VMs may be relatively more secure in this environment than others.

Further, the fact that we are sharing resources between tenants opens the door to potential Denial of Service (DoS) or Distributed DoS attacks between tenants (in the case of NFV and the "single-tenant/operator" scenario, this argument would devolve into inadvertent incompatibilities and bugs).

There is some rigor required around some of the virtualization operation tooling as well (eg, using snapshots to restore virtualized instances can inadvertently revert the instance to a less secure profile).

There is some exposure through file sharing systems so sharing between hosts and guests needs to be minimized and all storage access needs some sort of protection starting with encryption of access.

Given all the above, are containers as "relatively" safe as VMs (or safer)?[48]

At their root, containers are not the exact same abstraction as VMs.

Containers appear to have some intrinsic security via namespace isolation for network interfaces, file systems, and host processes (between host and container), resource allocation control provided via cgroups (assuming cgroups themselves are secure constructs) and limited callable system capabilities.[49] A lot of the security hinges on limiting filesystem access, but they do not have the benefit of hardware virtualization safeguards.

Docker is not totally unaware of the concerns,[50] and has been trying to add security feature to later releases—including seccomp profiles (a level of process control), user namespaces (allowing more granular access policies), and authorization plug-ins (managing access to the Docker daemon and API).[51] (Keep in mind that Docker is not the only container type.)

In addition, we have already mentioned a potential architecture or deployment scenario that removes VM visibility into the overlay (via the vSwitch) for the container in a VM/container hybrid. We have also touched on the hybrid of containers and ukernels (immutable operation).

Securing Linux

Intrinsic protections can be enhanced via further restriction of root/privileged capabilities (eg, no CAP_SYS_NICE) and mandatory access control via LSM policies (eg, Simple Modified Access Control Kernel (SMACK)[52]—using labels attached to system objects, or SELinux[53]). Illustrated in Fig. 7.8, LSM provides kernel hooks that allow system calls to be evaluated against security policies. But the fact that multiple security schemes exist add even more of a burden in the continuing theme around choice and supportability in this chapter. These schemes have been historically challenging to operate, particularly the use of access-list (like) constraints in allowing the right level of security without constraining utility.

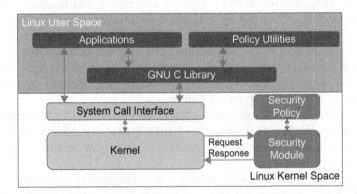

FIGURE 7.8

Linux Secure Module (LSM) framework.

These protections are equally applicable to VM environments and several vendors market "carrier-grade" or "hardened" Linux distributions that leverage these techniques, all of which should be evaluated against the previously-mentioned history.[54]

Just as with VMs, the container operation environment also requires security-focused vigilance. For example, there is a potential attack surface in the container image movement and verification (general operations for the environment).[55]

Not sharing

Beneath both hypervisor-based virtualization and containerization there exists the possibility of a class of bugs that allow for privilege escalation, allowing a malicious or suborned tenant to escape their private environment and gain access to the kernel or hypervisor, and from there other functions and possibly the rest of the network. This possibility feeds back into the "relative" security position of any shared host in the view of a security professional and potentially forward into the "reduced vulnerability surface" appeal of a minimized container-specific OS.

Looking forward, some of the networking optimization we need to discuss may also represent some tradeoff between security and performance. For example, the use of shared memory (as an IPC mechanism) has traditionally raised security concerns in the networking world. Many of the context-reduction techniques that adopt the use of shared memory (or, at the lowest level, shared processor cache) attempt to bound risk by limiting sharing to non-page-able memory and point-to-point (nonpooled) sharing.

NOT sharing might be the best advice.

That is, not allowing multiple tenants to share the same host. That does not mean the "end of virtualization" as a strategy for deploying NFV, but rather the adoption of the tenant segregation techniques employed by large cloud operators if your NFV solution is multitenant by design (eg, an NFVaaS infrastructure in which you allow resource slicing to enable multiple virtual providers).

SECURITY—THE LOWEST COMMON DENOMINATOR

Lying just below the surface of the argument around the relative security of the bare-metal, VM, container, or hybrid deployment model lurks a fundamental concern that everyone should have around NFV. This happens to exist for cloud computing environments as well. That is, whether shared computing systems and architectures can be *truly* secured or not, and whether or not virtualization, containerization or any other disaggregated system that runs on something other than a self-contained piece of hardware can be secured.

It has become clear that even on self-contained systems (ie, bare metal), that very low level components can be compromised including the BIOS, firmware, and hypervisor.[56]

Both Intel and the vendor community have responded by creating a trust model for cloud computing that starts with the hardware. The result will:

• Enable attestation as to the integrity of the hardware and images used.
• Enable compliance checking, policy, verification, and audit services.
• Enable hardware-based authentication of clients.
• Allow the provider to create trusted pools of compute that protect confidentiality and data integrity of the application.

Examples (nonexhaustive) include:

- Intel TXT, which is a hardware-based[57] solution that provides a traceable line of trust for the machine, its low level settings and the images loaded.
- Cavium provides a PCIE based "LiquidSecurity" Hardware Security Module to satisfy FIPS (Federal Information Processing Requirements) compliance and encryption needs (data protection) for government, finance, and other industries.

The ultimate solution to the problem of trust in virtualization will add even more complexity to the ETSI Management and Orchestration (MANO) components of the ETSI model particularly around resource management and VM placement policies, and change the fundamental requirements for NFVI.

CURRENT PACKET HANDLING

Processing packets in any network-centric software is a never-ending exercise in maximal forwarding performance optimization. This entails employing algorithms and "tricks" both in the firmware that executes on these devices and inherent in the hardware architecture. This task is made even more difficult when the hardware is not designed with these things in mind, as was the case with server network interface cards until a few years ago. Some of these "tricks" have unwanted side-effects, such as the use of poll-mode software drivers.

The IA uses optimizations that start with BIOS settings (NUMA, power mode, etc.), reaching through advanced NIC capabilities directly to the operation of the cache. For the best possible outcome, all of these optimizations (including their potential hardware dependencies[58]) are leveraged.

Using direct cache access (DCA is one of several accelerants that are part of Intel's I/O AT NIC technology), typical packet handling starts by directly writing packet info to the processor cache[59]:

- A processor RX descriptor write (a pointer to a filled buffer on a ring structure from the NIC, the size of which can also affect performance) is a trigger command on a DMA receive queue to begin the DMA transfer from a peripheral (NIC).
- The NIC reads a buffer (NIC descriptor read) and begins the DMA transfer; executing a header write, payload write, and status write all directly to the processor cache. This constantly churns the cache and the interplay introduces the need for coherency management (discussed later).
- The processor then does a complementing status read and header read from the cache. Then it does a payload read, which essentially is a zero copy operation.

If for some reason, there is no available cache line (ie, a cache miss) or the cache line is "dirty," indicating that contention or current use exists, the existing cache line will be "evicted" to clear the data for any current users. This leads to a subsequent access from system memory, which is a much slower proposition. This architecture is a bridge between the use of the cache and system memory. System memory is always updated regardless of the state of the cache. However, the trick is not to make the processor have to read from system memory very often because any such read incurs a decrease in performance.

The processor then makes a forwarding decision, implements features, does the header rewrite, outputs queue check, and adds this all to a TX descriptor (buffer). There really is no hardware transport management function (queue management) in this scheme. This would normally be handled by having an additional core resource assigned to a software forwarder handle this function.

Repeat. Repeat. Repeat.

Note that the provided acceleration (by reducing packet and packet descriptor access latency and memory bandwidth requirements) is just one part of the overall performance equation in getting packets from the NIC to the core and only applicable to receive side processing (transmit has a separate set of optimizations).

This description is for a single application on a host. Returning for a second to the NFV service-chaining model, it is easy to imagine the complications that may be introduced if and when more than one function in the chain is coresident on the host (and traffic has to traverse multiple VMs).

APPLICATION PROCESSING

The highest performing network applications will be micro-architecture sensitive (cache-friendly) and have few features (simple forwarding). Performance will be increasingly difficult to characterize as features are enabled (and additional CPU cycles consumed as we operate on the packet).

The performance required can be a bit daunting. To service a 10 Gbps connection, a service function would have to process approximately 15 million packets per second. While some vendors may claim that the average forwarding requirement is about 50 cycles per packet, that is largely applicable only to the most basic (and cacheable) L2 forwarding applications. Without some form of offload, prior knowledge that assists in prefetching[60] data or hardware acceleration, your mileage may vary.

In the compute/cache/memory sphere the application processing itself has a huge impact. Table 7.1 provides some back-of-napkin CPU cycle numbers for some common networking applications. (The point is not absolute accuracy, but relative number of cycles.) Your math may be aided by the knowledge that the generally available E5 family of processors is built for multiple applications and can clock in anywhere from 1.8 to 3.6 GHz. However, once you get into the 100s of cycles per packet, the ability to support 10 Gbps (per core) can be challenging.[61]

Table 7.1 Typical "First Generation" VNF Packet Processing Cycle Times. Firewall w/SSL Without Hardware Cryptography Offload	
Application	Approximate cycles per packet[a]
L2 forwarding	Many tens (~ 70)
IP routing	Few hundreds (~ 175)
L2-L4 classification	Many hundreds ($\sim 700-800$)
TCP session termination	Few thousands (~ 1500)
Stateful firewall	Many thousands (2000–3000)
Firewall w/SSL	Tens of thousands ($\sim 15,000-20,000$)
[a]YMMV, Your Mileage May Vary.	

BACKGROUND—CONTEXT SWITCH/DATA COPY REDUCTION

Setting aside the processor cycles required to actually act on a packet information (true compute—to actually perform the lookup and feature/application/function), a tax in the form of a context switch and data copying can be levied multiple times for every packet entering or leaving VNF, depending on how we have virtualized the environment.[62]

In general, a context switch will occur when we move between threads in a multitasking system, address spaces or protection domains (host-to-guest, kernel-to-user and the reverse or user to root and the reverse[63]), or handle external events (interrupts), exceptions, and system calls (these cause a trap to the kernel).

In the case of virtualized systems (particularly those virtualized with the Intel VMX technology), the major disruption occurs when a VM has to exit (VMExit). This occurs when the guest executes a privileged instruction, an I/O instruction, makes an access to the interrupt controller (APIC) or has to handle an external interrupt.

These actions are intercepted and lead to a save of the guest (VM) state into a control state or context memory, a load of host state from a similar memory, execution and then the reverse process. The operation can take many hundreds of CPU cycles. The TLB may be flushed and some indirect costs due to sharing of the cache may also be experienced.

Typically, when we virtualize a network device, the driver running in the VM puts a packet on a transmit ring and sets an I/O register (for this discussion, in the PCI address space). When the register is set, the software emulator receives a trap so that it can act on the contents. This trap or interrupt causes the context switch described above. This is just the first in a series of context switches and data copies on the way to the application in the guest OS (in a nonoptimized system).

By tracking the virtualized Task Priority Register (TPR), the VMM is supposed to know when it is safe to assert an interrupt. When a guest writes to this register, the VMM will cause a VMExit.

In general, optimizations attempt to bypass or augment the virtualization layer of the hypervisor and replace it with more sophisticated techniques. The performance gains in eliminating these perturbations can be greater than an order of magnitude in CPU cycle savings.

It would be preferable if we never had to do a data copy (possible, but with caveats). Zero-packet-copy claims rely a lot on the driver and on the implementation of some of the virtualization underpinnings. For example, the author of the hybrid virtualization project (described previously) found that virtio[64] in qemu/kvm 1.7.0 was not "precisely" zero copy because it creates a small fragment and then "pages in" the rest of the frame (from host to user space). The fragments persist and are returned by the same methodology to the host. If the driver does not fully support the fragmented frame API on the qemu side as the frame is being paged back, then the frame will be reassembled into a temporary buffer and passed as a single frame, not zero copy. In this release, no driver supported this paradigm in both directions (tap and hub have unidirectional support[65]).

This also meant that whatever you are running in user space that converses with kvm has to be able to operate on fragment lists shipped in the "iov" format. If not, a copy is required. The same limitation holds true for any application relying on legacy kvm kernel compatibility (eg, kernel defragmentation services).

It is important to note that the optimizations to eliminate packet copying and eliminate, coalesce or bypass the impacts of interrupt handling for network I/O are a continually moving target.

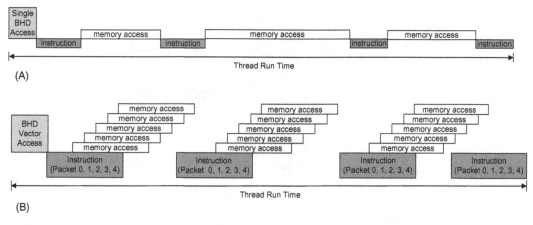

FIGURE 7.9

Vector processing amortizes load/use memory access latencies in (A) sequential code with nonoverlapping memory accesses and instructions by (B) loading a group/vector of packets and working on them simultaneously.

BACKGROUND—SCALAR VERSUS VECTORIZATION

Serialization of the packet transfers through context switches is an addressable problem. By putting multiple packets into a transmit buffer (safeguarding against triggering any traps) we can amortize the context switch over a number of packets. This switches the scalar operation to a vector basis, processing more data with fewer instructions and creating software parallelism (pipelining).

In Fig. 7.9, if the latency between the execution of the second and third group of instructions in the scalar example (A) is 100 ns, then the amortized value would be less than 20 ns in (B).[66] This is the root innovation behind some of the more advanced forwarders on the market. Efficiency improves with the size of the vector. In some cases, vendors have demonstrated a $256\times$ improvement (essentially, the scale of the packet vector).

"Vectorization" can have a positive secondary effect on cache efficiency (see Chapter 8: NFV Infrastructure—Hardware Evolution and Testing).[67]

ONGOING—INTEL ADVANCEMENTS (AND ACADEMIC WORK)

Intel has been acutely aware of network performance optimization for some time and actively are promoting acceleration through performance studies (which upstream their findings into new versions of DPDK and platform enhancements), recommended best practices and exposure of architectural performance changes/enhancements as new hardware becomes available, through open source tooling to make management and orchestration of their multiple generations less complicated and optimize-able.

Acceleration for packet transfers from NIC to guest started with changes to the I/O driver, which evolved from native trap and emulation, to include support for pass-through operation (SRIOV or PCIE direct) and virtio based paravirtualization.

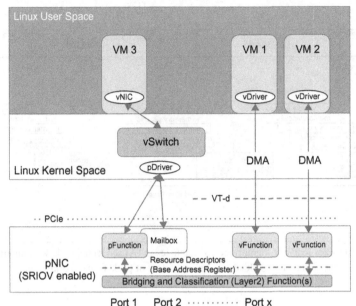

FIGURE 7.10

Intel VT-c and VT-d leveraged to support direct I/O into a VM (non-SRIOV supporting VM routes through kernel driver and hypervisor vSwitch).

Virtio-based solutions are evolving (recently from vhost-net to vhost-user) to shared-memory rings using large pages and the DPDK driver—bypassing the host kernel. The host stack is the last big bottleneck before application processing itself.

Intel offers a number of virtualization technologies in this area branded under the "VT-" umbrella (Fig. 7.10).

VT-x—added the previously-mentioned instructions specific to virtualization, starting with the VMX to the instruction set that enabled the VMM.

Intel VT FlexPriority support—removes the need for the VMM to track writes to the virtualized TPR, reducing the number of VM exits on context switches.

VT-d—(Directed I/O) allows the direct assignment of I/O devices to a specific guest via a dedicated area in system memory. VT-d performs address translation (and ensures separation of memory pages in different VMs) for DMA transactions between guest and host physical address. Smaller page sizes (4 KB) can result in inefficient mappings (lower coverage of the memory space in the TLB). A resulting miss can interrupt processing while the appropriate space is mapped and stored. VT-d addresses this with Extended Page Tables (EPTs) supported in the guest (1 GB). These techniques reduce copy-related behavior (staging of the data in separate host memory while performing the transfer) and are supported via a dedicated IOMMU.

VT-c—supports both VMDq (Virtual Machine Device Queues) and PCI-SIG SR-IOV (Single Root I/O Virtualization). VMDq is a NIC-based offload of some of the functionality common to the hypervisor (the hypervisor is a cooperative partner[68]) to enhance QoS and routing packets to VMs (queue mapping from hypervisor to NIC hardware queues).

SR-IOV—allows PCI devices that support these functions (eg, NICs and co-processors) to present themselves to the host as many virtual functions[69] that can be mapped directly to VMs (with varying bandwidth allocations). Its principal goal is:

to standardize on a way of bypassing the VMM's involvement in data movement by providing independent memory access, interrupts, and DMA streams for each virtual machine.[70]

SR-IOV allows sorting of the application traffic by tag, thus partitioning the resource and mapping them into the guests, eliminating copies that might have been incurred in the host to send/ receive the packet. However, SR-IOV does not emulate the port or cable (the individual logical links owned by the applications running in the VM), so there is some management information loss in the vNIC emulation.

SR-IOV can be considered an improvement over its precursor (PCI Device Assignment), which lacked vfunction mapping and thus dedicated the whole device to a VM/guest.

This optimization still places a burden on the DMA engine/controller (it uses Direct Memory Access to move the data).[71] Additionally, SR-IOV places some constraints on the movement of traffic between VMs on the same host, and thus needs augmentation/combination with non SR-IOV data planes (virtio based or entities like a DPDK-enabled vSwitch). And SR-IOV requires driver support in the VNF, which may be considered an operational burden if the driver needs to be continually updated/enhanced.[72]

Intel has a progressive strategy for minimizing memory copies involved both with virtio and SR-IOV data planes that include improvements to routines (a vectorized version of memcopy called rte_memcopy[73]), the potential to offload copies to dedicated cores (which is aligned with their general exploration of "pipelining" solutions for higher throughput) and the development of new/ stronger DMA engines.

Intel's DPDK libraries[74] (Fig. 7.11) enable a VM to take over network interfaces from the host OS using a PMD.

DPDK is a soft data plane that reduces context switches (PMD eliminates kernel interrupt context switching), reduces locks on queue structures (or optimizes them), and allows threads to be pinned to cores allowing packet processing to be isolated to a few cores. DPDK works well for fundamental frame movement but may be a more difficult programming model for complex features. To accelerate its use, Intel contributed an open source DPDK-enhanced version of Open vSwitch (initially their own version via 01.org but planned to converge with ovs.org at version 2.4.0—see drawing and explanation in Chapter 1: Network Function Virtualization). Communication is enabled through the use of shared memory ring structures between switch and VMs, its PMD, and the mapping of PCIe device base address space in host memory.

DPDK is the minimum/de facto optimization strategy for the VM and Intel oriented NFV architecture.

Intel's commitment to ongoing DPDK development should smooth out most of the negative observations around DPDK—adding interrupt support in addition to poll mode and changing threading operations (core mapping, thread type, and eliminating explicit declaration) to broaden DPDK adoption.

In fact, DPDK can be used in both the vSwitch data plane and/or the application data plane (examples of this arise in user space soft forwarders); other soft data plane proposals exist.[75]

These soft forwarders (with varying feature functionality) take similar advantage of DPDK and run in user space, relegating the vSwitch in the kernel to the role of patch panel—eliminating a great deal of overhead in exchange for the memory (normally a small footprint) and vCPU required to host its VM (illustrated in Fig. 7.12).

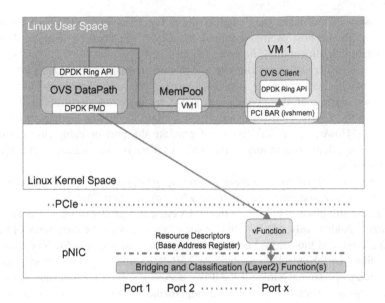

FIGURE 7.11

Intel's DPDK-enabled Open vSwitch, moves the switch construct to Host User Space.

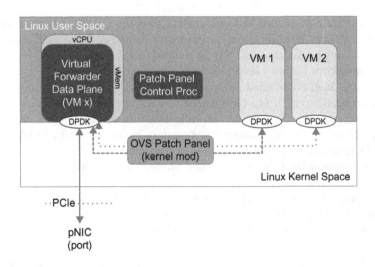

FIGURE 7.12

Alternative configuration of soft forwarder in user space and leveraging a thin driver in kernel (for the patch panel functionality) with a controller in user space.

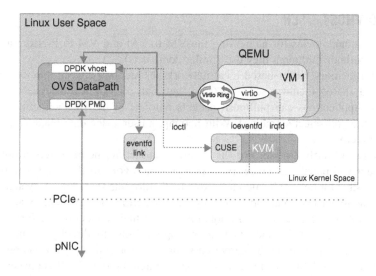

FIGURE 7.13

Intel's user space vhost implementation (errata—CUSE block represents the IO control routines for character devices).

In latter versions of DPDK (1.7), Intel attempted to accelerate the VM to VM and VM to physical connections through two mechanisms, both of which exploit a logical/virtual network device and user space forwarder: dpdkr/ivshmem (DPDK rings and shared memory) and us-vhost.

dpdkr/ivshmem uses host shared memory, making it less suitable for untrusted tenants. It also does not support live VM migration of the VNF but promises "zero copy" performance.

The us-vhost approach (Fig. 7.13) currently promises fewer data copies and context switches, but has the benefits of not requiring the VNF to be DPDK enabled (using the virtio driver—no new drivers required) and supports live migration.

The user space forwarder in both cases is the Intel provided DPDK enabled Open vSwitch, which uses a special netdev interface that bypasses the kernel. In the us-vhost case, the DPDK driver has capabilities similar to the kernel-based vhost-net (but in user space)—handling virtqueue kick events (on ioeventfd signals for guest-to-host and irqfd for host-to-guest) to put/pull data onto shared memory segments forged between the vSwitch and the guestOS (VM).

While the DPDK components include example applications, there is room for differentiation in custom forwarders (eg, feature completeness, performance at scale).

Intel typically publishes very high performance numbers on DPDK optimized platforms around low feature (L2 forwarding)—latest (version 1.7) claiming 59 Mpps on a core (at this rate, per packet time is 16 ns). While absolute numbers may be highly optimized, relative performance increases from release to release are generally believable and the CPU cycle reductions shown (greater than an order of magnitude over Linux stack) point to a reduction in context switching. Intel also introduced vectorization in version 1.3 (version 1.7 boasts intrinsic vector RX and TX support).

NETMAP AND VHOST-USER

There are other methodologies for addressing the VM to VM and VM to P-NIC transfer overhead than the DPDK methods (although they use similar constructs).

Netmap[77] is a memory buffer-based local network abstraction between applications. It consists of a kernel-based shared memory segment (ring) between the applications/guests (or application and host stack). Applications can pull/push packets onto/off of the ring without a context switch (it is explicit in the poll/select signaling). With netmap, a user space data plane can directly access memory/buffers (zero copy).

Synchronization is fairly simple. For the receive transaction, netmap uses a poll API and on transmit the writer will update the curser (new frames) and invoke ioctl to trigger a flush.

While it is possible for one application to inadvertently dirty the shared memory area, it is allocated from a restricted non-pageable area, and device registers and critical kernel memory are not exposed.

It is also possible to allocate separate pools for each virtual connection for further isolation and security. Netmap has a "pipe" mode that allows applications to directly connect via a shared memory ring (without Vale), using the kernel only for synchronization (again, via poll/ioctl).

Netmap can be used between applications (as pictured in Fig. 7.14), between the NIC and application/user space[78] (not pictured, we show DPDK as a common implementation in combination with Netmap) and between the application and the host stack (though for most networking applications bypassing the host stack is common).

Vale[80] (Fig. 7.15) is a complimentary system in the kernel that maps these netmap rings to each other. Vale scales the abstraction to multiple applications on the host.

Techniques like netmap can sometimes become dangerous in combination with test routines that are designed to exaggerate performance. An application distributed with netmap (pkt-gen) can generate 80 Mpps, but (typical of many speed-test applications) it can be used to set up a test that only manipulates rings of pointers to packets. Such unrealistic test scenarios can produce results unrelated to reality.

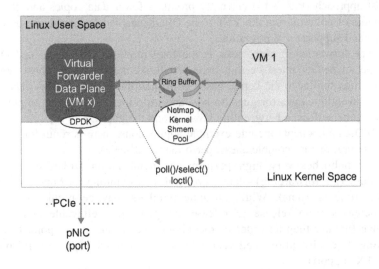

FIGURE 7.14

Netmap.[76]

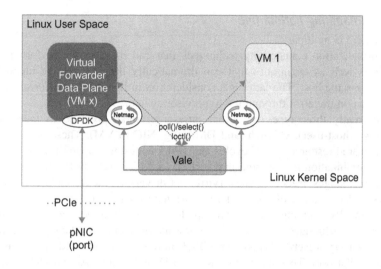

FIGURE 7.15

Vale.[79]

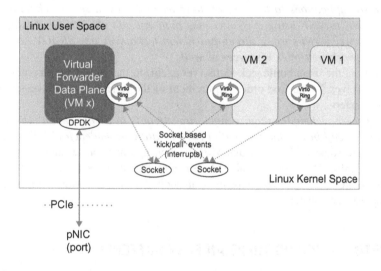

FIGURE 7.16

A virtual forwarder in user space leveraging DPDK and vhost-user.[81]

A generic forwarder in user space can also leverage user space vhost (vhost-user[82]) to forge user space shared memory rings between the guests and forwarder (as shown in Fig. 7.16), with the only remaining kernel based function being (socket) control, minimizing data copies.[83]

Using these methodologies in conjunction with a vector-based forwarder running in user space, we dramatically reduce the number of context switches to create a service chain (essentially one context switch for X-sized vector of packets traversing a virtual service chain on the box).

Software packet handling bottom line

The bottom line here is multipart:

There are virtualization connectivity techniques that can increase the performance of NIC to application I/O as well as techniques that can dramatically improve service chain (app to app) transfers within the same host. The latter is a consideration in light of the performance implications of the current focus on traversal through the hypervisor switch.

There are currently three types of virtual intraserver links involved in these optimizations: point-to-point (eg, vhost-user), vSwitch, and DMA (eg, NIC to VM). These are "bandwidth-less," but do consume shared resources (CPU cycles and DMA controller capability).

A promising combination is emerging that includes a NIC driven by DPDK, the VMs driven by vhost-user with no changes needed in guest (virtio net driver), and a vector-based virtual forwarder in host user mode. Performance of this model is expected to map well to containers.

DPDK is continually evolving with a roadmap already stretching beyond a 2.0 version.

Intel acceleration techniques like SR-IOV are not the only ones available, but tend to dominate as Intel presses their Open Network Platform (ONP) initiative. We focused on DPDK as part of an all-Intel reference platform. Techniques like Remote Data Memory Access (RDMA)[84] have been evolving in the High Performance Compute environment, but have yet to achieve the critical mass of SR-IOV (RDMA on DPDK is a potential future merge of technologies).

There are also implications to the uses of these technologies in service chaining. Whereas the switching from VNF to VNF using a vSwitch has platform and vSwitch bandwidth dependencies, switching to or between VNFs using direct-attachment techniques like SR-IOV can consume PCIe bandwidth and network controller resources as well.

Postoptimization, the main bottleneck shifts (yet again) to the guest Linux kernel and the service applications themselves.[85] The first order requirement of the functions would be to become vector-aware for data transfers.

Almost all of these techniques require support/awareness in orchestration (OpenStack), emulators (QEMU) and often library changes (eg, libvirt), creating dependencies of their own.

Finally, there are some applications that virtualization optimization techniques cannot completely address. A "true" Traffic Manager (verifiable QoS) is a (potentially) good example. Many VNF implementations that require "true" QoS will implement an additional core as a transport manager (TM)—creating a more sophisticated pipeline.

TURNKEY OPTIMIZATION (IS THERE AN EASY BUTTON?)

Given the possibilities for optimization and its ongoing architectural evolution (see Chapter 9: An NFV Future), Intel has cultivated an ecosystem of custom integrators,[86] some of which (notably 6Wind and Wind River) offer turnkey variants of the Linux OS with their own optimizations for the NFV VM environment.

Wind River[87] is an Intel company offering what their marketing calls "Open Virtualization Profile" that highly leverages Intel VT technologies (and DPDK) and purports an adaptive performance capability that allows the operator to prioritize throughput or latency.

They offer core pinning (for VMs) with some enhancements to enable dynamic core reassignment, NUMA awareness and isolation of potentially competing workloads, features that are pointed toward more intelligent orchestration. The environment also claims a greater degree of interrupt control and latency reduction that helps with context switching (VM exits)—notably by the passing of virtual interrupts to VMs and supporting EPTs that allow the guest OS to handle its own page table modifications and faults (again, leveraging VT technology). In short, they have incorporated the entire suite of Intel enhancements on Intel hardware.

The Wind River solution includes a proprietary optimized vSwitch and Linux distribution. While guest VNFs can benefit from the tuning of the basic offering without modification, incorporation of their driver in the VNF is required for the full benefit of the solution.

Wind River has put forward an ETSI PoC for the mobile RAN that accentuated the combination of interrupt reduction, SR-IOV enablement (Intel Ethernet adapter) and QuickAssist coprocessor support (for signal processing acceleration).

Many proposed "carrier grade" enhancements to KVM are (rightly) upstreamed over time. Other "carrier grade" NFV enhancements dealing with VNF management functionality are packaged as OpenStack plug-ins. This seems to place some of the functionality typically associated with a VNFM product, into the VIM (in ETSI terms).[88]

The 6Wind[89] 6WindGate solution (Fig. 7.17) focuses on host-to-guest bandwidth, vSwitch performance, and poor performance of standard OS networking stacks. The solution leverages DPDK (on Intel) and a 6Wind network stack (adding telecom-specific encapsulation support—eg, PPP, GTP).

Some of the stack modules are "FastPath" modules that can run on dedicated cores (scaling with the addition of cores) as FastPath Dataplane (eg, for TCP session termination, they go to parallel DPDK cores). Outside of FastPath, 6Wind provides some applications they call Transport services (eg, Routing). These address perceived shortcomings in the default Linux stack and some of the application cycle overhead noted earlier.

6Wind also includes their own Open vSwitch module that can be run on multiple cores and their own shared memory driver that is incorporated in both host and guest.[90] The specialized vSwitch points out what 6Wind sees as a problem with the standard OVS—performance does not scale linearly with additional cores (while the 6Wind accelerated switch claims to do this) and is available as a standalone product (6Wind Virtual Accelerator). Wind River similarly has a specially adapted vSwitch component.

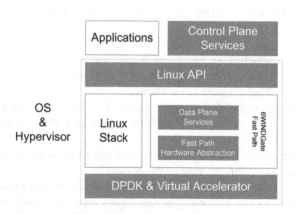

FIGURE 7.17

General depiction of 6WindGate architecture.

Turnkey environments offload the environment optimization problem (to some degree) to a vendor. Like the previously discussed optimizations, they can be architecture-specific (predominantly Intel). They do have their trade-offs:

- From a technology/business perspective, the operator depends on the vendor to follow the evolving software/hardware optimization curve (staying current)—potentially including support for evolving hardware that will get integrated into the architecture (looking forward to heterogeneous cores, etc.). This includes the support of containers and bare metal (which may create a tendency to mix solution pairings, as the optimized hardware virtualization provides little benefit).
- Generally, a high degree of vertical integration might limit the size of the ecosystem (third party products available for solutions).
- From a deployment/operations perspective, the operator may have to support an additional and specialized distribution of the Linux OS for network functions.
- From a development perspective, some turnkey environments may require augmentation of the development tool chain (eg, compiling a vendor's shared memory driver into your VNF/guest to take enable the advertised performance boost).

All of these need to be considered against the operational transparency NFV purports, and the significant amount of true open source that might eventually dominate the VIM and NFVI.

FD.IO (NONE OF THE ABOVE?)

By now you might have noticed a bit of a problem. Performance and functionality of virtual switches in the VM architecture have been bit slow to evolve and the forwarding paradigm for containers might be a bit immature. Proprietary solutions to the former seem to have fairly big trade-offs.

The Linux Foundation multiparty and multiproject fd.io (Fast Data) was launched to unify the approach to the data plane services. The scope of the project includes I/O, packet processing, and management agents.

As part of the project launch, Cisco Systems announced open sourcing of their Vector Packet Processor (VPP)[91] code, which may blunt the appeal of any proprietary accelerated vSwitch and provide a more suitable forwarder for the container environment in the short term and provide an extensible platform for other projects in the future.

VPP moves forwarding completely out of the kernel, for both containers and (because it can be configured to perform like a vSwitch) VMs. With a promised Neutron plug-in, it can readily replace OVS in OpenStack.[92]

Because of its independence from the kernel, the forwarder can be reset and return to forwarding in seconds without losing the electronic state of the device.

The basis of the VPP code has been used in some of Cisco's routing products (since 2002) and is arguably the progenitor of the vectorization techniques mentioned earlier. VPP acts as a user-space host router with stack, bypassing the need to use the host network stack in the kernel and unifies all IO (storage and peripherals) into a single platform.

A very high performer, the forwarder is capable of 14 Mpps/core and scales linearly with cores, supports extremely large tables and can run within an application container or in a container of its own.

VPP supports DPDK directly to (dVMQ) queues on the NIC as well as SR-IOV (though DPDK 2.0 is expected to replace SR-IOV over time).

Its modular code base allows developers to easily hang additional functionality off of the stack or support hardware accelerators (eg, encryption engines). VPP also supports flexible binding to a Data Plane Management agent, creating a great degree of deployment flexibility.

VPP has flexible plug-in support (Fig. 7.18). Plug-ins can alter the packet processing graph, introduce new graph nodes, and be added at runtime.

The project promises a CD/CI environment with a continuous performance test lab (to identify code breakage and performance degradation before patch review).

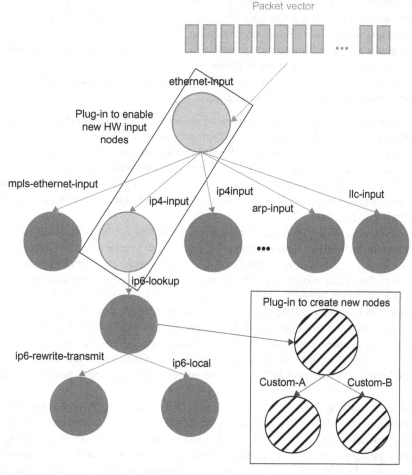

FIGURE 7.18

VPP supports a plug-in architecture.

CONCLUSIONS

It is hard to compress a discussion of virtualization performance issues and optimizations. This software-based component overview presents a portion of the future possibilities of high-performance NFV.

Awareness that performance can be an issue for NFV is good, but compulsion concerning performance details may be detrimental.

The focus on performance of a particular VNF or infrastructure component should not be a distraction from the broader and more long-term benefits of service creation.

Like the appliance market before it (which was already beginning to divert more towards generic processing platforms), the NFV infrastructure market will go through a continual innovation/optimization cycle. The network I/O performance of general compute architectures has progressed tremendously in the past two years and will continue to evolve. Vendors like Intel have a vested interest in raising awareness of these improvements and making them available as quickly and transparently as possible in orchestration.[93]

If innovation is a given and transparency inevitable, the NFV focus should be around integration and management of multiple generations of hardware capabilities.

The fluidity of NFV performance environment is typical of any early-stage phenomena like NFV. For now, some trends/patterns are emerging:

- *The demands of network I/O and attendant optimizations (pinning cores and mapping them to NICs, dedicating cores to virtual forwarders, dedicating cores to TMs) make it unlikely that virtual network appliances will be easily mixed with other applications in a general datacenter approach.*
- NFV systems will have multiple "generations," just like their integrated appliance predecessors (both in software and hardware). As we pursue performance optimization, we cannot forget the tie to the orchestration to properly align resources and avoid unnecessary bottlenecks in the overall solution architecture.
- Some of the more likely deployment architectures circulating for NFV in Telco environments show a "common forwarder" demarcation point between the service specific function and the network—a service-agnostic layer. This keeps "network operations" a traditionally separate entity (even in the virtual world) for debugging, performance monitoring, and provisioning. How well this approach integrates with evolving SFC/NSH (see Chapter 6: MANO: Management, Orchestration, OSS, and Service Assurance) remains to be seen.
- VNFs can approach the throughputs of dedicated network appliances, but (based on current trends) they will become hotter as they become more specialized for network I/O. Power efficiency will have to be taken into careful consideration at the solution architecture and design levels. The use of PMDs will have to accommodate some power savings potential.
- The VM-centric NFV architecture may not be the only packaging model going forward for all environments. MicroVMs, containers, and bare-metal all are emerging as alternative "packaging" models with varying risk/cost/benefit profiles. Security is only starting to emerge as a gating factor for shared infrastructure projects, and can be a key determinant in the packaging decision. "Compose-ability" of functions (a next generation potential for NFV enabled by SFC/NSH) may also be influenced by the packaging decision.

The potential shift in NFV from generic cloud compute toward network I/O optimized virtual appliances raises fundamental questions about some of the original premises behind NFV.

In particular, do the economics really work for NFV when the costs of specialization and power/Gbps are factored (now or in the future)? If not, can the overriding attraction of service creation, operational agility, and elasticity in NFV make the complications of specialization acceptable and keep NFV attractive (until the economics DO make sense)?

While it seems an assumption that the security risks associated with NFV are outweighed by the agility gains, the extent of that risk needs to be better understood and controlled. Security in an NFV environment should drive new opex spending, which has to be weighed into total cost in the balance of NFV.

There is an "easy button" being marketed, with a number of concessions to an entirely open and generic system. Organizational politics are often involved in the "easy button" decision. A traditional Data Center operator would forgo this level of customization and rely on the economies and availability of bulk compute services (and wait for these customizations to become part of the mainstream "COTS" purchase if they have long-term positive ROI). For a traditional Service Provider that offers wire line or wireless services, there may be political motivations to continue to own the delivery of services and deploy their own "service pods"—making the "easy button" attractive (reducing the need for inhouse virtualization expertise and giving the customer "one throat to choke" for NFV).

Additionally, the "carrier grade"-ing of solutions, while sympathetic to the concerns of traditional operators (particularly telcos), ignores the "pets" versus "cattle" thinking common in large-scale data centers. While some services might need some of the protections implied in "carrier grade," there is some substitution in terms when talking about software based services. VM "migration" for HA and "six 9s" may be replaced by the "service availability" and "resiliency" designed into today's web-scale applications instead of being baked into more expensive infrastructure.

The proliferation of NFVI-related optimization variables today may also be a short-term problem as the market determines the proper optimization tradeoffs going forward and/or as consumers opt again for the original NFV proposition (by deploying only what is commonly available or nonspecialized). This may sacrifice some short-term potential performance for longer-term operational simplicity.

The fd.io project may provide an open source consolidation of ideas and techniques that refocuses the disparate attempts to tune the data plane for the NFV environment.

In our next chapter, we will look at how hardware innovation (to solve the network I/O problem) exacerbates the potential complexity problems of NFV deployment and the need for standardized testing that is being driven by both hardware and software innovation cycles.

END NOTES

1. While general-purpose processors can include the Intel x86, ARM, and PowerPC architectures (and potentially the newer IBM/GlobalFoundaries OpenPower/Power8), the current de facto NFV target is the Intel x86. For the greater part of the performance chapters, the Intel XEON SandyBridge will be the exemplar because it is currently widely deployed.
2. *The microarchitecture of Intel, AMD and VIA CPUs*, by Abner Fog, Technical University of Denmark, 2013.

3. VMM—VMM is a layer of system software that enables multiple VMs to share system hardware. The applications can run without modification. The VMM runs in a special mode (VMX root is fully privileged while VMX nonroot creates the basis for the guest to run in Ring-0 deprivleged). The guest OS runs in Ring 0 deprivileged. Applications in the guest run in Ring 3 deprivileged.

4. http://www.linux-kvm.org, Kernel-based Virtual Machine.

5. QEMU is "a generic and open source machine emulator and virtualizer" (see http://wiki.qemu.org/Main_Page). QEMU can perform hardware-based virtualization.

6. http://docs.oasis-open.org/virtio/virtio/v1.0/csd01/virtio-v1.0-csd01.html.

7. There are other differences in the appearance of the memory space of the guest.

8. Introduced with the Xenon product family.

9. Note that scheduling happens outside the vSwitch context, which has implications on behaviors if the physical switch is oversubscribed (VM thinks it sent and is unaware of drops).

10. TLB is the physical-to-virtual memory mapper of the MMU.

11. Commonly by using an abstraction layer like *libvirt* (http://libvirt.org/).

12. The ETSI model also allows for "compound" VNFs, which may represent a complete service. Compound VNFs did not seem to provide the level of independence for application development and deployment that were goals of the ETSI architecture (as described by the end of Phase 1).

13. In some ways, this would mirror the Kubernetes distribution approach (pods) for containers.

14. While VM-to-VM connectivity of the time was not impossible (bypassing the vSwitch) it had accompanying marshaling and call overhead.

15. http://www.cc.gatech.edu/~qywang/papers/JackLiBigdata13.pdf is a good example of one of these studies. They have some interesting observations in Increasing Processing Parallelism and VM Placement (for Hadoop).

16. https://wiki.openstack.org/wiki/Ironic.

17. To realize some of these cross-operator use cases, federation of the NFVI and Orchestration systems might be required—an extremely "long pole" in the deployment of NFV.

18. http://user-mode-linux.sourceforge.net/.

19. *An Updated Performance Comparison of Virtual Machines and Linux Containers* Felter, Ferriera, Rajamony and Rubi <http://domino.research.ibm.com/library/cyberdig.nsf/papers/0929052195DD819C85257D2300681E7B/$File/rc25482.pdf>.

20. Non-Linux container environments do exist (eg, Solaris/Illumos zones, FreeBSD jails). The focus on Linux merely cuts down on an already large amount of environmental variance for our discussion.

21. https://www.kernel.org/doc/Documentation/cgroups/cgroups.txt.

22. https://www.docker.com/.

23. This is simply and clearly explained in the blog, http://tuhrig.de/layering-of-docker-images/.

24. https://github.com/jpetazzo/pipework.

25. http://www.socketplane.io/.

26. http://weave.works/.

27. http://kubernetes.io/.

28. http://www.redhat.com/en/about/blog/red-hat-and-google-collaborate-kubernetes-manage-docker-containers-scale. There are numerous additional tools that integrate around Kubernetes (eg, Mesos and Marathon).

29. http://blog.docker.com/2014/12/docker-announces-orchestration-for-multi-container-distributed-apps/.

30. http://blog.kubernetes.io/2016/01/why-Kubernetes-doesnt-use-libnetwork.html.

31. https://www.joyent.com/company/press/joyent-announces-linux-branded-zones-and-extension-of-docker-engine-to-smartdatacenter. Joyent is based on Illumos/Smartos zones.

32. http://www.coreos.com.

33. There are some hidden benefits to the smaller footprint as well if management schemes (including HA) require "snapshots" of memory to be taken.
34. https://www.opencontainers.org/.
35. http://martinfowler.com/bliki/ImmutableServer.html.
36. https://clearlinux.org/features/clear-containers.
37. http://osv.io/.
38. https://mirage.io/.
39. http://unikernel.com/.
40. https://medium.com/@darrenrush/after-docker-unikernels-and-immutable-infrastructure-93d5a91c849e-.cg821bgpl.
41. http://www.cisco.com/web/HR/ciscoconnect/2014/pdfs/QvBN-TechnicalOverview.pdf.
42. A microVM uses hardware-based virtualization with a very limited privilege based on task-based security and introspection. For an example, see Bromium http://www.bromium.com/products/our-technology.html.
43. User Mode Linux allows the operator to run a software-based secure VM (Linux in Linux). It is a Type II VMM equivalent (with a paravirtualized relinked kernel).
44. http://git.qemu.org/?p = qemu.git;a = history;f = net/l2tpv3.c;h = 21d6119ed40eaa6ef38765c5a4a22b3b27dbda98;hb = HEAD.
45. http://www.ncbi.nlm.nih.gov/pmc/articles/PMC4503740/pdf/pone.0130887.pdf.
46. A Xen hypervisor bug (disclosed in October 2014) required a number of reputable cloud computing providers to patch and reload systems (http://xenbits.xen.org/xsa/advisory-108.html). A KVM and Zen QEMU-related vulnerability (May 2015) https://access.redhat.com/articles/1444903 shows we may not be finished with possible escapes. Later failures of VMware's ESXi (printer hack), and other hypervisor failures have also paraded through the news recently.
47. http://www.bromium.com/sites/default/files/wp-bromium-breaking-hypervisors-wojtczuk.pdf is a good quick read to put the "relative" into your own view of virtualization security.
48. View http://seclists.org/oss-sec/2015/q2/389 and judge for yourself.
49. http://blog.docker.com/2013/08/containers-docker-how-secure-are-they/.
50. https://blog.docker.com/2013/08/containers-docker-how-secure-are-they/.
51. https://blog.docker.com/2016/02/docker-engine-1-10-security/.
52. https://www.kernel.org/doc/Documentation/security/Smack.txt.
53. http://selinuxproject.org/page/Main_Page.
54. The concept of Carrier Grade Linux has been around for some time and many of the protections/recommendations therein have been integrated into mainstream Linux versions (caveat emptor).
55. https://titanous.com/posts/docker-insecurity.
56. http://www.wired.com/2015/03/researchers-uncover-way-hack-bios-undermine-secure-operating-systems/.
57. It should be noted that Day Zero vulnerability in Intel architecture allowed a somewhat specialized exploit (the user needed access to Ring 0, which is privileged) of Ring 2 (System Management Mode) that would theoretically work around this level of security (http://www.bit-tech.net/news/hardware/2015/08/07/x86-security-flaw/1).
58. This is one of the funny paradoxes surrounding NFV. While most consumers want to use "open" and non-specialized hardware/software to avoid vendor lock-ins, they also seem to want the highest performance possible—which leads (at times) to deploying less-than-open systems.
59. http://web.stanford.edu/group/comparch/papers/huggahalli05.pdf provides a study of DCA with good descriptions.
60. Prefetch hinting was introduced (as part of DCA) to improve on write cache coherency transactions and reduce cache misses.

61. The approximate budget per packet would be less than 200 cycles for 10 Gbps. Naturally, moving to 40 or 100 Gbps drastically impacts that budget.
62. The simple packet processing routine described at the beginning of the section already contains some optimization (DCA).
63. There are OS dependencies here, so this is a generalization. The reaction to these perturbations can also be both OS- and architecture-dependent. For example, Intel provides both a hardware- and software-assisted functionality for domain crossing context switches, with the software-assisted method generally used to increase portability.
64. http://wiki.libvirt.org/page/Virtio.
65. The developer in this project was attempting to implement what was missing from qemu tuntap to see if they could improve this situation.
66. Locks are still required for multiprocessing.
67. The use of a packet vector reduces instruction cache thrashing.
68. VMDq works with VMware NetQueue and Microsoft Hyper-V Virtual Machine Queues. The combinations of hypervisor version and vendor NIC support should be researched if you want to use these features. Like SR-IOV, VMDq has resource limits—here, on the number of queues per port—that limit per-adapter scale for the function.
69. As a typical example, (in theory) a four port SR-IOV NIC can present four physical functions, each mapped to 256 virtual functions—for a total of 1024 virtual functions. In practice, since each device would consume system resources the supported numbers would be much lower.
70. http://www.intel.com/content/www/us/en/pci-express/pci-sig-sr-iov-primer-sr-iov-technology-paper.html.
71. Some SR-IOV implementations do not allow local delivery and SR-IOV is not entirely secure without an IOMMU.
72. This can arguably be generalized as a concern for any direct-device-attachment strategy.
73. http://dpdk.org/doc/api/rte__memcpy_8h.html.
74. PMD, ring library, timer library, hash library, memory zone library, mempool library, etc.
75. NTT's LAGOPUS (lagopus.github.io) and Microsoft's PacketDirect.
76. This is a simplification, normally there are two separate unidirectional rings—a TX and RX ring.
77. http://info.iet.unipi.it/~luigi/netmap/.
78. Solarflare open-on-load.
79. This drawing is also simplified as the rings are normally unidirectional pairs.
80. http://info.iet.unipi.it/~luigi/vale/.
81. This drawing is also simplified as the rings are normally unidirectional pairs.
82. http://www.virtualopensystems.com/en/solutions/guides/snabbswitch-qemu/.
83. The fd.io forwarder (discussed later in this chapter) is a generic forwarder in user space that goes further and even eliminates this kernel dependency.
84. http://www.rdmaconsortium.org/.
85. Each new service component in the netmap/vhost-user paradigm(s) can be a potential bottleneck, but parallel chains are basically additive for throughput—eg, multiple chains of one component have relatively linear scale.
86. http://networkbuilders.intel.com/ecosystem.
87. http://www.windriver.com/.
88. The term "carrier grade" or "six 9s availability" panders to traditional Telco sensibilities. As covered elsewhere, high availability in the cloud is achieved differently than it was on the traditional Telco appliances.
89. http://www.6wind.com/.
90. 6Wind can support VNFs that do not integrate their shared memory driver (obviously at comparatively reduced performance).

91. http://fd.io/.

92. According to their launch materials, the difference between OVS and VPP can be viewed as VPP being a platform on top of which a set of switching functionality similar to OVS can be easily created.

93. To their credit, Intel has been pushing updates to OpenStack to make NUMA and PCIE locality control available to automation.

NFV INFRASTRUCTURE— HARDWARE EVOLUTION AND TESTING

8

INTRODUCTION

Enhancements and evolution in NFV performance are not limited solely to software. In the previous chapter, we focused on how certain software components, in cooperation with advances in hardware, have rapidly accelerated the performance of NFV systems, especially on commodity hardware. In this chapter, we will look more closely at hardware evolution and projections going forward in future generations of commodity hardware.

Starting with the expected Intel "tick/tock" delivery and evolution of processor architecture improvements and Network Interface Cards (NICs), hardware advancements to make Intel platforms perform at ever higher rates of throughput will create a parallel track toward NFV enhancement to the software technologies of virtualization we covered in Chapter 7, The Virtualization Layer—Performance, Packaging, and NFV.

In this chapter, we will look in detail at the architectural evolution in the Intel Architecture (IA) for NFV including the increased dependence on cache efficiency for performance of NFV on CPU cores. Intel is also pursuing a strategy of hardware augmentation that is opening the market for complimentary hardware acceleration through PCIE expansion. This expansion is further leading to next generation NICs that allow third-party chips to be embedded on those platforms, as well as the use of Field Programmable Gate Arrays (FPGAs) and Graphics Processing Units (GPUs) for similar purposes.

The compute model amenable to the existing IA, its execution and memory models (including cache behaviors) have downstream effects on programming/development models. If the pursuit of performance leads to true parallelism in compute architecture, hybrid models of the IA will appear or new models altogether. This might lead the reader to question how strong a grip Intel has on the NFV market as it evolves.

When combined with the variability in software architectures, the evolution of hardware architectures and accelerators results in an explosion of the number of testable permutations for NFV deployment.

One of the core contributions of the ETSI PER WG was the realization that an iterative methodology for bottleneck identification would be required, but a more open verification environment is overdue. So, before we leave performance, we will also touch on testability and how any performance claim for NFV can be tested objectively.

EVOLVING HARDWARE

All the interest around network I/O performance has its root in a basic truth about COTS compute (when NFV became a use-case of interest). That is, both COTS compute architecture and system design, while providing a flexible programming environment were not particularly optimized for network I/O (the word "compute" is a clue to where the real emphasis lies—processing power applied to general computation). The design is biased more toward minimizing latency than optimizing throughput. Thus the generic x86 Intel server[1] (the presumed de facto NFV platform) needs some hardware tweaking and evolution to become a high-performance network appliance.

Just as we saw in virtualization software (via the use of vectors and shared memory transfers), there are a number of factors that can impact overall performance of a virtualized network function on existing CPU designs, including; I/O bandwidth, memory bandwidth/operations, processor operations, cache size (coherency and efficiency), context switching (data copying), the compute model (run to completion versus pipeline), multithreading, and coprocessing.

While it is possible to increase performance of the core pipeline (and system) by decreasing CPU cycle time (increasing frequency), optimizing instructions and applying a cache (all three are now in play in the IA) processor vendors have hit a ceiling on the first aspect (frequency).

Starting around 2003, increasing frequency started to show high cost (eg, increasing heat, error rate) and diminishing returns on performance (this process does not follow Moore's Law for all operational parameters).[2]

Instead of continuing to follow the steep/difficult processor speed curve, the approach to providing increased performance evolved into the creation of multiple execution pipelines and CPU manufacturers started making (generally lower clock speed) multicore and multisocket systems (exemplified by the Intel Sandy Bridge architecture shown in Fig. 8.1). This approach increases thread density and creates "some" hardware pseudo-parallel processing capability (although the underlying architecture and instruction set is still fundamentally designed for sequential execution and slowly adapting to exploit multicore).

CPU COMPLEX

In the IA, work of a thread (a process with its own call stack and program counter) is accomplished through a series of instruction and data fetch, decode, execute, and store actions.

Within a shared memory multiprocessor system, multiple threads can operate concurrently on different processor cores, or on a single core (via scheduler interleaving). These threads transform the sequential execution model to a concurrent one, but with added complexities (in part, due to the fact that they share memory/state).

On a single core, the Intel Sandy Bridge microarchitecture (shown in Fig. 8.2) can support the simultaneous execution of multiple nondependent operations (eg, one load, one store, one AVX floating point multiply). The scheduler supports multiple entries in two clusters of "ports." One cluster (the memory cluster) focuses on load/store operations allowing two simultaneous reads and one write per cycle (with an internal sequencer for queued requests) combined with masking these instructions.

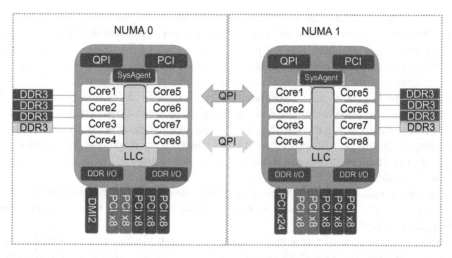

FIGURE 8.1

Sandy Bridge architecture has some variance depending on the model under discussion. The EN (2400) has an identical number of QPI links, memory channels, and PCI links as the EP (2600).

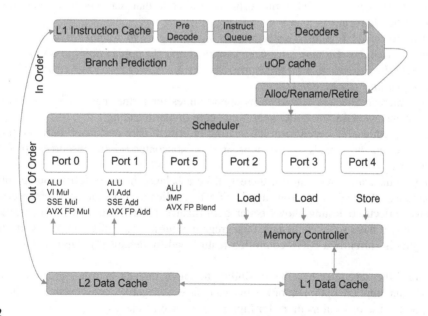

FIGURE 8.2

Sandy Bridge microarchitecture.

On more recent platforms, another (the execution cluster) optimizes some instructions by "packing" (Advanced Vector eXtensions, AVX)[3] into a larger operand size (256 bit), enabling (as an example) up to eight (32 bits) floating-point operations at a time (Single Instruction Multiple Data (SIMD) parallelism). As implied by the name, this is a vector strategy similar to the general packet buffer strategy covered earlier, but for arithmetic/floating-point instructions.

To maximize performance, the architecture supports hardware instruction pre-fetch and branch prediction (speculative execution). These speculative optimizations create instruction-level parallelism (ILP), but have penalties if they fail. These optimizations are algorithmic and depend on the loading conformance with predictive models. Because misprediction events have non-zero probability, recent changes in microarchitecture focus on increasing cache size and decreasing misprediction penalty.

If one of these optimized parallel instructions finishes before an earlier instruction, it will appear reordered[4] (eg, multiple "load" instructions may continue to stack and execute in the timeframe that other operations run).

The external appearance of sequential execution (through visible state created by dependent instructions) is enabled by resources/structures that augment the scheduler—the reorder buffer (ROB), load/store buffers, and the physical register files (in the case of Sandy Bridge) for integer and floating point instructions. Given that load/store operations can also be reordered, the programmer bears the responsibility of using given memory fencing techniques and locking to maintain proper ordering which leads us down the very deep rabbit hole on maintaining concurrency in the face of parallelism. This is a heavy burden for a programmer and is also *potentially* error prone. It also can lead to very platform-specific code that may not be optimal on the next generation of the platform.

Note that use of AVX require orchestration awareness as to whether a generation of cores supports the instructions that may have been compiled into the application (an AVXv2 set is slated for release with the Haswell microarchitecture, Skylake introduces an AVXv3 set and we can expect further changes with successive ticks).

The Intel microarchitecture also exploits opportunities for further parallel instruction execution through simultaneous multithreading on the same core (hyperthreading).

Because hyperthreading depends on the sharing of critical core resources[5] between threads it is most optimal when the threads access nonshared or noncontended for resources; otherwise one thread will block.

Like any virtualization mechanism, there will be a balance between full resource subscription and performance (that will vary from application to application). Resource oversubscription can have negative effects. If testing shows better performance for a function without hyperthreading, the operator might have some challenges in segregating out a subset of equipment with the feature turned off (this is currently a BIOS controlled feature and by default it is ON) specifically for the function.

By default, the scheduler has the flexibility to move threads between processor cores in a NUMA cell (an implicit optimization). This can have a negative consequence if the thread is depending on the use of local memory for high performance (cache).

Careful mapping of separate processes (and their threads) to cores (virtual or physical) can exploit the abundance of threads while minimizing conflict (at the core level).

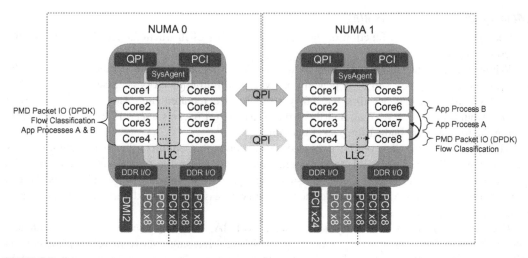

FIGURE 8.3

Run-to-completion (depicted on left) and pipeline execution models.[6]

Application and I/O processing can differ in application execution models (as depicted in Fig. 8.3)—run-to-completion or pipelining. The run-to-completion model is going to have an implicit requirement for flow load balancing to the cores associated with scale while the pipeline model can scale independent components.[7]

While it is possible to direct a flow to a core, "pinning" introduces load-balancing requirements and potential large flow HOL blocking problems.

At this point in time, another little-known effect is that the scheduler will still distribute kernel functions called by a pinned thread. Like all performance-related optimizations, this can be chased to yet another level. In this case, we will have to look at influencing the scheduler itself.

Individual programs can exploit these resources by becoming multithreaded and scaling across cores/threads.

Here, the complexity of the multisocket, multicore, paradigm percolates further up into design, development, and deployment by introducing concurrency management within the programs/applications (with compiler and CPU self-optimization dependencies).[8]

This assumes the individual program decomposes well into multiple concurrently running threads. Otherwise, enabling the ability to run more "copies" of the program may be beneficial, but the individual instances of the program might not be much more efficient.[9] There are some design limits when we use "sequential, imperative code to implement a parallel algorithm."[10]

While the multicore, multisocket paradigm (its accompanying instruction set architecture (ISA), cache and scheduler optimizations) provides some level of parallelism and resource sharing (through a combination of multithreading, SIMD, and ILP), performance inevitably suffers when the process has to actually access memory. While Intel has opened up bandwidth in memory access[11] *(memory technology has upgraded with every microarchitecture), latency is very hard to decrease for fundamental reasons.*

Memory access—cache is king

The compute capacity is a function of the aggregate number of instructions per clock cycle across the cores working on a process.

While it is possible to spread some of this work out across multiple parallel operations, the thread run time efficiency will be dependent on avoiding/limiting memory accesses.

Today's 10 Gbps network link has fairly strict service requirements. The smallest (64 byte) packets would arrive every 67 ns, and the larger (1518 byte) packets every 1230 ns[12]—effectively setting the timing/cycle budget for packet operations.

The typical router/switch vendor uses custom memories that optimize the small random access pattern (Fig. 8.4) associated with packet operations (smaller than the typical cache line size of a generic CPU at a higher rate).[14] Generally speaking, specialized Network Processing Units (NPUs) can perform over an order of magnitude more memory accesses per second than the current crop of general-purpose processors.

Even though memory technologies associated with IA, including the overall bandwidth and latency between CPU and memory, have been evolving,[15] fetching data from off-chip memory is still expensive in CPU clock cycles. Reasonable performance here is (currently) approximately 500 M access/second which includes bus turnaround and statistical bank conflict—multiple banks increase the "width" of access as long as simultaneous accesses do not attempt the same bank at the same time (with a variable delay of 10–100 s of ns). Increasing the number of cores is (generally) going to increase the number of memory accesses and bandwidth requirement. Further, (generally), the more bandwidth (read) provided the greater the chance of conflict.

There is also a memory bandwidth effect due to packet processing. The nonoptimized flow for a packet would be from NIC to memory, memory to CPU and the reverse (assuming the same core handled RX and TX)—creating a memory bandwidth multiplier per operation.

At higher port speeds, with nonoptimized access to data in memory, it becomes untenable to maintain line rate packet processing (for our example 10 Gbps interface). Memory partitioning per CPU, pinning, etc. can optimize the access to soften the impact on aggregate memory bandwidth. And, IA is moving forward in subsequent "ticks" to increase the number of channels and introduce "better" (faster, more power efficient) memory. For example, Haswell will introduce an option to use DDR4 versus DDR3 memory.

However, external memory access is the greatest bottleneck for network I/O performance because the processor will generally stall (for hundreds of cycles) during these reads (strategies like hyperthreading and out-of-order execution can somewhat mitigate the impact of stalling).

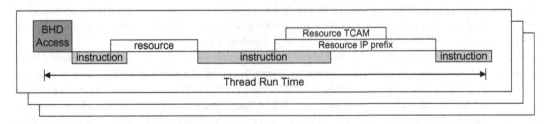

FIGURE 8.4

Multithreaded microcode and how it is used in traditional routers/switches.[13]

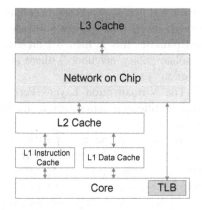

FIGURE 8.5

Typical/generic three-level cache structure for IA (c. 2013). L3 Cache (LLC) is shared resource. The L1 cache is depicted as separate data/instruction (not "unified").

Because of this, system design has moved to hierarchical chip caches (Fig. 8.5) and improving cache efficiency, mapping, and cache prediction.

In comparison with external memory, the shared last level cache (LLC) can be accessed at a significantly lower latency: the rate of one cache line every 26 clock cycles (on average ∼12 ns). The higher level caches operate even faster: L2 at 12 cycles (∼3 ns) and L1 at 4 cycles (∼1 ns or less with core pipelining). In general, the L1 cache can satisfy over a billion accesses per second with a variable (depending on cache state) but low latency.[16]

This is how we end up in the packet-handling scenario we painted earlier in the chapter. Optimizations[17] attempt to tweak the microarchitecture in such a way that, optimistically, all operations (data/instructions) remain in cache (keeping the cache "warm"), and the architecture performs (theoretically) at the access rate of the LLC.

However, cache is still a limited and shared resource, and it too has its own optimizations. Smaller caches can be oversubscribed (eg, hashing of real memory to virtual memory can lead to cache-line contention) and certain behaviors (as well as "sharing" between cores and peripherals) can cause interference (eg, read/write-back cycles can clash between CPU and device in the case of peripherals writing directly into cache lines), resulting in cache evictions and thrashing.

The complexities of multicore architectures extend into the memory controller and ultimately the cache controller, because locality of memory to processing can dominate latency. While preferable over off-chip memory access latencies, larger caches can introduce latency (of their own) and other management/design problems. Yet, for network I/O-centric applications, that is the direction that system design is taking (in both general size and cache line width).

In a three-level cache (depicted), the lowest level cache is inclusive—shared amongst all cores. Algorithms that partition or "share"[18] the cache to avoid interference between applications have been cropping up in academic research and have made it into the latest IAs.[19] Hyperthreading may add some complexity to allocation (requiring a finer granularity of allocation: the current allocation maps a core to a QOS class).

Until cache allocation is pervasive and useful or perhaps in conjunction with it, Intel offers potential cache conflict mitigation through cache management software.[20] Dynamic (external) resource monitoring and management (Intel proposes this in their SA architecture) enables management and orchestration entities to separate/isolate "noisy neighbors" (there is considerable academic research here as well on prediction and detection[21]).

As mentioned in Chapter 7, The Virtualization Layer—Performance, Packaging, and NFV, sharing of the LLC without hard partitioning introduces a number of security concerns when sharing in a multitenant environment.[22]

The layer 2 cache and the first level cache are specific to a core, but much smaller.[23] Dependency on this locality is a reason to avoid dynamic reassignment by the scheduler.

Some improvements in DPDK performance (version 1.7 over version 1.6) are attributable in part to newer processor chips assigning a bigger portion of L1–L2 cache to I/O (and DDIO allows the NIC to write buffer descriptors to that cache[24]). This creates a high degree of cache locality and size dependency for performance.

Obviously, not all is perfect in the reliance on caching for NFV. There is also a concern, dependent on the cache architecture, that network flows directed to a set of cores (from a NIC) may have little commonality (broader hash) increasing cache miss probability (unless you increase the cache size). Additionally, the combination of too large a data set being loaded by an application thread with either too small a cache, too busy a cache, or a small cache partition, will push strain back onto the memory bandwidth itself (which currently cannot be partitioned).

Beyond the problems introduced in the large shared cache, maintenance of the private caches introduced in the expanding number of cores introduces coherency issues (where updates to data shared by multiple processors do not propagate quickly enough to avoid invalid/stale reads make it harder to maintain proper ordering of reads and writes). The result of these pressures has been cache coherence strategies (eg, directories, snooping, and snarfing[25]) that have evolved over time to reduce bus transactions between processors, invalidations, and other sharing side effects of the various algorithms.

Although some performance-impacting cache behavior can be mitigated through compiler optimizations or by fastidious data structure design by the developer, the growth of caches in IA imply a very tightly coupled overall system design (where "system" implies "socket" and everything on that socket, including the on-chip network connecting the socket resources and reliability components, like coherency controllers). Coherence protocols (overhead) can dictate performance-related changes in cache architecture.[26]

Cache coherency will continue to play a role in the realization of concurrency and the synchronization and appearance of serialization necessary for multithreaded application design (the presentation of a consistent memory model for the developer). The recent "tick"/generation (Haswell) introduces coherence improvements to realize a form of hardware transactional memory (transactional synchronization extensions, TSX). TSX provides an abstraction for atomic transactions that can potentially avoid some of the pitfalls of more granular lock-based mechanisms.[27] As with almost *everything* we have talked about here, there are caveats in the use of TSX that might require additional optimizations.

Finally, beyond the simple system model (single socket) not all cache/memory access is the same—there is some concern around "locality" of memory. The QPI bus between sockets in the IA is a resource bottleneck for PCI traffic and NUMA node memory accesses.

A NUMA-unaware assignment of CPU resources (virtual and physical cores) to a VNF that straddles this bus will cause the application to be limited by the capacity and latency of the QPI bus.

PCIe—linking peripherals to the CPU

PCIexpress (PCIe) connections comprise the hardware path between peripherals, including accelerators and NICs and the CPU complex.

The current server and NIC market is comprised of a combination of older and newer PCI formats, splitting PCIe technology between version 2.0 and version 3.0 (Sandy Bridge EN/EP series now supports PCI 3.0).

The PCI SIG rates PCIe 2.0 at approximately 4 Gbps at 5.0 GHz[28] clock rate (in each direction).[29] PCIe 3.0 lanes are rated at approximately 8 Gbps.

The support for more/faster PCI connectivity has been scaling with the number of cores and sockets in the IA. For example, earlier versions of the Intel Xeon (E3—up to 10 cores in two sockets) supported 20 PCIe 2.0 lanes. The more recent E5(v2) versions come in two versions, 24 (EN) or 40 (EP) PCIe 3.0 lanes that could be configured in x4, x8, or x16 lane arrangements.[30] In the PCIe 3.0 configurations (x8), Intel can currently map up to 16 physical functions onto 128 virtual functions.[31]

The dominant 10GE NICs in the market are (currently) 8 lane PCIe 2.0 and the newer entrants are 4 lane PCIe 3.0 (40GE NICs are shipping that are 8 lane PCIe 3.0 and 100 Gbps NICs are shipping that are $2 \times 8 \times$ PCIe 3.0).

You really have to check the product literature for the controller to lane mappings. The E5v2 mappings are x4 on the DMI port (if you do not use DMI, it can be PCIe and they do not normally count these lanes in the total lane count). For most practical uses, there is (1) x8 lane and (1 or 2) x16 lane controllers, which can be subdivided logically further into 1, 2, or 4 ports (only on the 16 lane controller). This would set the maximum number of ports supported as well as their speeds— the ultimate limitation assuming you were going to use your PCIe bandwidth for no other peripherals.[32]

There is the potential to oversubscribe/undersubscribe the PCI bandwidth in a number of ways:

- A two-port 40GE NIC plugged into the 8 lane controller (PCIe 3.0) is technically oversubscribed (4 lanes or $\sim$ 32 Gbps would be allocated to each port).
- A one port 100GE plugged into a controller would underuse the PCI bandwidth of a 16 lane controller (128 Gbps), while a two port would seriously oversubscribe.

Some vendors are attempting to work around these static limitations by making PCIe control more programmable. Solutions normally introduce more hardware to create the appropriate mappings between peripherals and processors.

In mix-and-match systems the PCI connectivity (eg, a PCIe 3.0 NIC in a 2.0 system or vice versa) is going to throttle to the PCIe 2.0 rate (least common denominator). So, misalignment of your NIC and platform capability can be a potential handicap.

Just like NUMA awareness is required in vCPU/cache optimization, intelligent traffic distribution to those structures also has NUMA dependencies (each socket has its own I/O hub that aggregates peripherals). Proper alignment of PCI termination (creating an orchestrated channel from the NIC to function) requires architectural awareness—to avoid inadvertent use of the QPI bus (in current IAs).

Even with the advent of PCIe 3.0, PCI bandwidth can become a performance limitation on current Intel-based platforms. Additionally, we should expect PCI technology to continue to evolve to match Intel's product line.

In summary, performance claims may hinge on the availability and alignment of higher performance PCI technologies, and the introduction of PCI-connected accelerators may also stress this resource. PCI technology should see a next-gen evolution to keep in step with the changes in IA.

The bottom line for the digression into some of the hardware implications of the IA evolution is very basic—that Intel microarchitecture is on a constantly-changing course, including changes both subtle such as instruction set extensions, and profound including new memory technology, memory connectivity, cache size, upgraded PCIe support, inter-core connection, etc. Although other CPU vendors exist, the early dominance of Intel in NFV makes this easier (more documentation and available experience) to illustrate. We can by no means pretend that other microarchitectures are or will not follow similar trajectories. It is the fundamental awareness of this dynamic that is important to the discussion of NFV.

EXTENDING THE SYSTEM

Assuming that there is a knee in the productivity associated with additional cores or larger caches (particularly for network I/O focused applications), the pursuit of performance (throughput) via the hardware path enters into the arena of system augmentation. Most recently, the use of specialized silicon on the NIC and/or coprocessors (both off and on die) has started to garner attention.

Network interface cards

Capable NICs (via their drivers) can take advantage of Receive-Side scaling (RSS). This process creates many hardware-based receive queues for inbound processing distributing traffic (and interrupt requests, though this may require some tuning of the IRQ affinity) intelligently across physical cores (this has proven to be less effective with virtual cores). RSS also provides load-balancing support into these queues (though not for all protocols).

Intel has specific enhancements that are available on their NICs, including (part of their I/OAT technology):

- QuickData Technology—an on-chip DMA engine that enables data copy by the chipset instead of the CPU, and moves data in the background.
- Direct Cache Access (DCA)—alluded to earlier, allowing a device (like the NIC) to place data directly into CPU cache.
- Extended Message Signaled Interrupts (MSI-X)—distributes I/O interrupts to multiple CPUs and cores (has to be evaluated in your environment).
- Receive Side Coalescing (RSC)—aggregates packets from the same TCP/IP flow into one larger packet, reducing per-packet processing costs for faster TCP/IP processing.

NICs can also support encapsulation/decapsulation offload processing, reducing the CPU load for these hypervisor/vSwitch-based operations. These include offloads for the TCP/IP stack, checksum calculation, large segment support for transmit and receive (that shift the segmentation burden to the NIC) and tunnel header processing.

Often overlooked, the ability to offload simple network functions like VXLAN encapsulation can improve throughput (looking forward, the offload for the IETF encapsulation for service function chaining will see similar benefits).

These capabilities can be combined to direct packets to the appropriate DMA queue, aligned with the appropriate CPU for a specific VM and eliminate the need for hypervisor-related processing on the receive side. QoS-based queuing or traffic prioritization obviously plays a role in avoiding HOL (head of line) blocking.

Some of the turnkey environments for NFV boast their own (purportedly superior) load distribution algorithms.

The range of potential NIC coprocessing/offloaded functions is large. Netronome,[33] Cavium,[34] EZChip,[35] and Tilera[36] offer 100GE (or multiple 10GE) capable NICs that perform more like a traditional hardware switch with dense onboard core sets that can offload forwarding lookups, session termination, encryption, and other functionality.

With the new generation of NIC acceleration, there is an attempt to entirely avoid handling packets with socket cores. Because these accelerators are not in the primary processing socket, they will likely have a different development cadence (than the processor cores).

These NICs (generically depicted in Fig. 8.6) are essentially embedded NPUs.[37] These vendors go to lengths to point out how limited core processors and sequential operation is for networking

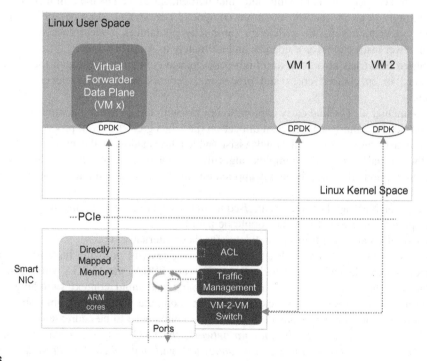

FIGURE 8.6

Smart NICs extend the network packet processing capabilities of core processors.

and how the migration toward heterogeneous cores (to provide parallelism) creates what their products already do (and how the data plane on the NIC and the control plane and application processing on the server CPU are more in tune with the SDN model).

With the number of cores they support (greater than 100 cores) they also pick on the need to dedicate cores for transmission management.

It seems natural that the smart NIC might be where dense, dedicated ARM cores might be leveraged against packet I/O processing. However, these solutions may not be restricted (over time) to use as an offload mechanism. EZChip has positioned its Tile-MX product line as not only an adapter but also as a standalone or blade-server NFV system (with hundreds of processors, they can support hundreds of VMs).

However, Intel is not staying still in the NIC market. They can (and will) integrate around their own switching silicon to create NIC appliance-like configurations with more offload(s), greater port densities and built-in hardware switching capabilities.

Heterogeneous cores

The multithreaded multicore processor designs of the IA with their large caches and superscalar (multiple instructions executed per cycle) or SIMD execution[38] have limits in achievable parallel processing and diminishing returns as cores are added.[39]

Detractors of this design/paradigm think that it cannot continue and point to the memory access issues, inter-chip connectivity bandwidth and other bottlenecks as well as the diminishing returns due to an increasingly large instruction set (more compound operations), slow compiler advancement, and lagging application software efficiency (atomicity guarantees, concurrence management and adoption of newer instructions) as evidence; and ultimately to Amdahl's Law.

A concerted effort has also gone into high-performance computation through the use of "dark," heterogeneous, or specialized cores and processors; network hardware coprocessors for feature acceleration.

The fundamental idea behind early exploration began with the idea that a nonuniform distribution of chip resources for a more task-efficient allocation (and thus greater overall processor speedup).

The original examples for Intel QuickAssist (which foreshadowed the need for coprocessing) included the "usual suspects"—complex algorithmic functions like QoS traffic management and IPSec encryption. But the vision for application of these cores amongst competitors is much broader.

In the case of NFV applications, scalar/sequential and parallel processing might be combined within the application (parallelize what should be parallel).

FPGA and GPUs are emerging as candidates for these alternative cores.

Like the assets on the "smart" NIC, these offload engines will probably have to be virtualized. The techniques used depend on the technology. For the FPGA, the vFPGA will most likely be realized through static or dynamic resource partitioning and rapid context switching. The GPU resource grouping is closer to the existing/generic compute model and amenable to virtual execution contexts (but limited resources like load/store units need to be addressed).

Until they are integrated into the on-chip network, the FPGA and GPU will be addressed as PCIe peripherals. The limits of the PCI bus bandwidth will make them less attractive than other offload technologies.

Intel has proposed an expansion of the DPDK API to address hardware acceleration.[40]

Parallel processing may require rethinking algorithms and programming approach (identify parallelism in the code), addressing weaknesses in hardware/software of existing hyper-sequential approaches. The potential to gain from this approach has large dependencies on how amenable the network I/O processing task is to parallelization (percentage of the overall work that can be parallel, predictability of data access, cache friendliness) and the return over existing tooling like SIMD. But the aforementioned challenges of the hypersequential approach may make it attractive to explore alternatives.

Field Programmable Gate Array

Historically, FPGA technology has been expensive and development tooling has been an issue and barrier to entry for use in the general compute environment.

FPGAs have long been used in specialized networking hardware because of their performance/programmability combination (more readily software reconfigurable than microcoded NPUs or ASICs). They also have seen some adaptation in the area of high performance compute due to their utility in parallel processing (eg, high frequency trading, oil/gas exploration, and genomics).

It is this latter, complimentary processing role that has NIC vendors adding them today (discrete FPGAs)[41] and CPU manufacturers planning put them into the socket (integrated) in the 2016 timeframe.

More than just a coprocessor, researchers are investigating the virtualization of the FPGA fabric as a shared resource (illustrated in Fig. 8.7).[42] It is possible that it could replace the vSwitch or vforwarder functionality entirely as well as augment processing in VNFs. Communication can take advantage of most of the previously covered copy and context reduction technologies (DPDK shown).

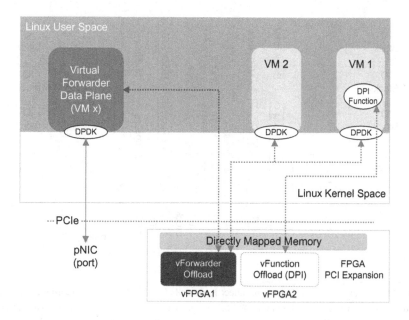

FIGURE 8.7

Discreet FPGA can be incorporated in the NIC or a plug-in coprocessor (leveraging PCI).

The FPGA is a collection of memory and logical/computation cells (lookup tables and flip-flops) that can be composed into logic blocks, block RAMs (ie, storage), DSPs, and Etherent/PCIe communication/IO cores. While not particularly strong on floating point calculation (like the GPU or via the Intel AVX instructions a GPU), they do have some resources specifically for this sort of calculation. In these cases, range and precision are controlled since they affect chip area and memory bandwidth. FPGAs are now commonly packaged like a SoC (ie, a system on chip), combined with multiple ARM or other processors as a common fabric.

Multiple systolic arrays (kernels) are created across these resources that enable stream processing—multiple computational steps with minimal memory accesses (storing intermediate results—memory is distributed along with the logic blocks)—illustrated in Fig. 8.8.

The speedup comes from the number of simultaneous operations that can be done per clock time. The pipeline takes data in and does the first logical operation/action in the array (first logic cell or block) then recycles the intermediate result to the next cell/block for the next operation on next clock edge while new data is hitting the original cell/block. Typical "data machines" are several hundred logical blocks long and input/output can be across multiple pins, generating thousands of simultaneous operations once the pipeline is full.

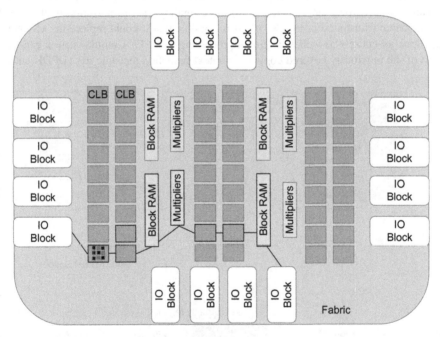

FIGURE 8.8

FPGA routing channels over a fabric that interconnect logic cells into logic blocks—creating a pipeline that includes resources like RAM access (RAM can be "block" or distributed), arithmetic logic (Multiplier), DSPs, or microprocessors (not shown). These systolic arrays connect to the outside world through the IO blocks (potentially entering and exiting through the same block/pin set).

Host memory provides source data. The accelerator is surrounded with shared memory for storing intermediate results between the accelerator and host, acting as a buffer. Memory choreography/synchronization is important and multiple incoming memory stream support is desirable.

Performance is a function of both the density (major vendors like Xilinx and Altera offer FPGAs with densities that exceed a million logical cells, thousands of DSP slices, support more than 50 Mbits of block RAM and implement enough transceivers to support multi-gigabit communication) of the cells/blocks and the efficiency with which the program is mapped to resources.[43]

FPGA acceleration is not automatic. The application is profiled to create a dataflow graph. From this, the compiler creates a dataflow machine used to reconfigure the FPGA. Dataflow machine size is limited by the size/area of FPGA, DRAM access, and pin bandwidth. Optimizations require a lot of effort and considerable tooling. Iteratively, successive dataflow graphs are generated and analyzed to derive a best fit on the available resources.

For a long time, the tooling required the use of specialized hardware description languages (Verilog, VHDL) and compilers and design was an art form. Recently, some vendors have come to market with higher-level language compilation and optimization support (eg, transforming runnable Java code into a data flow graph and optimizing that via kernel compilation to generate an FPGA structure[44]). These compilers can drive the orchestration of routine execution between a generic CPU (eg, Intel) running a specially adapted OS (eg, Linux) with a management program complement on the FPGA.

Nothing is static, and like the sequential processing solutions, FPGAs will also need to grow in capacity at a reasonable rate to provide more processing power.

In the end, the comparison of the ongoing growth cycles of CPU and FPGA technologies pits the growth in cell density of the FPGA versus core density growth of the CPU (at diminishing gains of clock rate). Similarly, it pits the dataflow mapping/special-compilation methodology of the FPGA versus the flow-mapping-to-core techniques and cache efficiency chase on the CPU. FPGA have advantages in power efficiency, particularly as the multicore paradigm has reached its efficiency "knee" (the point from which solutions take more power and generate more heat).

Integration of the FPGA in the CPU socket where FPGA is used as a heterogeneous core provides the mechanism for a synchronized tick/tock innovation cycle and eliminates a potential PCI bottleneck. Intel's acquisition of Altera has already manifested by the inclusion of FPGA on die in some Xeon variants and is expected to ship in 2016. It remains to be seen if integrators will take advantage of it.

Finally, although new tooling exists for FPGAs, there is still limited choice. Solutions are still needed on the software development side to soften the cost of development and additional tooling.

Graphics processing unit

GPUs are potential accelerators and have been used in research like Packetshader.[45] Like FPGA, they are used in High Performance Computing and have consumer applications (eg, gaming).

While the GPU was originally developed specifically for graphics processing (rasterization, shading, 3D, etc.), it has evolved to a more general-purpose programming model (GPGPU) that allows the GPU to be treated like a multicore processor (with an equally large, independent memory space). Many universities have curricula that include parallel programming techniques and include the use of CUDA,[46] a domain-specific language for NVIDIA GPUs.

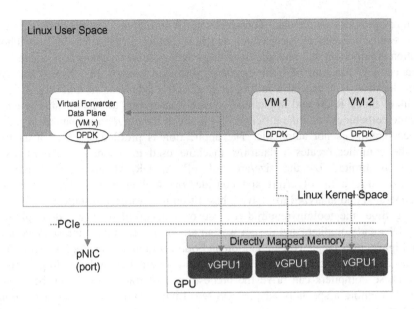

FIGURE 8.9

Graphics processing unit.

As generically illustrated in Fig. 8.9, the virtualized GPU processors could be directly mapped to VMs/containers possibly reducing their host resource requirements or used as standalone machines. Like the connectivity in the discreet FPGA, a number of copy/context saving mechanisms could be leveraged to provide access between the GPU and other cores. Most notably, this can result in the use of incoherent shared memory.[47]

Makers like NVIDEA[48] and AMD[49] offer products designed for more general compute tasks (parallel compute focus) with multiple streaming multiprocessors (SMs) on a die—each with 32 or more ALU (currently driving total core-equivalent density well into the hundreds)—illustrated in Fig. 8.10. Overall performance of these products is measured in many hundreds of GFLOPS (10^9 Floating Point Operations per Second). Be forewarned, not all GPU architectures are the same, even within the same manufacturer (they have application-focused designs).[50]

GPUs also use caching as arbitrage against memory access, though they currently are being designed with significantly greater memory bandwidth that may ultimately decrease this dependency.

As with the FPGA, SoC architectures with integrated GPP cores are emerging. (Intel's Haswell has an integrated GPU with up to 40 "execution units." Sandy Bridge and Ivy Bridge had models with up to 12 or 16 "execution units," respectively.) This is still a much smaller size than is seen in designs mentioned earlier.

It remains to be seen if a large enough, on-socket GPU will evolve to be a serious network I/O off-load processor. Power consumption and resulting heat may make this a difficult design point. Until then, the use of the GPU as a PCI peripheral for this purpose will probably NOT be the best

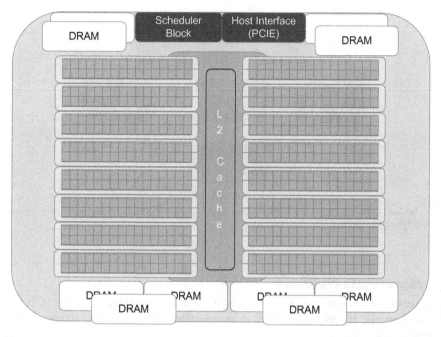

FIGURE 8.10

A high-level view of GPU architecture, with its many multicore streaming processors (16SM × 32ALU depicted), thread scheduling and data caching.

solution for this application because of limitations imposed both by PCI bandwidth and round-trip latency from NIC to GPU.

In addition, GPUs have also proven to be more difficult to virtualize/share than the cohort of competing technologies covered in this chapter.

The GPU cores are optimized for threads with long running series of computations and devote more area to this than is seen in the design of a generic processor architecture (lA).

Basic GPU programming technique creates a "kernel"—the computational component of an algorithm. Note that this is not the same concept as an OS kernel. Applications or libraries can have one or more "kernels." After compilation, the "kernel" can be many threads, which execute the same routine. The threads can then be assembled into "blocks" of greater than a thousand threads, limited by scheduler capability to execute on an SM. This creates opportunities to share memory. In the case of NVIDEA, execution is in groups of 32 threads within the SM (ie, a "warp")—even though in some cases, the number of ALUs in an SM is only 16 due to a higher clock rate for the ALUs. The GPU can also switch in and out of applications in tens of microseconds. All of which can be used to create large scale parallel processing such as multithreaded SIMD.

GPUs support their own ISAs and have their own unique development environments. These products support higher-level languages like C, C++, Java, and Python.

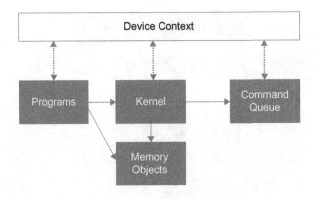

FIGURE 8.11

OpenCL model (generalization).

Heterogeneous compute challenges

Hardware diversity introduces complications, and a number of challenges emerge in heterogeneous compute environments, particularly tooling, core selection, and application steering (almost all of them borne by the developer).

From a tooling perspective, OpenCL[51] is emerging as an API set and kernel specification for describing and programming heterogeneous compute models.

OpenCL is a very large idea; first, it is open source and second it is trying to provide a description language for multiple processor types. It is an abstraction of the underlying hardware.

For a developer, the chip manufacturer needs to stand up a product-specific OpenCL SDK, and a large number already have (NVIDIA, Altera, Intel).

The OpenCL model (Fig. 8.11) starts with inventory of the OpenCL capable devices on the host creating what OpenCL dubs a "context." Per-device programs are created, driven from the context associated devices. The basic unit of work is analogous to a function or the "kernel" in FPGA. These kernels are grouped as the equivalent of a program. OpenCL makes the analogy of a dynamic library with runtime linking.

Kernels are queued along with data transfers to different context elements for in-order or out-of-order execution. The individual kernel/functions are the equivalent of a thread and these can be grouped to create beneficial behaviors common to a "core" (eg, sharing local memory). OpenCL 2.0 allows the queueing control to be decentralized. OpenCL devices can queue kernels to themselves iteratively.

OpenCL also has to grapple with the concepts of shared virtual memory if and how the host and the accelerator pass data back and forth, language atomics support, and synchronization.

The kernel queuing above does raise some questions about scheduling optimization. Conventional thread scheduling is fairness/priority/affinity-centric in its algorithm(s). Some prior work is available around scheduling with monotonically increasing homogeneous processors such as different power/capability or the same ISA. That aside, with heterogeneous cores and accelerators, tasks will run on different processors with different efficiencies and modalities (SIMD or SPMD) requiring specialized processing distribution strategies.[52] Some vendors outside of the OpenCL project are already suggesting "middleware"-like schemes for the SoC network to enable "demand scheduling." Academic research is also beginning to investigate this problem.

There are some preliminary performance studies using OpenCL versus vendor-specific languages to program GPUs for a specific application such as video, but for a wider field of use performance has not been explored and what would be the basis for comparison. OpenCL cites a number of benchmark routines that leverage OpenCL, but the application is still largely video.

It remains to be seen if OpenCL will successfully address the development challenge in heterogeneous computing (programming for parallel processing requires not only new tools but an arguably different mindset/approach). They do boast support (via language extension, wrapper, compiler directive, etc.) in a number of tool chains, incorporation in a wide range of projects, and university-level courseware availability and adoption—all good signs of traction in the industry.

Nor is OpenCL the ONLY alternative here, as both OpenGL[53] and OpenMP[54] are attempting to promote their own communities with the same general ideas with slight variances in focus.

All the potential for tooling aside, it is unclear whether heterogeneity may still introduce software portability problems. It will certainly make scheduling more complex—even if we can overcome the first-order problem of effectively dividing the work into schedulable units.

There may also be some general/high-level impact from the use of heterogeneous cores and smart NICs on VM migration, which (for some) is required for NFV elasticity/HA. Similarly, upstream (orchestration) impacts on packaging and image management will also need to be ironed out.

In the end, further venture down this road might make the casual observer ask "aren't you building a dedicated appliance . . . again?"

ARM

This chapter focuses primarily on IA based solutions. But, as noted earlier, there are other multicore CPU makers in the market.

The 64-bit ARMv8[55] (and accompanying ISA) has become a credible alternative, with many traditional CPU manufacturers developing ARM complements to existing products or ARM standalones.

This camp obviously backs the extension of COTS compute to do network services, but currently offers lower power consumption than the IA. The first commercial 8-core were touted by some to have a 50% greater power efficiency compared to equivalent Intel SoCs, but apples-to-apples comparison is difficult.[56] ARM also offers what it markets as a better virtualization and security environment (TrustZone).

Hidden more deeply are architectural differences between ARM and Intel around concurrency with specific bearing on multicore systems. ARM supports a relaxed memory model that comes into play when multicore systems perform a "load" operation. The more-strictly-ordered Intel environment enforces a synchronization step between the cores to make sure one has not written to the cache location the load will access. Newer lock-free/wait-free algorithms can take advantage of the relaxed memory model of ARM, but do not have the same advantages on Intel.[57] There are also subtle differences in core-interconnectivity (fabrics) and coherency strategies.

The potential problem with the use of ARM in NFV (and the complement or heterogeneous core environments just discussed) is the need to support two ISAs and their tool chains (for application developers). This may become less onerous over time as ARM is dominating in distribution of tablet computers, phones, and smaller devices—making the support of ARM development inevitable.

Linaro[58] provides open source tools, compilers, and Linux support to ARM.

Turnkey (or "easy button") deployment environments (eg, 6Wind) are also available for ARM.

ARM designs have the luxury of a large presence in non-server compute markets, particularly in smaller form-factor products like mobile phones and IoT devices, that allows them to continue to evolve a server solution competitive with Intel.

PERFORMANCE MEASUREMENT

How can a vRouter vendor claim "120 Gbps of throughput per socket!" yet realize only 10 or 20 Gbps throughput on the multisocket server in your lab?

At a recent conference, an attendee asked a multivendor panel "is there any standardized measurement of performance for NFV?" By this point, the reader should realize how difficult the answer to that question might be. With the fluidity of virtualization architecture driven by ongoing software and hardware based network I/O evolution, there are multiple variables that can control the outcome. The latter evolution will directly affect the standalone performance of a service function, while the former will affect the performance of a service (multifunction). Further, depending on the evolution of metadata passing for SFC, specific services may perform better overall if the components pass metadata while that capability might be inconsequential to a standalone test.

It is not hard, however, to see why the answer is so desperately needed for consumers. Not surprisingly, prior to any real standards existing for NFV or SFC, vendors are already publishing performance claims for specific functions. As usual for our industry, these claims typically "hero" tests measuring port-to-port throughput without application operations—essentially, pipeline speed. In short order, as multiple vendors adopt the same virtualization methodologies, software tricks and base hardware, these claims all normalize except for some lingering and possibly purposeful ambiguity about how a vendor "counts" throughput.

So, how DO you measure performance?

MEASURING PERFORMANCE

Expectations for performance testing for virtualized service can get quite complicated.

However, establishing the formal testing methodology is the beginning of potential test work—as it can then be applied across a number of viable deployment permutations.

The test should start by aligning the physical and virtual resources appropriately for the microarchitecture (eg, avoiding NUMA and PCI problems).[59] This consideration can be simplified somewhat by not fully loading the host (ie, "fully loaded" may be a separate scale test case).

The test permutations would include, roughly: the forwarder by itself, the VNF by itself, the forwarder and the VNF, a forwarder and multiple VNFs on the same host with parallel streams and a forwarder with multiple VNFs in a service chain. The virtual forwarder can be placed in the host or guest OS. There can be have multiple sometimes combined, acceleration techniques and virtualization environments (VMs, containers, hybrids).

A comparative test might also iterate through forwarders (eg, OVS, VPP, Snabbswitch[60]) and potentially multiple similar applications from different vendors. Should the test include service chains, the permutations of multiple vendor products would also have to be factored.

While it seems like the permutations are endless, by starting with an agreed-upon methodology, time and automation favor a solution. The very process of testing will eliminate or at least define the appropriateness of different permutations—and over time, noneffective ones will phase out (we learn more through comprehensive testing). The process will also end the period of wild but either inappropriate to deployment or unverifiable vendor performance claims.

The testing might be feature-, role-, or service-specific. Academic tests or shallow L2 port-in-port-out tests may not give an accurate view of performance and scale. Role-based tests are more expensive to craft and standardize, and agreed upon (existing) standardized role tests may need adaptation to a virtual environment.

Anecdotally, RFC 2544 methodology proved to be nondeterministic when applied to vRouter applications without some changes. It did this by showing a binary search in this context to provide maximum throughput for a specific loss tolerance and packet size. A methodology that extends RFC 2544 for NFV involves multiple runs that statistically smooth out behavior can lead to consistent results (eg, using a linear step method around worst/best measurements).

Numerous IETF proposals around this methodology exist. The vNet-SLA methodology proposed by Cisco Systems applies this idea (and was presented to OPNFV).[61]

A second round of problems will have to be addressed when comparing different hardware acceleration methodologies, once they become widely available.

This is a problem that directly confronts an organization like OPNFV, which they will attempt to pursue through their VSPERF work.

Meanwhile, several vendors have resorted to external testing for validation (Cisco and ALU have both gone to EANTC).[62,63]

POWER EFFICIENCY

Up to this point, there have been hints in the book that something unexpected might happen when an operator "switches to NFV" for their services. The unexpected impact is in power efficiency.

If the model for COTS compute for NFV is the general data center web application, then the operator might expect the average power consumption quoted for a particular server in that environment, where performance guarantees and power efficiency trade-offs, while orthogonal on the x86 platform are well understood.

The big difference for network I/O centric applications lies in the poll mode driver (as compared to an interrupt-driven mode) of some of the proposed performance enhancements. If you do not poll and use the built-in system power management (automatic frequency adjustment, idle sleep, etc.) the CPU clock will vary (eg, from 2.5–3.2 GHz to 400–800 MHz) and at very low clock rates, memory clocks may drop on some chipsets as well. Obviously, performance guarantees are no longer possible, but longer box life and lower power consumption are great trade-offs/compensations.

On the other hand, an implementation which operates strictly in poll mode, polls network devices constantly and feeds into a run-to-completion software stack which returns control to the poll loop until more data becomes available. Such an operation will consume the maximum power budget $24 \times 7 \times 365$ by design and, for some designs, could exceed the maximum thermal limits of a rack, row or datacenter altogether.

Right now, relief in this paradigm is hard to find. Perhaps, it may be possible for the polling mode drivers (such as DPDK) to be enhanced to do the power management themselves (work in post 2.0 DPDK on the RX thread may provide opportunities), eg, reducing the CPU clock-speed and/or turning cores off based on multiple successive polls that return no data.

At first blush, adding GPUs and FPGA to an existing generic processor can also be expensive from a power perspective, but studies show that they are both more energy efficient for a unit of work.[64] Both have power efficient operational modes (eg, hibernation) but could be as compromised as those in the generic processor unless the pipeline is empty. PCIE based cards can consume several hundred Watts, and directly adding FPGA/GPU will not make the generic CPU die operate any cooler. On-die accelerators will be a smaller form factor compared to their card-based counterparts with different overall capability and thermal impact. However, the longer impact may be more cost-efficient as the use of the GPU or FPGA could significantly decrease the number of required CPUs overall in a pure CPU environment.

CONCLUSION

It is a little ironic that the continuing cycle of hardware refresh that was the bane of network operations in the past, is now one of the accepted assumptions of anyone wishing to operationalize NFV or its related concepts. Hardware changes are thankfully less subtle than those in software. However, just as we saw with software enhancement for NFV, hardware enhancement needs to be quickly integrated into orchestration schemes and systems so that it is managed in operational environments appropriately. Resource management complexity needs to be managed in order to avoid recreating the equipment/inventory management challenges associated with the "dedicated appliances" environment that NFV is promising to replace.

The good news is that NFV has, and will continue, to motivate CPU vendors to push optimizations in cache design, additional core capacity including the number of sockets and cores per socket, new core types and internal communications bus technologies and strategies to address network I/O bottlenecks. NIC vendors similarly will continue to offer alternative or complimentary relief strategies including localized processing power offloads and hardware assists. Both traditional and new vendors may offer heterogeneous cores or exploit GPUs to achieve these continuously improving goals.

Our quick but detailed examination of the hardware evolution also leaves us with some questions:

- To repeat the question from the software performance chapter, will the economics really work for NFV when the power and cost of hardware performance enhancement are factored in? Are we factoring in the cost of continual integration of new/improved solutions?
- *How is adding an I/O accelerator ultimately any different than building a dedicated appliance? If operators build a "Telco DC" full of I/O specialized platforms in support of NFV, how many*

variants are supportable before the idea of "theoretically substitutable infrastructure" mentioned in Chapter 2 is not recognizable?

- Will Intel be able to continue to evolve their architecture for NFV in a cost-effective way, or will the architecture splinter into a number of potential solutions (specialization)? If so, see the preceding questions.
- We need to focus on repeatable and standardized tests or benchmarks to assess performance/cost trade-offs and make accurate comparisons. Can OPNFV or some other forum provide an objective way to do this?

The overriding attraction of service creation, operational agility, and elasticity in NFV may still make the complications of performance enhancing specialization acceptable if it is pursued, and keep NFV attractive.

The proliferation of solutions today may also be a short-term problem as the market determines the proper optimization trade-offs going forward and/or as consumers opt again for the original NFV proposition by deploying only what is commonly available or nonspecialized. This may sacrifice some short-term potential performance (cost) for longer-term operational simplicity.

END NOTES

1. Most analysis through the end of 2013 involved the Intel Sandy Bridge micro-architecture.
2. http://deliveryimages.acm.org/10.1145/2190000/2181798/horowitz_fig7.png.
3. Introduced with Sandy Bridge micro-architecture. By no coincidence, Sandy Bridge cores have multiple ALUs.
4. The CPU itself and the compiler can also perform optimizations that induce reordered instructions. Depending on development language and compiler, developers use constructs like locks, memory fences, and atomic instructions to avoid reordering at the CPU or compiler level.
5. Besides the L1 and L2 caches (which can lead to invalidations as they clash) and the TLB, the threads share the FPU, integer math unit and other structures; even the optimizing resources like the ROB and (ultimately) the instruction bandwidth itself. There can also be affects related to power management.
6. Run-to-completion typically uses an RSS-capable NIC to distribute flows to multiple cores (enhanced flow distribution algorithms can be a feature of turn-key environments discussed earlier), each running the complete suite of tasks. The "pipeline" model directs the flow to sequential cores (or vCPU), each executing specific tasks in the application.
7. "First-generation" network application functionality (rough theoretical) processing workload: packet receive/transmit (22%), 5-tuple classification (15%), forwarding lookup (33%), and the remaining 30% for the actual value-add application processing.
8. One of the early negatives associated with the multicore approach was the lack of robust "parallel" software development methodology and tools.
9. Amdhal's Law.
10. https://existentialtype.wordpress.com/2011/03/17/parallelism-is-not-concurrency/.
11. For a device dedicated to packet I/O, memory access bandwidth can become a multiple of port speed. This could be two to three times, if not more for read, write, refresh—including inefficiencies and excluding the obvious multiplier that replication might invoke (multiple reads).
12. *Direct Cache Access for High Bandwidth Network I/O*, Huggahalli, Iyer, Tetrick Intel Corp. 2005.

13. Many NPUs are composed of extremely dense/numerous packet processing engines creating high thread densities and optimize memory access parallelism within a packet. Hardware resources (TCAM, TBM) provide atomic operations for features (eg, policing, ACL, prefix look-up).

14. From a hardware perspective, the differences between the network-specific processor and the generic compute processor boil down not to density of transistors but to the use of those transistors. From a software perspective, NPUs have transport management advantages—for example, they do not require the overhead of a descriptor mechanism (direct mapping).

15. Server memory enhancements have historically focused more on size/bandwidth/channel density and less on latency.

16. Absolute numbers are going to vary by architecture (these numbers reflect a specific architectural arrangement as a reference), what is important here is the *relative* penalties for accessing memory versus different cache levels.

17. Some of the DPDK library optimizations, particularly the memory libraries and the use of huge pages, are designed to improve cache and TLB performance. Pragmatically, data length should be aligned with cache line length.

18. people.csail.mit.edu/sanchez/papers/2013.jigsaw.pact.pdf.

19. Intel's cache allocation offering is based on QoS. In reality, it's currently limited and not for the faint of heart. See https://github.com/01org/intel-cmt-cat and the referenced software development manual.

20. Not all Intel SKUs support both CMT and CAT. As a generalization, these were introduced with the E5 2600 v3 series (Broadwell). See http://www.intel.com/content/www/us/en/communications/cache-monitoring-cache-allocation-technologies.html.

21. Great background can be found in http://csl.stanford.edu/~christos/publications/2015.heracles.isca.pdf.

22. Another deep rabbit hole for the curious; this is particularly well demonstrated in some of the presentations around cryptologic research (stealing your keys is one potential side effect). See https://eprint.iacr.org/2015/898.pdf for a nice start on the subject.

23. For example, on a four core Xeon system (c. 2013), the L1 cache would be 64 KB, the L2 would be 128 KB and the L3 could be up to 20 MB. As the number of cores has ramped, the L3 cache has continued to grow. The size of the L3 cache essentially limits the size of the overall dataset that can be cached, which can have more effect on performance than the number of cores.

24. Direct Cache Access (implemented as DDIO) is made possible through changes in Intel's cache management (over time) to support a combination write-allocate and write-update cache policies that are highly optimized for packet I/O. Write-allocate enables fetch-on-write, which has obvious advantages in skipping a memory read when the packet is received. Write-update is a greedy way of assuring concurrence if a cache block is updated. On the off-chance that another thread on another processor accessed the same data location/block (from the cache or from memory), any local update is broadcast to all caches containing a copy.

25. http://www.numascale.com/snooping.html.

26. Cache coherency does not guarantee "safe" concurrency, because the CPU architecture can reorder load/store operations (so the burden of "safe" concurrent development remains with these multicore architectures). Cache coherency protocol overhead also increases with core count. Although a rather deep rabbit hole, http://www.microarch.org/micro40/talks/3B-1.pdf is a reasonable start.

27. The original implementation had a defect that pushed a usable implementation into the Broadwell release ("tick"), though the Haswell EX models were not affected.

28. Some older NICs ran at a 2.5 GHz clock rate, so you effectively halved the throughput.

29. There is an art in quoting performance numbers when it comes to networking. Often, quoting aggregate bandwidth capability implies that if traffic were not uniformly bidirectional the excess capacity can be

used to support greater bandwidth one way. This is only true if the resource limitation is shared (eg, processing), but in the case of communication links, the resource is often not shared—the bandwidth of the link itself (constrained by signaling speed). Thus, there is a difference between the terms "bandwidth" and "forwarding performance."

30. The PCIE mapping change required to support some of the new-to-market 100 Gbps NICs may require a BIOS change to support 2x8 PCIEv3 landing.
31. As mentioned in this chapter, there is a difference between theoretical mapping and practical mapping limits.
32. That means technically, on the current EN or EP you will not be able to get more than 192/320 Gbps (respectively) per socket (theoretically—there will be signaling overhead that drags this down as well).
33. http://www.netronome.com.
34. http://www.cavium.com.
35. http://www.ezchip.com.
36. http://www.tilera.com was acquired by EZChip.
37. The NPU is not ALWAYS a pipelined ASIC but may instead be a managed bank of small microprocessors—essentially, arrays of "cores" that can be dedicated through specialized microcode to specific tasks.
38. Superscalar provides ILP.
39. This statement is apropos to the spread of a single workload over multiple cores (like the example of vRouter scale in Chapter 1: Network Function Virtualization) than the traditional multitenant cloud compute environment (discrete workloads on discrete resources).
40. https://networkbuilders.intel.com/docs/aug_17/Future_Enhancements_to_DPDK_Framework.pdf.
41. Until "integrated," if the FPGA functions as a "coprocessor" it is connected to the core socket via PCIe. This is not as much an issue if the function is as "preprocessor"—implying the need for a lower bandwidth connection (more of a control channel).
42. http://www.ntu.edu.sg/home/sfahmy/files/papers/asap2013-khoa.pdf.
43. Just as we saw with the COTS multiprocessor, data/memory locality is critical. The FPGA memory dispersion and dataflow mapping appears (at a high level) as a more strict application of data/memory locality requirements.
44. http://www.maxeler.com.
45. http://www.ndsl.kaist.edu/~kyoungsoo/papers/packetshader.pdf, Packet Shader: a GPU Accelerated Software Router (Han, Jang, Park, Moon).
46. CUDA (https://developer.nvidia.com/about-cuda) has evolved into an open parallel programming project (openMP) (see http://openmp.org/wp/).
47. Coherent memory is possible if the FPGA or GPU share a common socket, on-chip network, memory and memory controller.
48. http://www.nvidea.com.
49. http://www.amd.com.
50. http://www.nvidia.com/content/PDF/kepler/NV_DS_Tesla_KCompute_Arch_May_2012_LR.pdf. The Kepler architecture for High Performance Compute (NVIDEA).
51. https://www.khronos.org/opencl/.
52. Of course, the compute device in question has to be modeled as a resource.
53. https://www.opengl.org/.
54. http://openmp.org/wp/.
55. http://www.arm.com.
56. http://www.extremetech.com/extreme/146850-facebook-arm-x86-and-the-future-of-the-data-center.
57. http://concurrencyfreaks.blogspot.com/2013/12/the-rise-and-fall-of-x86.html.
58. http://www.linaro.org/.

59. Of course, the test could be less performance-oriented and more deployment-oriented, in which case the OpenStack distribution (and patch set) intended for deployment will do whatever placement optimization is possible.
60. http://snabb.co/.
61. http://events.linuxfoundation.org/sites/events/files/slides/OPNFV_VSPERF_v10.pdf.
62. http://www.lightreading.com/nfv/nfv-tests-and-trials/validating-ciscos-nfv-infrastructure-pt-1/d/d-id/718684.
63. http://www.lightreading.com/ethernet-ip/new-ip/validating-nokias-ip-routing-and-mobile-gateway-vnfs/d/d-id/720902.
64. An older, but good, paper on the subject: http://research.microsoft.com/en-us/people/erchung/heterogeneous.pdf.

AN NFV FUTURE

INTRODUCTION

Throughout this book, we have tried to bring the reader along on the evolution of thinking about Network Function Virtualization and in the process instill an understanding of both its potential problems (as realized today) and potential future benefits for network operators.

We have introduced the basic problems in service creation that provided the impetus for a change in paradigm. We moved through a monolithic physical hardware service solution, through aggregates of appliances to the proposition that service functions could be disaggregated and chained together as if a collection of Lego blocks. This latter state is what is commonly referred to today as Network Function Virtualization and the corresponding connection of these virtualized functions Service Function Chaining.

We have discussed the involvement of various groups in defining the conversation, technical details, Standards applicable, and best practices around NFV.

We have taken a look at some of the solution components defined by operators and implemented by vendors through the lens of an open source project, specifically the big ETSI architectural blocks of NFVI and MANO.

We have described the evolution of virtualization techniques, target hardware, and solution packaging: an ever-changing landscape.

By the time of the printing of this book, the world will have already moved forward in the evolutionary process of NFV by some four-to-six months. Given the rate of change we have described and our numerous observations on avenues for further evolution, our conclusion has to be that the material we surveyed above is by no means the end of the road for this topic.

But if this is not the end of the road for NFV, where do we go from here? We could start by working on the current NFV model, because it does not seem to make sense economically (yet).

In this chapter, we will summarize the major points from the past, paint a brief picture of the present and set a course for the future. Our final chapter is not the end of a story. Like SDN before it, NFV has a long way to go.

WHAT IS NFV (RESTATED)?

In our first chapter, we defined NFV as a concept that builds on some of the basic and now salient concepts of SDN and the evolution of virtualization technology to realize network functions on commodity (COTS) hardware platforms. These include control/data plane separation, logical centralization, controllers, application awareness, and application intent control.

We also said NFV was about service creation and that its true value would be realized through a combination of SFC and OSS modernization (the latter reemphasized in the Chapter 6: MANO: Management, Orchestration, OSS, and Service Assurance).

From a business perspective, NFV is more than these things. NFV is an exercise in massive organizational change as much as technology.

THE CURRENT NFV MODEL

We are in a phase of NFV that is destined to change.

The starting point for NFV—the ETSI mandated architecture—is a familiar movie for anyone familiar with the telco world. They can easily draw comparisons with the specification of IMS.[1]

It is the habit of telco engineers to specify a solution in a manner that there are many ambiguous interfaces that are impossible to extract and implement singly. So, vendors ultimately implement the functionality in one big integrated bundle. We already see some customers already drifting that way.

Because of, or in spite of, its appeal and necessity, NFV exists in a currently chaotic environment. ETSI is continually working on its model, trying to distance it from the fates of models like IMS. Will additional interface models fix fundamental problems?

The implied open source focus of the participants has led to a confusing number of initiatives to expand, define, and develop NFV. Everyone (and we mean *everyone*) is trying to take the beach so to speak, and declare that their approach—open source or otherwise—can completely and utterly address the ETSI base architecture in the best way. Truth and promises compared to reality are still a little different—quite a bit in some cases.

There are positive signs. NSH is showing the first signs of being adopted (a service is no longer a single function) and some providers are now talking with more about microservices and complex virtual network functions (VNFs) (particularly those with mobile-oriented use cases).

But, as we have hinted throughout the latter part of the book, the question is whether we are following the right model. We are three years into PoCs and early implementations and it's still not clear.

One of our reviewers posed the question differently:

Web scale providers are executing over-the-top (OTT) services without the strictures of the ETSI architecture and have been for years. Why are we bound to this architecture if it's not clear that it's a winner?

THE COST OF NFV

Stepping back a bit, it is important to note that one of the often-cited premises of NFV was a massive reduction of OPEX and CAPEX costs around network services.

Certainly, there will be an architecture that delivers on the goals of NFV for which costs and saving cross the threshold of our expectations and needs. But, it is difficult to pinpoint where that horizon in which NFV CAPEX and OPEX savings combine—against the balance of the cost of transition, declining costs in existing solutions, increased OPEX spend on security and NG-OSS— to deliver on that premise.

We have referenced repeatedly the troubling lack of a comprehensive and compelling financial model. We have talked about the cost of infrastructure (including new OPEX in increased ongoing power costs, orchestration, and security) that will be incurred to implement NFV-based services and the implied reductions in operations expense (OPEX).

The simple equation below might help with some basic reasoning around such a model.

TC_non-virt >> TC_NFV (virtualized)

Total Cost (TC) = cost of CAPEX + cost of OPEX over service lifetime

The equation above illustrates a hard reality around virtualization regardless of the mechanisms as described earlier in Chapter 5, The NFV Infrastructure Management; Chapter 7, The Virtualization Layer—Performance, Packaging, and NFV; and Chapter 8, NFV Infrastructure—Hardware Evolution and Testing, as well as whether or not the virtualized component is considered "aggregated" or "disaggregated." What it says simply is that the total cost of both acquiring and operating a service built from virtualized components must be *quite a bit less* expensive than the equivalent nonvirtualized version. This implies that it can be made more profitable too, but that depends on the business and its operations in question, so we will not consider that for the moment.

Thinking about the equation above, one will observe that the complexity of TC_NFV component and the obscurity of existing service-related OPEX for the existing methodology make it harder to state definitively that the equation is true—that NFV "works."

To start with, there are potentially so many more moving software parts in the NFV go-to-market operational configuration. In contrast to an nonvirtualized version of a physical device—say a popular routing platform (with its attendant orchestration)—the operational cost considerations of a comparable aggregated virtualized solution must now not only include the traditional EMS/NMS and orchestration (our MANO/OSS layer) used to commission, manage, and de-commission services, but must now *also* include a potential virtualization layer (the hypervisor, perhaps less so if a container is used in a pure container environment, but virtualization is not "free"), VNF and infrastructure lifecycle management system (our VIM, eg, VMware or Openstack), including service chaining, resource optimization, and security components in order to operate effectively at scale.

While the cost of the actual VNF might be cheaper than the physical equivalent or at least be consumable dynamically on an at-needed basis, the overall or total cost of ownership (TCO) currently may NOT be running away from the costs of the existing physical model.

Granted, there are encouraging signs (for the CAPEX parts of the sum) that value engineering is already occurring in the platform and optimization of the virtualization aspects of the original ETSI NFV architecture.[2] Beyond the continual tick/tock of Intel hardware delivery making per socket density increase and incorporating some of the I/O centric offload technology, this is shown through the increasing focus on containers (smaller footprints), ukernels (packaging), and new networking paradigms (fd.io).

However, as we have pointed out in several chapters, the real difference in the virtualization strategy and resulting economics for NFV versus general "cloud" is the load type—NFV applications are predominantly network I/O centric. If we reduce the equation solely to a measure of network service throughput, for example, a 10 Gpbs "equivalent" for a virtualized service—eliminating the potential overhead of virtualization, will even the simplification *TC_non-virt CAPEX >> TC_virtualized CAPEX* be compelling?

With a "your mileage may vary" caveat (your discounts for both the virtualized and nonvirtualized platform basis of the equation), the answer TODAY probably will be "no"—particularly if your virtualization platform is of the variety (highly available, five 9s, fully redundant) being peddled for Telco DC.[3]

Assuming that 10 Gbps/core is achievable throughput for your service function with no restriction on PCI bus throughput and mapping of adapter port to that core,[4] what are you paying per core compared to the same 10 Gpbs on an established vendor's "service edge" platform these days?

Keep in mind that the design of most virtual service connectivity can also carry some implicit connectivity overhead that is not always in the not-virtualized variant. In the simplest scenarios, we may have added an additional Ethernet port per 10 Gbps flow equivalent to the cost. For example, instead of entering the platform on a downstream port and exiting via an upstream equivalent (typical of edge and aggregation), the customer connection now must detour somewhere in the path through at least one additional port dedicated to the virtualization platform. It is expected that these "unloaded/commodity" ports are cheaper than those of the vendor service edge platform, but they are part of the overall cost of infrastructure and should be counted.

A potential to draw ROI closer to existing network platforms may lie in building a network I/O "race car" using additional hardware. At that point, we would posit that you have then changed "NFV" to be a "white box appliance" play—and that may be truly what lies under the current generation of NFV. But it is not exactly the same model of COTS compute as applied to massively scaled data centers.

And, if you are really going to do the math on the CAPEX ROI part fairly, remember two things about the "old way of doing things":

First, vendors of existing network service platforms have not stopped innovating.

In this landscape both orchestration for and the pricing of traditional physical network functions (PNFs) have not been stagnant since the emphasis on NFV began. (Whether the NFV focus can be credited for this or normal "learning curve" economics are taking place is a separate conversation.)

Another way of putting this is that the revolution in orchestration was going to happen ANYWAY. Several vendors had already stepped into this void and the push for model-based services and APIs will only accelerate the pace.

The continued evolution of PNFs and their management can push out the horizon in which both the agility and the cost-effectiveness of the virtualized counterparts undercut traditional offerings— even a self-constructed white-box appliance.

Second, and as a further complication, for most of the parties involved—both vendors and operators—NFV is not their only operational focus. NFV is not a cliff; it is a transition.

Like SDN, NFV will not occur in a vacuum. Both vendors and operators will continue to produce, consume, and support products to support existing services until customers are migrated— creating a very "long tail" for both. And there are additional carrying costs for everyone implied in that "long tail." How do we quantify THOSE?

The truth today is that we seem *heavily dependent on OPEX reduction* for the current NFV architecture and vision for services to work economically.

The OPEX savings COULD be tantalizing. In our experience, most operators are not very forthcoming about the exact allocation of operations costs. The public record can *sketch* the potential. For example, looking at Verizon's 2014 year-end public financial report,[5] the cost of services and sales were almost US$50 billion (this part includes the lion's share of service OPEX). Selling, general and business expense was US$41 billion. Aggregate customer care costs, which include billing and service provisioning, are allocated between the two buckets. This was not ALL of their yearly operational expense, but probably is the part most directly related to service. By comparison, total capital expense was only US$17.2 billion.

With that in mind, for many operators an OPEX:Revenue ratio reduction of even one percent can mean hundreds of millions (if not billions) of dollars of profitability. For most, tangible results will probably be realized through a reduction in headcount as an expression of efficiency.

Still, how much of that OPEX is NFV supposed to save exactly?

Given the uncertainty of potential savings, is there anything else can we do to optimize the cost of NFV solutions? Or do we just wave our hands and say it does not matter because the *potential* OPEX savings is so large?

A FIRST ORDER CHANGE

While the potential for a degree of agility is present in the current realization of NFV and there has been some increase in competition due to NFV (which is bound to be of benefit to the provider), there has been no fundamental change in service architectures themselves.

The ability to change the service architecture beyond replacing the physical with the virtual is the first order change required for success.

There is still a lot of functional duplication between VNFs and we still cobble them together to make services, like we used to cobble together dedicated appliances.

So, there is an opportunity for further optimization in the approach to NFV in front of operators—to change from emulation to new paradigms.

For some services, providers need to think like an OTT even though it may seem unnatural to do so.

NFV may push operators to the cusp of the network becoming "transport centric" with some services going completely OTT—which may not be a bad thing IF it is the operator themselves adopting the OTT ethos. And that is the fundamental lesson for the next NFV phase for operators:

This does not leave the network operator out in the cold. First, there is a profitable future for value-engineered transport and that CAN theoretically be leveraged to add some "binding power" (think optimized paths) to OTT services. Second, the operators can adopt the OTT ethos in their own offerings (or sell through some other OTT party's solution).[6] Third, there is a great deal of automation/OPEX reduction either way.

Of course, along the way, we will have to get a grasp on some of the troubling unknowns in NFV (outside of the economic model itself). Among these, at the highest rank, include what security compromises will be made in the NFV environment.

We need to figure out whether everything can and should be offloaded to COTS compute, and what a hybrid VNF/PNF solution architecture and its economic model look like.

If we really care about the CAPEX component of the solution we need to figure out whether the complex VNFs that cannot be approached as an OTT service (and are just now coming to market) might evolve to be combined VNF/PNF deployments.

Take the NFV service creation model to a new level—think PaaS.

The ultimate new paradigm may be to think of NFV and service creation as a PaaS problem (as introduced in Chapter 5: The NFV Infrastructure Management). Reduce the functionality required into microservices and use development and deployment frameworks that allow more flexible combining, extension, and innovation in creating new services. With these changes comes the opportunity to address the currently very long production-consumption-deployment cycle that hinders agility in the current model (and is perpetuated by simply converting monolithic physical service appliances into monolithic virtual service appliances).

THE ROLE OF STANDARDS AND OPEN SYSTEMS

Throughout the book we have illustrated different SDO approaches to NFV, particularly major contributions (or potential contributions) from ETSI and the IETF.

In ETSI, we saw an example of "forum seeking" behavior by a user group which resulted in a study group but no Standards.

With the IETF, we saw the slow and somewhat restrained response of an SDO with a recognized mandate that applies to pieces of the NFV puzzle. The result is focused and not as sweeping architecturally, but important to NFV.

We could continue from here to explore more Standards bodies that are now "studying" or "developing standards" for NFV, but that will not add much more to the conversation. As with SDN and cloud computing before NFV (and probably the "Internet of Things"—the next breaking technology wave), many other SDO bodies (eg, the TMF, ITU, ONF, MEF, BBF) exhibit common behaviors regarding rapidly emerging technologies. They generally start work late after relevance to the industry is established, often straying from their original mandate or purpose to form study groups and pursue Standards in these areas.

You could argue that the restraint and less-than-agile process of the IETF probably contributed to the establishment of the ETSI forum in the first place.

As we pointed out in Chapter 1, Network Function Virtualization, this has been discussed publicly and can hopefully be addressed through structural and evolutionary changes in the IETF and partnerships with Open Source projects relevant to new technology.

While interoperability with legacy systems is paramount to enable a smooth transition to NFV-driven services, traditional standards are no longer the only avenue to achieve interoperability between the management systems or functional parts of complex architectural specifications like NFV.

A bloom of API generation and publication (some using modeling mechanisms described earlier) is attempting to address the gap between legacy and new systems. APIs are also a proposed binder between competing and complimentary Open Source projects pursuing solutions in the SDN and NFV space.

While the ability to create, publish, and maintain an API is a GOOD thing, too many APIs and the inability to agree on a standard API definition for a function can lead to additional costs.

For example, creating a market for API brokerage (eg, the Enterprise Service Bus alluded to in the silo-creating, multidomain approach to resource control mentioned in Chapter 6: MANO: Management, Orchestration, OSS, and Service Assurance). Not surprisingly, an open organization has sprung up to try and insert some neutrality into the API description format (https://openapis.org/).

Open source can be a powerful tool for collaboration and to unlock the stranglehold on captive markets. This advance in the general software engineering space has left a lasting mark on how NFV can potentially achieve its goals is the growing trend of implementation in highly collaborative environments. In many cases there are multivendor open source environments. This is impacting how NFV components are standardized, packaged, and very rapidly getting to the marketplace where network operators now have many choices on how to deploy these services.

While open source has accelerated the pace of innovation in NFV, and open source has been an objective of NFV proponents, it has not been without drawbacks. The open source environment related to NFV was described earlier as "chaotic" because:

- Older projects like OpenStack have started to spread their focus as they attempt to address more desired functionality. Some of the older projects have slowed in their rate of innovation. They can begin to suffer some of the same organizational drawbacks that are pointed to in SDOs.
- In response, new projects are starting up with a more specific focus on individual areas of functionality related to NFV (eg, the fd.io project mentioned in Chapter 5: The NFV Infrastructure Management). So, while an open source framework may endure, not all of its projects might. Over time, the community or the market will move to fill gaps.
- This is exacerbated by a general tendency to "open wash" existing products or generate new projects with questionable governance. This will "muddy the water," as some companies and individuals jockey to control the "open" conversation or particular pieces of functionality (normally through a tightly regulated API).
- A misconception plagues those unfamiliar with open source—that open source is "free." This is normally coupled with the idea that there is no way to add value to the functionality.

Without doubt, a great deal of the NFV architecture will be open source. But until open source projects offer the full functionality of vendor integrated and maintained products, there will be legitimate areas in which the operator might purchase "value-added" functionality (eg, orchestration in the MANO space).

The integration and maintenance of architectures with many parts, some vendor provided and some open source presents a great complexity problem for service providers venturing into NFV. These are only compounded by the potential security problems we discussed in Chapter 8, NFV Infrastructure—Hardware Evolution and Testing.

In Chapter 1, Network Function Virtualization, we mentioned a discontinuity between "readiness" and "willingness" in the NFV target customer base. Unless they can "shift" to becoming leaders in their open source projects of choice, that is, self-supporting in this environment, this sort of integration and its ongoing maintenance will have to be obtained by paying a trusted partner.

When we are doing the economic model for NFV, we have to honestly address the systems integration costs and ongoing maintenance costs of the NFV solution.

CONSUMER BEHAVIOR

Because NFV is a cultural change, organizations are approaching it in different ways - often reflecting their internal hierarchies and political realities related to service creation and delivery. Across the spectrum of network operators, different organizations end up leading the NFV purchase decision (and architecture). This has three basic NFV consumption/purchasing patterns:

- Use-case-led consumption driven by individual business verticals within carriers (eg, consumer, wireless, broadband access, security). This top-down approach tends to pick vendor-provided turnkey solutions (that may or may not have open source components). Since the early ETSI NFV architecture work was heavily driven by a large number of use-cases, this orientation is not unexpected. Further, it allows network operators to absorb NFV without necessarily crossing organizational boundaries. Ultimately, consolidation of infrastructure may make this purchasing pattern fade. *This pattern does lead to the architecture (and its problems) described in Chapter 6, MANO: Management, Orchestration, OSS, and Service Assurance—effectively "punting" the stitching of domains to a higher level orchestrator and potentially recreating the OSS proliferation of the past.*

- Infrastructure-focused purchasing, led by network and data center infrastructure teams, is becoming more common (potentially overtaking use-case driven purchasing behaviors). Traditional operator engineering relates very well to hardware speeds-and-feeds, infrastructure tasks and control paradigms. These teams' first NFV decisions revolve around choosing a common VIM—platforms, virtualization strategy, and SDN controller. VNFs and orchestration (potentially selected on a use case basis as previously described) have to integrate those components. Here the approach and focus is much more aligned with the "NFV economics come from DC economics" driver originally propelling NFV. *This particular purchasing center is often diverted towards "telco data center," which has different requirements, focus and costs than the traditional, high-volume IaaS data center (driving the network I/O focus covered in this chapter and also in Chapter 8: NFV Infrastructure—Hardware Evolution and Testing).*
- Orchestration-focused consumption is something of an outlier, but some providers have started with a use case and consolidated around the orchestration system involved, driving all future purchases. Some providers have also made relatively recent investments in more modern orchestration from vendors to automate and drive end-to-end network services (MPLS pseudowire or MEF Ethernet-based services). This purchase would ideally become the high-level orchestrator for their NFV strategy. Here, the provider network management and OSS groups first select a MANO solution with which VNF vendors and service solutions have to integrate. *This can be problematic if the orchestration system selected is not open and/or does not provide the tooling for the customer (or their agents) to easily add support for other vendor's products or interface with other systems (ie, emulating the behavior of older OSS systems).*

We are not implying that there is any right/wrong way to begin with NFV. Rather, that every organization will have a different focus/anchor for their architecture depending on their individual internal power structures. These strategies might all be transients as the NFV model and focus change.

CHANGING YOUR SPOTS

Automation and a software-driven approach to services CAN lead to new efficiencies that allow huge organizations to trim down—and *that is the plan.* A good view of this was presented in a recent NY Times article[7] (its subject, AT&T, is not alone in their views).

One of the thrusts of NFV was to enable a new vendor ecosystem in which solutions are produced by software and equipment vendors in a more agile and rapidly developed and deployed model. The idea of making releases of relatively major functions available at a pace of weeks or months and not years has played an important role in the NFV vision.

To this end, in order for traditional service providers to play in this evolving world, they need to adopt and accept these new delivery models. In fact, they need to *become part of* the new delivery model and begin doing some software development on their own. This directly challenges the status quo in their operations departments by forcing network operations people to evolve their skill sets to learn *DevOps* skills and even some mild software engineering. The mantra of their future is clear: *change or be changed.*

As to the genesis of a new ecosystem, at ONUG 2014, a panel group of investment bankers (three technology investors for mainstream banks and one venture capital representative) was asked if the stated direction of the AT&T Domain 2.0 publication[8] (relatively new at the time) would lead to opportunities for startups—a new vendor ecosystem. Except for a caveated response by the venture capital representative (if THEY are not bullish, you know there is a problem), the rest of the panel was negative. They cited service provider habits in procurement and vendor management (long cycles and heavy resource demands) as negative environments for fostering a startup. Tellingly, they preferred to back products that appealed to Enterprise and exploit any overlap with service provider sales—and this was echoed by the products being discussed at the meeting (overlay VPN tools for enterprise and enterprise data center infrastructure tools).

The implication is that the organizational changes required for such an NFV vision go well beyond operations and engineering.

PARTING THOUGHTS

Even though we are over three years into the NFV cycle, NFV is at a very early point in its realization. Unlike the SDN wave that preceded it, NFV is potentially on a much steeper adoption curve. The anticipation is that IF NFV does not succeed for the companies that have publicly declared transcendence via NFV—the financial results for shareholders could be calamitous. Although SDN and NFV are often coupled in conversation and analysis, as we have stated several times throughout the chapters, NFV is a MUST for traditional network operators.[9]

Operators face tremendous pressures from two sources—retaining or expanding customers/business and reducing costs.

For the former, OTT service offerings from competitors in wireline services and a rapid embrace of MVNO architectures in wireless threaten to upend existing hierarchies and relationships.

The often cloud-based OTT offerings can "cherry pick" important large enterprises through their self-serve, multi-operator, customer managed service models (with strange parallels to how CLECs threatened incumbent telcos years ago).

The MVNO architecture slices the network to create a wholesale/retail split such that the transport/infrastructure provider no longer has direct access to the customer.

In both scenarios, the infrastructure provider is commoditized, disintermediated, or disintegrated.

For the latter, investor pressures to reduce costs, streamline operations and become more agile at introducing new services (this also plays into customer retention) mean changes in both labor force and the traditional approaches to providing services.

Unlike our prior book on SDN, we do not feel compelled to convince a readership of the value and place of NFV[10]—it is obvious. Nor do we feel compelled to encourage the reader to experiment, because experiments abound.

Both of us are bullish on the future of NFV; maybe not on the ETSI architecture and implementations of today, but definitely on the need for operators to become more agile, break their OSS bonds and evolve both as value engineered transport providers and service providers.

The catastrophic scenario in NFV is that OTT vendors take all services away from telcos over time. While the ubiquity of outsourcing the Enterprise to the OTT vendors (eg, AWS) is debatable (see articles that imply much of their growth is due to startups—ie, venture capital driven revenue vs "true" Enterprise) the trend to do so cannot be ignored. These companies are much more adroit in a software world and are slowly becoming credible business partners to the Enterprise. For some OTTs, their back-end analytics capabilities can potentially allow them to derive even greater value from network service offerings by increasing the value of other products (e.g. advertising).

The biggest question is whether the NFV road we are on ultimately leads to the agility required of traditional operators in time to avert that outcome.

NFV is definitely another paradigm shift in the networking industry—the second in the past six years. The rapid succession of these changes is an indicator that networks are important not only for what we used them for in the past, but for what we envision for the future.

Stay tuned...

END NOTES

1. https://en.wikipedia.org/wiki/IP_Multimedia_Subsystem-/media/File:TISPAN_IMS_Reference_Architecture .png
2. You COULD argue that NFV itself is a "value engineering" project for existing services.
3. We fully understand that the operator CAN buy an OCP-specified platform from an ODM at a much-discounted price, but (so far) we have not seen any of them actually do this at volume, like their OTT contemporaries.
4. Note well—these are a LOT of simplifying assumptions and you will likely achieve far less throughput for EVERY core in a system as a result.
5. https://www.verizon.com/about/sites/default/files/2014_vz_annual_report.pdf
6. See Verizon's announcement of their sell-through of Viptella services.
7. http://www.nytimes.com/2016/02/14/technology/gearing-up-for-the-cloud-att-tells-its-workers-adapt-or-else. html?_r = 0
8. https://www.att.com/Common/about_us/pdf/AT&T Domain 2.0 Vision White Paper.pdf
9. Arguably, SDN concepts have been discussed for 6 or more years now with a low degree of implementation (thus far). There was a lot of academic and vendor-led promise for SDN, but carriers did not stake their future financial outcomes on SDN.
10. While we framed SDN as useful in that it was about network programmability (which is part of the automation and optimization of networks required for operation at scale), we had proposed that the cover of THAT book be a unicorn because of overhype of SDN utility.

Index

Note: Page numbers followed by "*f*" and "*t*" refer to figures and tables, respectively.

A

Abstract Syntax Notation One (ASN.1), 92
Academic tests, 211
Access to interrupt controller (APIC), 172
Advanced Vector eXtensions (AVX), 194
Amdahl's Law, 202
APIC. *See* Access to interrupt controller (APIC)
Application
  processing, 171
  versioning, 164
Architectural diagram reference points, interpretations from, 134
ARM, 209–210
ASN.1. *See* Abstract Syntax Notation One (ASN.1)
AVX. *See* Advanced Vector eXtensions (AVX)

B

Base header, 82, 83*f*
Base use case, 32
Baseband radio-processing unit (BBU), 61
BESS, 77
Birds of Feather (BoF) meeting, 77
BNG. *See* Broadband network gateway (BNG)
BoF meeting. *See* Birds of Feather (BoF) meeting
Branching service chain, 20, 21*f*
BRAS. *See* Broadband Residential Access Server (BRAS)
Broadband network gateway (BNG), 25, 25*f*
Broadband Residential Access Server (BRAS), 37
Brownfield partnership, reimagining OSS/BSS, 131–132
"Brownfield" networks, 112–113
"Brownfield" of dreams, 44–45
Business Support Systems (BSS), 55
  OSS/BSS block, 129, 130*f*
    ETSI GAP analysis, 130–131
    interpretations from architectural diagram reference points, 134
    reimagining OSS/BSS—Brownfield partnership, 131–132
    reimagining OSS—opportunities in SA, 132–133

C

Capital expense (CAPEX), 2, 4
  costs, 218
Cat with the prosthetic unicorn horn, xxi
Caticorn. *See* Cat with the prosthetic unicorn horn
Central Office Re-architected as Datacenter (CORD), 117

Cinder code, 106–107
CLI. *See* Command line interface (CLI)
Cloud computing, 3
CloudVPN project, 38
Command line interface (CLI), 25, 91
Commercial off-the-shelf (COTS), 1, 23, 155
Composite function, 86
"Config-drive", 141
Configuration complexity, 27
Consumer behavior, 223–224
Containers, 8, 160
  application versioning, 164
  CoreOS, 163–164, 163*f*
  Docker networking, 163
  layering/separation, 162
  LXC, 161, 162*f*
  network namespace, 161
  NFV, 165
  resource scale, 160
  UML and container hybrid, 166*f*
  VMs and, 161*f*
Content layer, 93
Context header format, 83*f*
Context switch/data copy reduction, 172
Controller architecture, 112–113
Conventional thread scheduling, 208–209
CORD. *See* Central Office Re-architected as Datacenter (CORD)
CoreOS, 163–164, 163*f*
Corporate/enterprise/IT applications, 19
COTS. *See* Commercial off-the-shelf (COTS)
CPE. *See* Customer Premise Equipment (CPE)
CPU complex, 192
  I/O processing, 195
  Intel Sandy Bridge microarchitecture, 192, 193*f*
  memory access—cache, 196–199
  multicore, 195
  PCIe, 199–200
  run-to-completion and pipeline execution models, 195*f*
  virtualization mechanism, 194
CRUD operations, 56
Customer Premise Equipment (CPE), 37

D

Data Center Network, 105–106
Data center-oriented draft, 84
Data machines, 204

Data plane I/O and COTS evolution, 9—11
Data Plane Management, 183
Dataplane Development Kit (DPDK), 3, 9, 175, 177, 180
DCA. *See* Direct cache access (DCA)
Decomposition, varying approaches to, 32—35
   IMS "merged" decomposition proposition, 34*f*
   IMS decomposition, 33*f*
   PCSCF function split decomposition, 34*f*
Denial of Service (DoS), 167
Deployment, 49, 55
Digesting ETSI output
   architecture, 53—55
     big blocks and reference points, 55—58, 56*f*
     domains of Orchestration and SDN controller products, 57*f*
     high level ETSI NFV architecture, 54*f*
   gap analysis, 65—67
   output, 52
   POC observations, 67—68
   terminology, 53
   use cases, 59—62
   virtualization
     in mobility applications, 61*f*
     requirements, 62—65
Direct cache access (DCA), 170, 200
Distributed DoS, 167
Distributed Management Task Force (DMTF25), 65
Distribution management scheme, 164
DMTF25. *See* Distributed Management Task Force (DMTF25)
DNS servers. *See* Domain Name Service (DNS) servers
Document Type Definition (DTD), 92
Domain Name Service (DNS) servers, 7
DoS. *See* Denial of Service (DoS)
DPDK. *See* Dataplane Development Kit (DPDK)
DTD. *See* Document Type Definition (DTD)

E

Elasticity, 63
Element Management System (EMS), 128—129
EN. *See* European Standard (EN)
Endpoint services, 44
EPL. *See* Ethernet Private Line (EPL)
EPTs. *See* Extended Page Tables (EPTs)
Ethernet Private Line (EPL), 136
ETSI. *See* European Telecommunications Standards
     Institute (ETSI)
ETSI NFV ISG group, 49
   contribution, 49
   digesting ETSI output, 52—68
   future directions, 70—71
   organization, 51—52
   organizational structure, 51*f*
   3GPP, 52
   white paper 3, 69—70

European Standard (EN), 49
European Telecommunications Standards Institute (ETSI), 19,
   49—50
   ETSI GAP analysis, 130
Evolution and Ecosystem Working Group (EVE), 72
Extended Message Signaled Interrupts (MSI-X), 200
Extended Page Tables (EPTs), 174
Extending system, 200. *See also* Network Function
     Virtualization (NFV)
   FPGA technology, 203—205
   GPUs, 205—207
   heterogeneous compute challenges, 208—209
   heterogeneous cores, 202—203
   NICs, 200—202
External Network, 105—106
"Eye in sky" management, 137—138

F

Fast Data (fd.io), 182—183
Fault Management, Configuration Management, Accounting
     Management, Performance Management, and Security
     Management (FCAPS), 127
Feature velocity friction, 26
Fiber to the home (FTTH), 61
Fiber-to-the-cabinet (FTTC), 62
Field programmable gate array (FPGA) technology, 191, 203
   data machines, 204
   discreet FPGA, 203*f*
   host memory, 205
   memory and logical/computation cells, 204
   new tooling for, 205
   routing channels over fabric, 204*f*
Firewall, 53
First order change, 221—222
First Segment, 89
"First-generation" of service, 41
Fixed Access Network Virtualization, 62
Flags, 89
Flow classification function, 39
FPGA technology. *See* Field programmable gate array
     (FPGA) technology
FTTC. *See* Fiber-to-the-cabinet (FTTC)
FTTH. *See* Fiber to the home (FTTH)

G

Gap analysis, 65
   INF WG, 65
   MANO WG, 65
   NFV architecture mapping, 66*f*
   NFV Security and Trust Guidance document, 67
   PER WG, 66
   REL WG, 66

SEC WG, 66–67
SWA WG, 67
GBP. *See* Group Based Policy (GBP)
General-purpose programming model (GPGPU), 205
Generations, 25
GiLAN, 39
Glance code, 107
GPGPU. *See* General-purpose programming model (GPGPU)
GPUs. *See* Graphics processing units (GPUs)
Granularity, 43–44
Graphics processing units (GPUs), 191, 205–207, 206f
  high-level view of GPU architecture, 207f
Group Based Policy (GBP), 109
Group Specification (GS), 49

H

Hardware evolution, 192. *See also* Software evolution
  ARM, 209–210
  CPU complex, 192
    I/O processing, 195
    Intel Sandy Bridge microarchitecture, 192, 193f
    memory access—cache, 196–199
    multicore, 195
    PCIe, 199–200
    run-to-completion and pipeline execution models, 195f
    virtualization mechanism, 194
  extending system, 200
    FPGA technology, 203–205
    GPUs, 205–207
    heterogeneous compute challenges, 208–209
    heterogeneous cores, 202–203
    NICs, 200–202
  Sandy Bridge architecture, 193f
Head of line (HOL) blocking, 201
Header Ext Length, 88
HEAT Orchestration Template (HOT), 143
Heterogeneous compute challenges, 208–209
Heterogeneous cores, 202–203
Hierarchical caching, 90, 90f
HMAC fields, 89
HOL blocking. *See* Head of line (HOL) blocking
HOT. *See* HEAT Orchestration Template (HOT)
Hybrid virtualization, 165–167
Hyperthreading, 197
Hypervisor, 57–58, 156, 160

I

I2RS working group, 77
IA. *See* Intel Architecture (IA)
IaaS. *See* Infrastructure-as-a-Service (IaaS)
IDS. *See* Intrusion Detection System (IDS)
IEEE. *See* Institute of Electrical and Electronics Engineers (IEEE)

IETF. *See* Internet Engineering Task Force (IETF)
IFA. *See* Interfaces and Architecture (IFA)
ILP. *See* Instruction-level parallelism (ILP)
Image Service API, 107
Industry Study Group (ISG), 49
Infrastructure (INF), 13
  INF WG, 65
Infrastructure-as-a-Service (IaaS), 106. *See also* Platform as a Service (PaaS)
Infrastructure-focused purchasing, 224
Inline carriage, 35
Institute of Electrical and Electronics Engineers (IEEE), 96–97
Instruction set architecture (ISA), 195
Instruction-level parallelism (ILP), 194
Integration, 23f
Intel, 155, 169–170, 202
  advancements, 173
    configuration of soft forwarder, 176f
    DPDK, 175, 177
    DPDK-enabled Open vSwitch, 176f
    Intel VT-c and VT-d, 174f
    SR-IOV, 175
    us-vhost approach, 177
    user space vhost implementation, 177f
    Virtio-based solutions, 174
  platforms, 191
  Sandy Bridge microarchitecture, 192, 193f
  VT FlexPriority, 174
Intel advancements, 173–177
Intel Architecture (IA), 155–156, 191
Intellectual Property Rights (IPR), 50
Interfaces and Architecture (IFA), 72
Internet Engineering Task Force (IETF), 19, 77
  BoF meeting, 77
  NETMOD workgroup, 91–98
  NSH header, 82–88
  relationship to NFV Standards, 77
  SFC, 78–88
  SPRING workgroup, 88–91
  workgroups, 77
"Internet of Things", 222
Intrusion Detection System (IDS), 29
IPR. *See* Intellectual Property Rights (IPR)
ISA. *See* Instruction set architecture (ISA)
ISG. *See* Industry Study Group (ISG)

K

Kernel(s), 204, 207–208

L

Last level cache (LLC), 197
Layered controller model, 114f

Library operating systems (libOS), 165
Life Cycle Management, 141
Linux, 3–4, 161
Linux Branded Zones (LXz), 163
Linux containers (LXC), 161, 162*f*
Linux Foundation, 139, 182
Linux Secure Module (LSM) framework, 168*f*
LLC. *See* Last level cache (LLC)
Logical limits
    anonymized propagation delay of real network, 43*f*
    "brownfield" of dreams, 44–45
    NFV/SFC, 45–46
    granularity and extra vSwitch or network transitions,
        43–44
    service chains, 43*f*
    speed of light, 41–43
    standardization above network layer, 44
    subset of fiber map of United States, 42*f*
Loosely coupled solution, 26–27. *See also* Tightly integrated
    service solutions
    configuration changes, 27
    configuration complexity, 27
    Gi-LAN of wireless network service center, 26*f*
    IDS, 29
    operational costs, 27
    overlay/tunnel technology, 29
    passing clue problem, 27
    proprietary/internal methodology, 27
    SDG, 27, 29
    VLAN stitching, 28, 28*f*
LSM framework. *See* Linux Secure Module (LSM)
    framework
LXC. *See* Linux containers (LXC)
LXz. *See* Linux Branded Zones (LXz)

M

Management and Orchestration (MANO), 13, 103, 127, 170
    architecture, 128*f*
    architecture on steroids, 150–151
        multidomain silos, 152*f*
    descriptors, 135–136
    NFV orchestration, 134
        generic resource and policy management for Network
            Services, 137–138
        MANO descriptors, 135–136
        Network Service Catalog, 136–137
        Network Service descriptors, 135–136
        Network Service graph, 135*f*
        service graphs, 134–135
        VNFM demarcation point, 138
    open orchestration, 138
        Open MANO approach, 148–149
        Open-O organization, 147–148

OpenBaton, 149–150
    Tacker, 139–147
OSS/BSS block, 129, 130*f*
    ETSI GAP analysis, 130–131
    interpretations from architectural diagram reference
        points, 134
    reimagining OSS/BSS—Brownfield partnership,
        131–132
    reimagining OSS—opportunities in SA, 132–133
VNF Domain, 128–129
WG, 65
Management Network, 105–106
MANO. *See* Management and Orchestration (MANO)
MD Type. *See* Meta Data Type (MD Type)
MD-SAL. *See* Model-Driven Service Abstraction Layer (MD-
    SAL)
MEF. *See* Metro Ethernet Forum (MEF)
Memory access—cache, 196
    external memory access, 196
    memory bandwidth effect, 196
    multithreaded microcode, 196*f*
    NUMA-unaware assignment, 199
    performance-impacting cache behavior, 198
    in three-level cache, 197
    typical/generic three-level cache structure for IA, 197*f*
Memory Management Unit (MMU), 157
Merchant, 15
Messages layer, 93, 95
Meta Data Type (MD Type), 82
Metadata, 35–36
Metro Ethernet Forum (MEF), 96–97, 136
"Middlebox" studies, 12
Minimization of context switching, 13
MMU. *See* Memory Management Unit (MMU)
Model-driven approach, 113
Model-Driven Service Abstraction Layer (MD-SAL), 115
MPLS label mechanics, 88
MSI-X. *See* Extended Message Signaled Interrupts (MSI-X)
Multilevel virtualization, 166
Multiple systolic arrays, 204

N

NETCONF protocol. *See* Network Configuration (NETCONF)
    Protocol
Netmap, 178, 178*f*
    software packet handling bottom line, 180
    Vale, 179*f*
NETMOD workgroup. *See* Network Modeling (NETMOD)
    workgroup
Network Configuration (NETCONF) Protocol, 91, 93–94
    base, 94*f*
    conceptual layers, 94*f*
    NETCONF/YANG, 136

Network controllers, 111
  controller architecture, 112–113
  layered controller model, 114*f*
Network Function Virtualization (NFV), 1, 4–5, 14–15, 19,
    120, 217. *See also* Open orchestration
  academic studies, 12
  analysts predicting big growth for, 15*f*
  architecture mapping, 66*f*
  background, 1–3
  base case, 6–8, 7*f*
  changing our spots, 224–225
  consumer behavior, 223–224
  current NFV model, 218
    cost of NFV, 218–221
    first order change, 221–222
  data plane I/O and COTS evolution, 9–11
  enabling new consumption model, 15–16
  at ETSI, 12–14, 50–51
  evolution, 1
  hypothetical vRouter, 10*f*
  innovations make NFV compelling, 2*f*
  marketplace, 11–12
  orchestration, 134
    generic resource and policy management for Network
        Services, 137–138
    MANO descriptors, 135–136
    Network Service Catalog, 136–137
    Network Service descriptors, 135–136
    Network Service graph, 135*f*
    service graphs, 134–135
    VNFM demarcation point, 138
  PaaS on, 121–123
  parting thoughts, 225–226
  Performance & Portability Best Practises document, 63
  redrawing NFV and missing pieces, 3–4
  SDN, 5, 217
  SDN–NFV–Merchant cycle, 16*f*
  Security and Trust Guidance document, 67
  services through microservices and PaaS, 122*f*
  without SFC, 46
  standardizing NFV architecture, 11
  standards and open systems, 222
    economic model for NFV, 223
    in ETSI, 222
    open source, 222–223
    "value-added" functionality, 223
  strengthening "NFV as SDN use case", 8
    improving virtualization, 8–9
    taxonomy for virtualizing services, 9*f*
  2013 depiction of drivers, 3*f*
  virtualized EPC, 6*f*
Network Function Virtualization Infrastructure (NFVI), 53,
    103–104, 127
  architecture, 104*f*

hardware evolution, 192
  ARM, 209–210
  CPU complex, 192–200
  extending system, 200–209
Intel platforms, 191
network controllers, 111
  controller architecture, 112–113
  layered controller model, 114*f*
NFV, 120–123
ODL, 114
  AKKA-based clustering, 115
  ODL Project, 115
  and OpenStack collaboration, 116–117
ONOS, 117–120, 119*f*
OpenStack, 105
  fork or not fork open source distributions, 111
  IaaS building blocks, 106*f*
  infrastructure networking, 105*f*
  Management Network, 105–106
  ML2 plugin architecture, 108*f*
  Neutron, 107
  Nova and Neutron interaction in VM creation, 109*f*
  OPNFV picture of OpenStack multisite use case, 110*f*
  plugins, 107–108
  software projects, 106
  stretching, 109–111
OpenStack, 120–123
PaaS, 120–123
performance measurement, 210
  measuring performance, 210–211
  power efficiency, 211–212
VIM, 103
Network Interface Cards (NICs), 191, 200–202
  network packet processing, 201*f*
Network Modeling (NETMOD) workgroup, 77, 91. *See also*
    Source Packet Routing in Networking (SPRING)
    workgroup
  message layer, 95
  NETCONF protocol, 93–94
  operations, 94–95
  public Github Yang repository, 96–98
  RESTCONF protocol, 96
  secure transports, 96
  Yang data modeling language, 92–93
Network Operators Council (NOC), 50
Network Platform Context, 83–84
Network Processing Units (NPUs), 196
Network Service, 19
  descriptors, 135–136
  generic resource and policy management for, 137–138
  graph, 135*f*
Network Service Catalog, 136–137
Network Service Chaining (NSC), 23
Network Service Descriptors, 150–151

Network Service Header (NSH), 5, 82, 134–135
  base header, 82, 83*f*
  data center-oriented draft, 84
  DC-specific proposal, 84
  dominant draft, 82
  Fixed Context Header block detail, 84*f*
  guidelines, 83–84
  lookup, 85–86
    SFC example using NSH, 86*f*
    SFF NSH mapping example, 86*f*
  MD type, 82
  MD Type 2 Variable Length Context Header, 85, 85*f*
  using metadata to enhancing reliability, 88
  Network Platform Context, 84
  Network Shared Context, 84
  NSH Data Center context header allocation, 84*f*
  Service Platform Context, 84
  Service Shared Context, 84
  SFF NSH mapping example, 85*f*
  SP Header, 83, 83*f*
  SPI, 83
  TLV Class field, 85
  worked example, 86–87
Network Shared Context, 83–84
"Network underlay" domains, 51
Network Virtualization Overlays (NVO3), 77
Neutron, 107
  project, 109
Next Generation OSS (NGOSS), 132
Next Header, 88
NFV. *See* Network Function Virtualization (NFV)
NFV Infrastructure as a Service (NFVIaaS), 59, 60*f*
NFV Orchestrator (NFVO), 56, 127
NFVI. *See* Network Function Virtualization Infrastructure (NFVI)
NFVIaaS. *See* NFV Infrastructure as a Service (NFVIaaS)
NFVO. *See* NFV Orchestrator (NFVO)
NGOSS. *See* Next Generation OSS (NGOSS)
NICs. *See* Network Interface Cards (NICs)
NOC. *See* Network Operators Council (NOC)
Nonuniform memory access (NUMA), 161
Northbound interfaces, 129
Nouns, 96
Nova code, 106–107
NPUs. *See* Network Processing Units (NPUs)
NSC. *See* Network Service Chaining (NSC)
NSH. *See* Network Service Header (NSH)
NUMA. *See* Nonuniform memory access (NUMA)
NVO3. *See* Network Virtualization Overlays (NVO3)

O

OAM. *See* Operations and Management (OAM)
ODL. *See* OpenDaylight (ODL)

ONOS. *See* Open Network Operating System (ONOS)
ONP. *See* Open Network Platform (ONP)
Open Daylight controller, Tacker integration with, 144–145
Open MANO. *See also* Management and Orchestration (MANO)
  approach, 148–149
  Orchestrator, 149, 149*f*
  VNFM, 149
Open Network Operating System (ONOS), 117–120, 119*f*
Open Network Platform (ONP), 180
Open orchestration, 138. *See also* Network Function Virtualization (NFV)—orchestration
  Open MANO approach, 148–149
  Open-O organization, 147–148
  OpenBaton, 149–150
  Tacker, 139
    integration with Open Daylight, 144–145
    ODL integration, 145*f*
    and service function chaining, 144
    SFC functionality, 145*f*
    Tacker VNF Catalog, 140, 140*f*
    Tacker VNFM, 141
    Tacker/Openstack system, 144*f*
    TOSCA template, 142*f*
    TOSCA templates and parser, 142–143
    TOSCA/HEAT translator, 143*f*
    VNF auto-configuration, 141
    VNF monitoring, 141–142
    workflow, 146–147, 146*f*
Open Platform for NFV (OPNFV), 69–71, 71*f*
Open Virtualization Format (OVF), 65
"Open Virtualization Profile", 180
Open vSwitch (OVS), 3, 107, 158
Open-O organization, 147–148
"Open-washing" of products, 3–4
OpenBaton, 149–150
  dashboard, 151*f*
OpenCL model, 208–209, 208*f*
OpenDaylight (ODL), 104, 114, 132
  AKKA-based clustering, 115
  ODL Project, 115
  and OpenStack collaboration, 116–117
  Project, 65
OpenFlow, 118
OpenStack, 105, 120–121
  fork or not fork open source distributions, 111
  IaaS building blocks, 106*f*
  infrastructure networking, 105*f*
  Management Network, 105–106
  ML2 plugin architecture, 108*f*
  Neutron, 107
  Nova and Neutron interaction in VM creation, 109*f*
  and ODL collaboration, 116–117
  OPNFV picture of OpenStack multisite use case, 110*f*

plugins, 107–108
software projects, 106
stretching, 109–111
OpenStack Foundation, 105
OpenStack Project, 65
Operational expense (OPEX), 2, 4, 218–219
Operations and Management (OAM), 52, 82
Operations layer, 93
Operations Support System (OSS), 4, 55, 127
OSS/BSS block, 129, 130f
ETSI GAP analysis, 130–131
interpretations from architectural diagram reference
points, 134
reimagining OSS/BSS, 131–132
reimagining OSS, 132–133
OPEX. See Operational expense (OPEX)
OPNFV. See Open Platform for NFV (OPNFV)
Or-Vnfm, 137
Orchestration, 5
and management, 64
orchestrated overlays, 4
orchestration-focused consumption, 224
OSS. See Operations Support System (OSS)
OTT. See Over The Top (OTT)
Out-of-band models, 36
OVDK, 9, 10f
Over The Top (OTT), 2
services, 218
Overlay, 78
Overlay/tunnel technology, 29
OVF. See Open Virtualization Format (OVF)
OVS. See Open vSwitch (OVS)

P

PaaS. See Platform as a Service (PaaS)
Packet Gateway (PGW), 26–27
Packet handling, 170
application processing, 171
context switch/data copy reduction, 172
fd. io, 182–183
first generation VNF, 171t
Intel advancements, 173–177
Netmap, 178–180
scalar vs. vectorization, 173
system memory, 170
turnkey optimization, 180–182
vector processing, 173f
vhost-user, 178–180
Passing clue problem, 27
PCIexpress (PCIe), 199–200
PCRF. See Policy and charging rules function (PCRF)
Performance (PER), 51
measurement, NFV, 210

measuring performance, 210–211
power efficiency, 211–212
PER WG, 66
PGW. See Packet Gateway (PGW)
Physical network functions (PNFs), 220
Physical NIC (pNIC), 157
Pinned thread, 195
Platform as a Service (PaaS), 44, 120
on NFV, 121–123
NFV services through microservices and PaaS, 122f
PMDs. See Poll-mode drivers (PMDs)
PNFs. See Physical network functions (PNFs)
pNIC. See Physical NIC (pNIC)
PoC. See Proof-of-Concept (PoC)
Policy and charging rules function (PCRF), 35
Policy List, 89
Poll-mode drivers (PMDs), 167
Portability
chain, 57
requirements, 63
Power efficiency, NFV, 211–212
Proof-of-Concept (PoC), 49, 67–68
Proprietary/internal methodology, 27
ProtoBufs, 92–93
Protocol agnosticism, 112
Public Github Yang repository, 96–98
Public Yang Repo, 97, 97f

Q

QEMU hardware emulator, 156
QuickData Technology, 200

R

Radio access network (RAN), 52
Receive Side Coalescing (RSC), 200
Receive-Side scaling (RSS), 200
Redrawing NFV, 3–4
Reliability (REL), 51
REL WG, 66
Remote procedure calls (RPCs), 92
Rendered Service Path (RSP), 80
Reorder buffer (ROB), 194
Repatriation/ISG2. 0, 71–73
Representational State Transfer (REST), 96
Residential Gateway (RGW), 61
Resiliency/resilience, 82
requirements, 63
Resource management, 13
Resource oversubscription, 194
REST. See Representational State Transfer (REST)
RESTCONF protocol, 96
ReSTful interfaces, 112

RFC 5539, 96
RFC5717, 95
RFC6022, 95
RGW. *See* Residential Gateway (RGW)
ROB. *See* Reorder buffer (ROB)
Role-based tests, 211
Route Reflection, 7
RPCs. *See* Remote procedure calls (RPCs)
RSC. *See* Receive Side Coalescing (RSC)
RSP. *See* Rendered Service Path (RSP)
RSS. *See* Receive-Side scaling (RSS)
Run-to-completion and pipeline execution models, 195, 195*f*

S
SA. *See* Service assurance (SA)
SDG. *See* Service Delivery Gateway (SDG)
SDN, 1, 111
    drivers of NFV use case, 3*f*
    NFV, 5
    SDN–NFV–Merchant cycle, 16*f*
    strengthening "NFV as SDN use case", 8–9
Se-Ma reference point, 134
SEC. *See* Security (SEC)
Second-generation functions, 41
Secure Sockets Layer (SSL), 93
Secure Transport layer, 93
Secure transports, 96
Securing Linux, 168–169
Security (SEC), 51
    lowest common denominator, 169–170
    SEC WG, 66–67
    trade-offs, 167
        DoS, 167
        not sharing, 169
        Securing Linux, 168–169
Segment List, 89
Segment Routing for IPv6 (SRv6), 88, 91
    forwarding example, 89*f*
    header extension format, 88*f*
    hierarchical caching application using, 90*f*
Segments Left, 89
Service assurance (SA), 64, 130
    opportunities in, 132–133
Service Chain, 20, 20*f*
Service continuity, 64
Service creation, 19
    problem, 22
    quick history, 22
        COTS, 23
        functions, 23
        integration and virtualization, 23*f*
        loosely coupled solution, 26–29
        network services, 23

NSC, 23
    tightly integrated service solutions, 24–26
    virtualized elements, 23
Service Delivery Gateway (SDG), 27
Service function chaining (SFC), 1, 19, 29–35, 78, 165
    architecture document, 79–82
    CloudVPN project, 38
    Control Plane, 82
    CPE, 37
    dedicated BNG functionality, 37*f*
    dynamic and elastic nature, 41
    fledgling deployments, 40
    flow classification function, 39
    GiLAN, 39
    high availability of stateful service functions, 32*f*
    mobile network, 39
    network edge environment, 36
    NFV without, 46
    problem statement, 78–79
    providing NAT for legacy IPv4 devices in IPv6
        network, 39*f*
    Proxy, 81–82, 81*f*
    second-generation functions, 41
    service chains with separate paths, 30*f*
    service offerings, 41
    step-wise deployment/expansion of service offering into
        new market, 40*f*
    Telefonica, 37
    TeraStream CloudVPN, 38, 38*f*
    virtualization, 38
    vRouter, 38
    vVPN function, 38
    workgroup, 78
Service Function Forwarder (SFF), 80–81, 80*f*
Service Function Path (SFP), 80
Service functions (SFs), 19, 78
Service graphs, 32, 32*f*, 134–135
Service Index (SI), 83
Service Instance, 20*f*, 21
Service Level Agreement (SLA), 41–42
Service models, 65
Service Path, 20*f*, 21
Service path ID (SPI), 81, 83
Service Platform Context, 83–84
Service Repository, 136
Service Shared Context, 83–84
Service Template, 22
Set top box (STB), 61
SFC. *See* Service function chaining (SFC)
SFF. *See* Service Function Forwarder (SFF)
SFP. *See* Service Function Path (SFP)
SFs. *See* Service functions (SFs)
Shallow L2 port-in-port-out tests, 211
SI. *See* Service Index (SI)

SIMD. *See* Single Instruction Multiple Data (SIMD)
Simple Modified Access Control Kernel (SMACK), 168
Simple Network Management Protocol (SNMP), 92
Single Instruction Multiple Data (SIMD), 194
64-bit ARMv8, 209
6Wind, 180–181
  6WindGate solution, 181, 181*f*
SLA. *See* Service Level Agreement (SLA)
SMACK. *See* Simple Modified Access Control Kernel
  (SMACK)
SMI. *See* Structure of Management Information (SMI)
SMIv2, 92
SMs. *See* Streaming multiprocessors (SMs)
SNMP. *See* Simple Network Management Protocol (SNMP)
Software Architecture (SWA), 13, 51
  SWA WG, 67
Software evolution, 156. *See also* Hardware evolution
  containers, 160–165
  hybrid virtualization, 165–167
  hypervisor maps physical resources, 158*f*
  KVM execution and QEMU emulation, 157*f*
  QEMU hardware emulator, 156
  security trade-offs, 167–169
  security—lowest common denominator, 169–170
  UML and container hybrid, 166*f*
  Unikernels, 165
  VM-centric model, 158–160
Software network, 155
Software packet handling bottom line, 180
Source Interface ID, 84
Source Node ID, 84
Source Packet Routing in Networking (SPRING) workgroup,
    77, 88. *See also* Network Modeling (NETMOD)
    workgroup
  demonstration, 90
  First Segment, 89
  flags, 89
  header, 88
  Header Ext Length, 88
  HMAC fields, 89
  MPLS label mechanics, 88
  Next Header, 88
  Policy List, 89
  Routing Type, 88
  Segment List, 89
  Segments Left, 89
  SRv6 proposal, 88, 88*f*, 91
SP Header, 83, 83*f*
Speed of light, 41–43
SPI. *See* Service path ID (SPI)
Split decomposition, 33, 34*f*
SPRING workgroup. *See* Source Packet Routing in
    Networking (SPRING) workgroup
SRv6. *See* Segment Routing for IPv6 (SRv6)

SSL. *See* Secure Sockets Layer (SSL)
Standardization above network layer, 44
Standards and open systems, 222
  economic model for NFV, 223
  in ETSI, 222
  open source, 222–223
  "value-added" functionality, 223
STB. *See* Set top box (STB)
Steroids, architecture on, 150–151
  multidomain silos, 152*f*
Streaming multiprocessors (SMs), 206
Structure of Management Information (SMI), 92
SWA. *See* Software Architecture (SWA)
Swift code, 106–107
System memory, 170

T
Tacker, 139
  integration with Open Daylight, 144–145
  ODL integration, 145*f*
  and service function chaining, 144
  SFC functionality, 145*f*
  Tacker VNF Catalog, 140, 140*f*
  Tacker VNFM, 141
  Tacker/Openstack system, 144*f*
  TOSCA template, 142*f*
    and parser, 142–143
  TOSCA/HEAT translator, 143*f*
  VNF
    auto-configuration, 141
    monitoring, 141–142
  workflow, 146–147, 146*f*
Task Priority Register (TPR), 172
TC. *See* Total Cost (TC)
TCO. *See* Total cost of ownership (TCO)
Technical Steering Committee (TSC), 51
Telefonica, 37
TeraStream CloudVPN, 38, 38*f*
Terms of Reference (ToR), 72
Testing, Experimentation, and Open Source Working Group
    (TST), 72
Third Generation Partnership Project (3GPP), 50
  impact on, 52
"Tick-tock" cycle, 9–10
Tightly integrated service solutions, 24. *See also* Loosely
    coupled solution
  BNG, 25, 25*f*
  feature velocity friction, 26
  generations, 25
  implementations, 24–25
  internal connectivity, 25
  operational concerns, 24
  operators, 25

Tightly integrated service solutions (*Continued*)
  purchasing leverage, 24
  revenue opportunities, 24
  vendor lock-in, 26
TLB. *See* Translation Look-aside Buffer (TLB)
TLS Protocol. *See* Transport Layer Security (TLS) Protocol
TLV Class field, 85
TM. *See* Transport manager (TM)
TM Forum (TMF), 129
TMF. *See* TM Forum (TMF)
Top-down approach, 223–224
Topology and Orchestration Specification for Cloud
        Applications (TOSCA), 65, 136
  template, 140, 142*f*
    and parser, 142–143
ToR. *See* Terms of Reference (ToR)
TOSCA. *See* Topology and Orchestration Specification for
        Cloud Applications (TOSCA)
TOSCA/HEAT translator, 143*f*
Total Cost (TC), 219
Total cost of ownership (TCO), 219
TPR. *See* Task Priority Register (TPR)
Translation Look-aside Buffer (TLB), 157
"Transport Derived SFF", 82
Transport Layer Security (TLS) Protocol, 96
Transport manager (TM), 180
Transport-tied solutions, 79
TSC. *See* Technical Steering Committee (TSC)
TST. *See* Testing, Experimentation, and Open Source
        Working Group (TST)
Turnkey optimization, 180–182

U

UML, 166
  and container hybrid, 166*f*
  kernel across multiple customers, 167
Underlay, 78
Unikernels, 165
Universal resource identifier (URI), 96
URI. *See* Universal resource identifier (URI)
Us-vhost approach, 177
Use-case-led consumption, 223–224

V

vCPE. *See* Virtualized residential service CPE (vCPE)
vCPU. *See* Virtual CPUs (vCPU)
VDUs. *See* Virtualization Deployment Units (VDUs)
Vector Packet Processor (VPP), 182
  plug-in architecture, 183*f*
Vendor lock-in, 26
vEPC. *See* Virtual Evolved Packet Core (vEPC)
Verbs, 96

vFW. *See* Virtual firewall (vFW)
vhost-user, 178
  software packet handling bottom line, 180
  user space vhost implementation, 177*f*
  Vale, 179*f*
Vi-Vnfm, 137
VIM. *See* Virtual Infrastructure Manager (VIM)
Virtio-based solutions, 174
Virtual Cache use case, 62
Virtual CPUs (vCPU), 157
Virtual Evolved Packet Core (vEPC), 53
Virtual firewall (vFW), 38
Virtual Infrastructure Manager (VIM), 56, 103. *See also*
        Network Function Virtualization Infrastructure (NFVI)
Virtual Machine Extensions (VMX), 157
Virtual machine manager (VMM), 156
Virtual machines (VMs), 8, 21, 54, 105, 134, 157
  VM-centric model, 158
    ETSI NFV architecture, 158
    ETSI workgroups, 160
    vGiLAN, 160
    VM distribution, 159*f*
    VM migration, 159
Virtual Network Function Component (VNFC), 53
Virtual Network Function Manager (VNFM), 56, 127
  demarcation point, 138
Virtual network functions (VNFs), 51, 53, 218
  auto-configuration, 141
  Domain, 128–129
  monitoring, 141–142
  Set, 53–54
Virtual Network Functions as a Service (VNFaaS), 59
Virtual NIC (vNIC), 157
"Virtual router", 7
Virtual service creation, 29–35
Virtual switch (vSwitch), 43–44, 157
Virtualization, 23*f*, 38, 155
  connectivity techniques, 180
  current packet handling, 170
    application processing, 171
    context switch/data copy reduction, 172
    fd. io, 182–183
    first generation VNF, 171*t*
    Intel advancements, 173–177
    Netmap, 178–180
    scalar *vs.* vectorization, 173
    system memory, 170
    turnkey optimization, 180–182
    vector processing, 173*f*
    vhost-user, 178–180
  elasticity, 63
  energy requirements, 64
  evolution, 156
    containers, 160–165

hybrid virtualization, 165—167
    hypervisor maps physical resources, 158*f*
    KVM execution and QEMU emulation, 157*f*
    QEMU hardware emulator, 156
    security trade-offs, 167—169
    security—lowest common denominator, 169—170
    UML and container hybrid, 166*f*
    Unikernels, 165
    VM-centric model, 158—160
ISG REL WG, 64
of Mobile Core Network and IMS, 59
NFV Performance & Portability Best
    Practises document, 63
orchestration and management, 64
performance, 63
portability requirements, 63
requirements, 62
resiliency requirements, 63
security and maintenance sections, 64
service
    assurance, 64
    continuity, 64
    models, 65
work groups, 63
Virtualization Deployment Units (VDUs), 140
Virtualized residential service CPE (vCPE), 61
VLAN
    segmentation, 21
    stitching, 28, 28*f*, 38
VM to exit (VMExit), 172
VMM. *See* Virtual machine manager (VMM)
VMs. *See* Virtual machines (VMs)
VMX. *See* Virtual Machine Extensions (VMX)
VNF Descriptions (VNFDs), 140

VNF Platform as a Service (VNFPaaS), 59—60
VNFaaS. *See* Virtual Network Functions as a Service
    (VNFaaS)
VNFC. *See* Virtual Network Function Component (VNFC)
VNFDs. *See* VNF Descriptions (VNFDs)
VNFM. *See* Virtual Network Function Manager (VNFM)
VNFPaaS. *See* VNF Platform as a Service (VNFPaaS)
VNFPool, 66
VNFs. *See* Virtual network functions (VNFs)
vNIC. *See* Virtual NIC (vNIC)
vPE termination (VPN), 38
VPN. *See* vPE termination (VPN)
VPP. *See* Vector Packet Processor (VPP)
vRouter, 38
vSwitch. *See* Virtual switch (vSwitch)
VTEPs, 108
vVPN function, 38

W

White paper 3, 69—70
Wind River, 180
Wireless operators, 2
Wireline operators, 2

Y

Yang models, 14, 78, 93, 96
    usage, 99—101
Yet Another Next Generation data modeling language,
    92—93, 115

Z

Zero-packet-copy, 172

Printed in the United States
By Bookmasters